Unsocial l

Unsocial Europe

Social Protection or Flexploitation?

Anne Gray

Pluto Press

LONDON • ANN ARBOR, MI

First published 2004 by Pluto Press
345 Archway Road, London N6 5AA
and 839 Greene Street, Ann Arbor, MI 48106

www.plutobooks.com

British Library Cataloguing in Publication Data
A catalogue record for this book is available from the British Library

ISBN   0 7453 2032 5 hardback
ISBN   0 7453 2031 7 paperback

Library of Congress Cataloging in Publication Data applied for

10   9   8   7   6   5   4   3   2   1

Designed and produced for Pluto Press by
Chase Publishing Services, Fortescue, Sidmouth, EX10 9QG, England
Typeset from disk by Stanford DTP Services, Northampton, England
Printed and bound in the European Union by
Antony Rowe Ltd, Chippenham and Eastbourne, England

Contents

Tables, Boxes and Figures

TABLES

BOXES

FIGURES

Acknowledgements

Thanks are due, in the first place, to all the research partners in the project 'Minima Sociaux et Condition Salariale' on which parts of this book are based: Cathérine Lévy (coordinator), CNRS, Paris; Estelle Krzeslo, Université Libre de Bruxelles; Stephen Bouquin, VUB, Brussels; Martin Gueck, University of Heidelberg. Secondly, to the European Commission for financing that project. Thirdly, to London South Bank University for hosting the author while doing the research. Fourthly, to the four unemployed workers' centres who hosted focus groups and helped to contact unwaged people to take part: The Crossing, Lowestoft; Norwich Unemployed Workers' Centre; Brighton and Hove Unemployed Workers' Centre; and Derbyshire Unemployed Workers' Centres, Chesterfield, who also organised a survey of New Deal participants. Likewise to the Vocational Training Initiative, Waltham Forest, and to New Deal training staff in Bradford, for helping to set up focus groups. Fifth, the author thanks several individuals for their comments on particular chapters: Regan Scott, Les Levidow, Pauline Bradley, Richard Chilvers and Alec Johnson. Sixth, much appreciation to Katy Andrews for her comments and editing support on the whole manuscript, and for sorting out the bibliography. Any errors and omissions remain entirely the responsibility of the author.

Abbreviations

ALE	Agence Locale d'Emploi
ALMP	active labour market programme
ANPE	Agence Nationale pour le promotion de l'Emploi
DWP	Delors White Paper
EC	European Commission
ECHP	European Community Household Panel
ECSC	European Coal and Steel Community
EEC	European Economic Community
EIRO	European Industrial Relations Observatory
EMU	European Monetary Union
EPL	employment protection legislation
ERT	European Round Table
ETUC	European Trade Union Confederation
EU	European Union
GATS	General Agreement on Trade and Services
GDP	Gross Domestic Product
HZA	Hilfe zur Arbeit
ILO	International Labour Organisation
IMF	International Monetary Fund
JSA	Jobseeker's Allowance
MDRC	Manpower Demonstration Research Corporation
NAPs/incl	National Action Plans on Inclusion
NJTS	New Job Training Scheme
OECD	Organisation for Economic Cooperation and Development
PARE	Plan d'Aide au Retour à l'Emploi
RMA	Revenu Minimum d'Activité
RMI	Revenu Minimum d'Insertion
SUD	Solidaire, Unitaire, Démocratique
TUC	Trade Union Congress
UNICE	Union of Industrial and Employers' Confederation of Europe
WPSP	White Paper on Social Policy
WTO	World Trade Organization

1
Introduction

WELFARE, WORK AND GLOBALISATION

This book attempts to address two gaps in the literature about international comparison of welfare systems. Firstly, the way in which benefits systems, changing forms of work and labour regulation interact with each other, especially in the context of globalisation and the progress of European integration. Secondly, the testimony of unwaged people themselves on how welfare systems and labour market policies affect their daily lives, as they struggle with employers and benefit rules, living on a pittance or in and out of short-term jobs. The dry bureaucratic language of 'active labour market measures', 'availability for work testing' and 'wage flexibility' is transformed by their accounts from the front line into a human reality; the 10 per cent of Europe's citizens whose voices are too rarely heard.

Globalisation, the merging of national economies towards one giant playing field for large companies, is distinctively different from the 'internationalisation of capital' through investment flows that has been going on for over 150 years. Globalisation involves greater opportunities for companies to shift production anywhere, so that European bank customers can be served by call centres in India, and car plants can move to cheap-labour countries. This process is assisted by the breaking down of trade and investment barriers, and by technological change especially in communications and transport. Globalisation has had a profound impact on Europe's economies and social policies. Companies who can move or outsource production across the world have far less interest in preserving and nurturing a particular national labour force than the Krupps or Rowntrees of the nineteenth century. 'Regime shopping' for the most business-friendly tax and regulatory environments becomes common. Taxing profits to provide a 'social wage' whether in cash or in services is no longer so easy. But nor is it so difficult as often maintained; widely differing levels of business taxes persist between countries. The tendency towards international equalisation of rates of profit, which supplies the apparent constraint on tax policies, is expressed only in imperfect capital markets, leaving considerable differences in rates of return and business investment horizons. Globalisation has also impeded freedom of manoeuvre in macro-economic management, through the greater scale and unpredictability of international capital movements. Keynesianism in one country becomes more difficult than ever. But Keynesianism in a large bloc, such as the European Union, should surely have some prospects. The current policies of the EU, with very tight limits on public spending and borrowing, seem to be a missed opportunity. The Maastricht framework has put an international seal of approval on the pessimism with which many European governments had begun to regard Keynesian policy instruments, pushing them further towards neo-liberal supply side policies to deal with unemployment that throw the responsibility more on to unemployed people themselves than their governments. This is perhaps an example of a third impact of globalisation: the emergence of a supranational level of economic policy coordination, which is beyond democratic control and susceptible more to the influence of the right than the left. But this supranational level goes much further than a presumption against Keynesianism. There is a similarity between the policy prescriptions of the OECD and those of the European Commission that can barely be accounted for by mere consensus among technical experts; it is the consensus of those whose brief it is to maintain, without reference to the shifting class forces of national politics, the foundations of the capitalist system. Hence a profound fatalism in these institutions that the rate of profit and the apparent 'needs' of employers can rarely be challenged

Since the recession of the 1980s, the quality of jobs in Europe appears to be declining for the unskilled and most of all for those struggling to find employment. Some experience a brutal downgrading of their careers owing to the impossibility of finding jobs as good as those they lost. The rise in the share of temporary and part-time jobs, and the disappearance of reasonably paid positions for the unskilled, results from pressures in each of the economy's three main sectors. In manufacturing, employers' response to stiffer international competition both within the 'developed' countries and from newly industrialised economies has been to shrink operations, to replace people with machinery, and to a quest for 'throwaway labour' in the form of under-unionised casual workers who can be sacked easily when times are hard. In many private sector services, which now account for the bulk of employment growth in Europe, labour requirements have always contained a high share of temporary, part-time or low-paid work. In the public sector, budget constraints have led to an increasing share of temporary jobs, and privatisation has transferred many posts into an arena of keen, sometimes internationalised, competition between contractors eager to minimise and casualise their labour force. Temporary and part-time jobs are less unionised and lower-paid. All of these changes lead towards a two-tier labour market, with the less fortunate facing a shrunken stock of quality jobs for lower-skilled people, and likely to be trapped in a cycle of alternating short-term work and unemployment.

A demand for freedom to hire short term has been driven both by privatisation and by increased uncertainty for many private employers in the face of intensified international competition. Their response has often been to reduce long-term payroll commitments, relying more on fixed-term contract employees and agency workers. Labour is wanted by many modern companies in a form more like water, a resource to be turned on and off at will. The policies of European governments have been largely to 'go with the flow' of employers' pressure to change the nature of jobs, drawing their labour laws closer to the American model of near-complete employer freedom to hire and fire. In the 1980s and 1990s, most European states have encouraged 'flexibilisation' of labour contract forms in the hope of promoting more jobs – removing regulatory barriers to temporary and part-time hirings – as well as 'flexibilisation' of working time patterns (removing barriers to shift-working, night work, variable or annualised working hours). Restrictions on employers' freedom to dismiss workers have often been eased. Collective bargaining arrangements have often been 'flexibilised' too – decentralising to permit flexibility at local or company level, sometimes making wide exceptions to normal wage rates for newly hired unemployed (as in Germany), and in extreme cases, like Thatcher's Britain, making savage attacks on trade union rights. The 'flexibilisation' of labour markets impacts most on those with least bargaining power as individuals – the low-paid, less well-educated and less experienced workers. Flexibilisation, for them, means an intensification of exploitation – *flexploitation*, to coin a term that is central to this book.

While flexploitation is in part a direct result of globalisation, privatisation and the shift of European economies from manufacturing to services, it also results from deliberate deregulation of labour markets and from the decline of union power. Casualisation is made easier where unions are weak, and makes them weaker still. In pressing for greater flexibility of labour markets, the European Commission argues that flexibility can and should be balanced with security; Denmark, where workers change jobs frequently but do not appear to feel insecure, is upheld as a model. It is rarely recognised that a high degree of unionisation, and a strong trade union presence in all aspects of labour market governance, is at the heart not only of the Danish model but of the concept of 'social dialogue' on which EU-level regulation of labour markets has been built. Consequently a downward spiral of casualisation and reduced union power threaten the basis of the 'social dialogue' model.

The evidence on the benefits of flexibilisation for employment growth is in any case contested. One view is that some erosion of rights for workers – in terms of lower job security and greater employer-driven flexibility of working hours, is inevitable as a way of enabling national economies to compete in global markets. Another is that the constraints are exaggerated and that, in practice, neither deregulation of labour contracts nor erosion of minimum wage levels have much positive impact on employment growth. If so, the fatalism of current economic orthodoxy is misplaced, even within a capitalist framework. There are choices to be made between policies that increase inequality, power and wealth towards employers, and those that uphold high labour standards and quality opportunities for all.

Running contrary to the theme of flexibilisation is a degree of reregulation of labour contracts. Several national governments in the 1990s have introduced new laws affecting temporary work agencies, some relaxing old restrictions, others introducing new ones to equalise conditions of agency workers with those of others. Likewise some of the European Union labour directives are intended to control and limit the outcomes of flexibilisation, by securing equality of certain conditions across different types of labour contract, and providing for cross-national workers' representation in multinational companies. They try to prevent deregulation from being used to gain a cost advantage for particular national economies within the single European market. But while the EU labour directives have made important gains in certain areas, like the rights of women, they fall short of aiming for upward harmonisation of minimum wage levels, rights to time off and fringe benefits, or trade union rights. This invites the question, what is the future of labour market regulation in Europe? A new concern with 'job quality' has emerged in meetings of the European Council since the Lisbon summit of 2000. This may offer a platform to push for new workers' rights, or it may fade under pressure from employers' lobbying groups and those governments that listen to them most.

WHITHER 'SOCIAL EUROPE'?

'Social Europe', the project of a common policy framework across the EU to address poverty and promote 'social dialogue' between employers and trade unions, emerged in the early 1990s as the expression of a social-democratic vision for a form of European integration that was rather more than an integrated market. Uncomfortably grafted on to an essentially capitalist project that was under increasing influence from powerful multinational companies, it has taken back stage in the later 1990s as EU policies have increasingly responded to employers' needs. The macro-economic policy framework established by the Maastricht Treaty tended to shrink the state sector and severely limited state spending as a source of job creation. Those member states that might have chosen such a solution were pushed instead towards policies that tried to 'clear' the labour market by making labour cheaper. This meant flexibilisation of labour markets, making labour easier to hire and fire on employers' terms and giving free rein to employers' increasing preference for temporary labour in certain situations. It also involved flexibilisation of the unemployed, by recasting benefit systems to induce less resistance to offers of casual work or jobs well below the claimants' former status. Thus 'social protection' – the ensemble of benefit rights and rights at work – has come under increasing pressure in many countries from neo-liberal policies to mobilise a low-cost labour supply and reduce wage pressure. The shift from the idea of unemployment benefits as a right to a regime closer to American 'workfare' in many variants is taking place across Europe. Workfare and stricter benefit regimes are used to chase unemployed people into low-paid, temporary or part-time jobs associated with the new 'flexible' labour market. 'Active' labour market policies are encouraged by the European Commission as part of a neo-liberal approach to the management of the labour market, as a complement to greater flexibility of working conditions and of 'hire and fire' rules. In this state strategy for 'flexploitation' of the labour force, obligations for unemployed people are increased, while those of employers are often reduced.

Where trade unions have had a strong role in the management of social insurance (in France, Belgium, Sweden, and Denmark, but not Germany or the UK) they have tended to place unemployed benefits relatively high on their bargaining agenda in tripartite 'deals' with the state and with employers at national level. An exception may be Spain, probably because having the highest level of unemployment in Europe keeps benefits at the forefront of workers' demands despite the state management of the benefit system. But a key factor in raising the profile of unwaged people's needs in the late 1990s was the development of unemployed people's own social movements, coordinated internationally through the Euromarches and with a strong presence in the series of 'counter-summit' meetings and marches that have pursued successive meetings of the European Council from 1997 onwards.

Trade unions' attitudes to active labour market programmes are often cautious; likewise to wage subsidies intended to assist the reintegration of the unemployed. They fear 'cheap labour', ever mindful of the ways in which such programmes may be used to provide a labour supply that undercuts established wages and conditions. This is part of a wider issue about the way in which the 'reserve army of labour', as Marx described it, influences the price of labour power. 'Cheap labour' is not merely an issue about subsidised or 'scheme' workers taking away jobs from those for whom the employer pays a full normal wage. There is a continuity of purpose between workfare and benefit rules that channel jobseekers into low-paid or otherwise unattractive work, often forming a planned sequence of interventions in the individual's job search that are intensified as unemployment lengthens. 'Workfarism' or 'work first' is the name given here, following Peck and Theodore (2000), to the ensemble of benefit rules and employment service practices that are designed to mould jobseekers' aspirations to available jobs. Strict rules apply about what level of wage unemployed people must accept help to slot ex-miners into hotel kitchens, ex-car workers into the cash desks of supermarkets, young graduates who have fallen out of a professional ladder into call centres and casual farm work. Those who used to earn good money suffer 'the cost of losing a job' – in many cases a substantial drop in living standards.

Unemployed people need not only more jobs but better jobs. However, improving job quality requires a break with the 'deregulation' agenda and the mobilisation of the 'reserve army' to drive down labour costs. Within the limited arena of labour market policy, the challenge for Europe in the twenty-first century is how to avoid the flexploitation of the dual labour market and break with the workfarist policies for managing unemployment that tend to intensify and encourage it. Unemployed people demand better training, not just for mere 'employability' in the lowest-level jobs, which is all they tend to be offered in some national systems, but training for new careers to break out of the 'flexploited' layer of jobs. But in the nature of the globalised economy, with short horizons for attachment to any local labour force or local market for subcontracted labour, employers are more reluctant than ever to invest in training.

Some unemployed people, however, are beyond the reach of mere skills training or an increase in the number and quality of vacancies; there are other problems to be addressed. The need for childcare for working mothers is the easiest, already much better tackled in Sweden, Denmark and France than in Britain and itself a source of job creation, but still requiring extensive public funds. More intractable is racial discrimination, which requires a significant change in employer attitudes. The most difficult is the issue of disability, affecting a significant minority of jobseekers, not infrequently because of mental health rather than physical health issues. If they get jobs at all, it may be the worst jobs, which increase stress and barely improve their income. The challenge is how to integrate them into quality employment in a non-stigmatising way.

All of this requires a regrowth of state investment in education and training, and in collective services (if not provided by the state, at least and perhaps preferably by NGOs). This in turn requires redistribution of wealth and income to turn private profit into collective funds. Here we confront the limits of capitalism – particularly in its latter-day, globalised form.

COUNTRY COMPARISONS AND EVIDENCE FROM RESEARCH WITH THE UNEMPLOYED

Among other sources, this book draws on unemployed people's own accounts of their experiences of benefits, 'welfare to work' measures and the jobs to which they lead in a selection of four European countries: the UK, Germany, France and Belgium. Chapters 5 and 6 tell their stories of the job market as seen from the dole queue, illustrating the qualitative dimensions of the 'work incentives' problem, including the fear of deskilling or being trapped in low-paid casual work that pays barely more than benefits. Chapter 8 looks at their experience of active labour market programmes.

The evidence on unemployed people's experiences comes from a comparative project in which the author's work in the UK was mirrored by that of research partners in France, Germany and Belgium. Funded by the European Commission under the TSER Programme,[1] its French title translates as 'Minimum-Income Benefits and Waged Work: Europe seen from Below'. In the text of this book it is referred to as the 'Minima Sociaux' project, and the project reports appear in the bibliography under the joint names of the five research partners: Cathérine Lévy (coordinator) in France, Martin Gueck in Germany, Estelle Krzeslo and Stephen Bouquin in Belgium, and Anne Gray in the UK. The UK fieldwork had three stages: focus groups in the summer of 1999, involving altogether 98 claimants found through unemployed workers' centres and training schemes in six locations: London, Chesterfield, Brighton, Norwich, Lowestoft and Bradford; individual questionnaires for the same people at that time and by post 18 months later; and thirdly a survey of 84 participants in the New Deal in Chesterfield, in spring 2000. In Germany, survey work along similar lines covered over 200 people. A more ethnographic approach involving around 30 people in each country was used in France and Belgium.[2]

The author joined the planning of this international project at a late stage when the countries had already been chosen. With hindsight, it would have been valuable to include a south European country and at least one Scandinavian country, to examine the full spectrum of welfare systems and labour market policies across the European Union at the turn of the twentieth century. (To cover the enlarged EU of 2004 might have been too ambitious a task.) It was therefore decided that the book should include secondary material on Sweden and Denmark, as examples of what Esping-Andersen (1990) describes as 'social-democratic' welfare systems, and to Spain, as a case study of the south European variant of a 'corporatist' or insurance-oriented welfare system. Sweden and Denmark have both been included because they have some important differences described in Chapter 7, which form the backcloth to differences in welfare developments. Sweden has a highly regulated labour market while Denmark, in the matter of employers' freedom to fire, is upheld by the OECD (1999b) as a model of flexibility.

SUMMARY OF CONTENTS

Chapter 2

A brief overview of the history of income maintenance and labour market policies examines how and why these systems were established, and how they have changed in the last 20 years, with a short narrative portrait of each of the seven countries and some comparative statistics on the evolution of national labour markets. The history of income maintenance can be examined in the light of Esping-Andersen's classification of welfare regimes and the debates around it. Unwaged benefits are seen a means of 'de-commodification' of labour; they protect the unwaged from the full blast of the market, which treats their labour as a commodity. Esping-Andersen (1990) made 'de-commodification' a key dimension in his typology of welfare states, which has survived a wide range of criticisms and modifications to become a cornerstone of welfare state analysis in the 1990s. Developments in welfare-to-work and labour market policies in recent years introduce new dimensions to Esping-Andersen's classification, and indeed cut across it. One is the extent and nature of active labour market programmes, and the nature of tests and conditions imposed on unemployed people about the way they are looking for work. Another is the degree to which trade unions have been involved in the development and management of benefit systems, and how this influences the style in which claimants are treated. A third is the extent of labour market flexibilisation and how it is regulated.

While several writers have concluded that there is little 'convergence' between different welfare state types within the EU, each of Esping-Andersen's types largely maintaining its specificities, the analysis of changing benefit systems in Chapters 5 and 8 questions the convergence hypothesis. There is clearly some convergence of policies towards the unemployed, in a 'workfarist' direction, encouraged to some degree by the coordination of employment and social policies at EU level. Sweden and Denmark have sometimes been upheld as models of 'activation' of benefits systems. There is some controversy over whether elements of their active labour market policies should be regarded as workfare or workfarist. Chapter 8 argues that they are moving in that direction, but retain differences from workfare of the neo-liberal type.

Chapter 3

Globalisation presents a threat to the welfare state on three fronts, all of which have potentially severe consequences for the unemployed. Footloose production and the possibility of outsourcing across the globe pose a threat to labour standards. Globalisation also impedes macro-economic management; it is harder than ever to have Keynesianism in one country. Companies may move their production to locations with lowest taxes and least regulation. However, the evidence that social expenditures have fallen in response to globalisation is patchy and inconclusive. In so far as pressure to reduce welfare budgets exists, globalisation may not be the key factor. Antedating globalisation are long-standing concerns about a 'fiscal crisis of the state' from internal causes: the incapacity of the mature capitalist economy to generate enough taxable surplus to meet all the demands placed upon the welfare state, including those of an 'ageing society', which have attracted considerable attention in the late 1990s. The theory of the Keynesian policy model turning into a 'workfare state' in response to both globalisation and fiscal pressures is unconvincing when it posits a *functional necessity* to cut and transform unemployed benefits. Certainly there are tensions and pressures; but how they are resolved is a matter for debate and struggle.

Chapter 4

This chapter gives an account of 'Social Europe', the attempt associated with the Delors presidency (1985–95) to temper the market forces of a customs union with some gains for workers' rights and with a commitment to employment growth and gender equality. It then traces the later EU policy developments of the 1990s, in which neo-liberal policies have dominated, committing the EU to a supply side, workfarist approach to unemployment and to flexibilisation of the labour market. The framework for economic integration laid down by the Maastricht Treaty of 1992 favoured the demands of employers' lobbies, and introduced supranational rules for macro-economic management, which gave governments an externally located excuse for restricting wage growth and public expenditure, as well as for imposing stricter work discipline on the unemployed. After the Amsterdam Treaty (1997) the economic guidelines entrenched the policy goals of tighter benefit conditions and labour market flexibility. Lately there has been some concern with job quality, but the EU's economic policy guidelines continue to emphasise 'wage flexibility' and acceptance of job insecurity as conditions of employment growth.

Chapter 5

Unemployed benefit systems across Europe have undergone a transformation since the recession of the late 1980s, from having a mainly social protection function to becoming an instrument for managing the unemployed labour reserve. The ideal of 'de-commodification' – the term developed in relation to social security by Gøsta Esping-Andersen (1990) and perhaps exemplified in the Danish system of the 1980s, one of the most generous on record – meant providing an income for as long as the claimant reasonably needed to find another job comparable to the old one, or retrain, albeit with certain safeguards against abuse of the system. Increasingly in the 1990s, benefit systems have moved away from 'de-commodification', with reduced rights to reject undesirable jobs, greater obligations to demonstrate active job search, more use of sanctions and more compulsory labour market programmes. These new 'workfarist' policies play a key role in damping down jobseekers' expectations to match the low-paid, part-time or temporary nature of many of the jobs now being created.

Unwaged people report many unpalatable experiences of jobs they have taken out of desperation, sometimes under actual or implied pressure from employment service officials, sometimes under actual threat of losing benefits if they refused. Employers can easily take advantage of people in these situations. Low pay, work being withdrawn unexpectedly after a few weeks, long and unpredictable working hours, even poor health and safety conditions, are common among jobs they have had and lost. Those with longer and better experience can sometimes trace a degradation of conditions in their habitual occupation. There is also an issue of wasted potential where some people can be downgraded for years as a result of some mistake or personal disaster – a sacking, a divorce, an illness – after which they must accept the first job available regardless of previous experience.

Workfarist benefits appear to have been a deliberate policy choice to engineer acceptance of the low-quality jobs thrown up by the process of 'flexibilisation' of labour markets. The pros and cons of the alternatives are also discussed: wage supplements such as tax credits, opportunities to combine casual or part-time work with benefit receipt, and the demand for an unconditional basic income often made by unemployed people's movements. None provide an entirely adequate solution for jobseekers faced with flexploitation, and the wrong kind of benefits system can make the problem worse. Low pay and job insecurity need to be tackled at source.

Chapter 6

This chapter attempts to document the 'bad jobs' problem and how it affects the careers of the unemployed. European (and other OECD) countries have seen a huge growth of part-time and temporary jobs in recent years, often with worse pay and conditions than full-time permanent workers. Many of these have become the lot of youth, women returners, migrants and people re-entering work after unemployment. Inequality among labour incomes has also grown, with stagnant or falling real wages in the lowest layers of the wage distribution. The ratio of vacancies to jobseekers has risen in most countries, partly because some jobs offer too little to be of interest except to the most desperate. Growth of temporary work agencies has been particularly rapid. They have become key forces in moulding the job opportunities available to the unemployed, who form a large share of agencies' labour supply. Although employment service officials press home the message that any job is better than no job, unemployed people themselves ardently dislike temporary work. Not only is the wage/benefit ratio too low to provide much incentive in many cases, but temporary jobs often appear to lead nowhere except back to the dole queue.

Chapter 7

The trade-off between the number of jobs and the level of wages or job security is an ever-present theme both in debates about macro-economic policy and in trade union negotiations, whether at employer, industry or national level. One question is how high minimum wages can go without choking off the growth of employment. Employers' demand for labour rises faster in upswings if they can hire workers on the terms they want, with regard to working time (and its variability), length or security of contract, freedom to fire and the extent to which they have to compensate dismissed workers. But if it encourages hiring, flexibilisation also makes workers easier to fire, so that taking booms and recessions together, the effect on overall unemployment seems to be neutral. If deregulation reduces long-term unemployment, it does so by increasing labour turnover, and the greater job insecurity resulting from flexibilisation creates different problems. The first of these is the labour market dualism that increases inequality and poverty of life chances; the second is a severe erosion of trade union strength; a third is that the more 'flexible' are labour contracts, the greater the risk of workers needing to call on unemployed benefits, as well as other forms of state support for low-paid and part-time workers.

Yet the backcloth to the struggle about labour rights is one of some steps forward as well as some steps back. The period since the late 1980s has seen extensive 'deregulation' of labour markets across the EU, tending towards reduced job security rights, increased freedom for employers to hire temps and agency staff, and sweeping away of restrictions on working time patterns. To prevent competitive deregulation from becoming a 'race to the bottom', a series of labour rights directives have been laid down by the European Union. Those concerning fixed-term contracts and agency work must be seen as ways of controlling the process of labour flexibilisation and making it more palatable to trade unions. Certain other directives – for example on working time and parental leave – serve to prevent competition within the integrated market from undercutting established workers' rights in certain member states. A third group, on gender equality, has secured valuable advances in the rights of women, although a cynical view would attribute this goal to the need of capital to increase the low-cost female labour supply in order to put pressure on men's wages. The implementation of EU labour directives presents several exemptions and loopholes, especially in the UK, which has 'transposed' them into national law in relatively weak forms. Moreover, the enforcement of labour rights depends on trade unions, whose strength has been undermined not only by flexibilisation itself but also by changes in labour law in some countries. In Britain, where trade union rights were emasculated during the Tory years and have not been fully restored, this is an especially acute problem.

Chapter 8

Government programmes to integrate unemployed people have placed less emphasis than previously on Keynesian-style job creation, and more on getting jobseekers to make do with jobs that are on offer. National and European Commission policy documents describe 'active labour market programmes' of whatever kind – training, advice sessions and work experience – as constructive. No doubt some are, but to assume this without question is to side-step the issues of whether they are compulsory, to what extent unemployed people welcome certain programmes, and how these affect wages and conditions in the labour market as a whole. A proportion of low-paid and temporary jobs are created or encouraged by measures to promote hiring of the unemployed.

Workfare, broadly defined as work that unemployed people must take on pain of benefit sanctions, and which is paid with a less than normal wage, is present to some degree in six out of the seven countries discussed here. Following the example of the USA, where its benefits for the taxpayer have been somewhat overrated, several EU member states have introduced measures of this kind in recent years, but with considerable variations in the scale and nature of the programmes, which are also coloured by their political context. Workfare has been accused of undermining 'normal' jobs by 'cheap labour', but its significance is much more as one element of a 'workfarist' benefits package that mobilises the unemployed labour reserve to reduce wage pressure. Workfare is widely unpopular with unemployed people, and many do suffer benefit sanctions rather than take part. In so far as workfare reduces unemployment, this is more because of its 'deterrent' effect, driving people into open market jobs, than because of positive outcomes of the programmes themselves.

Those who fail to respond to the 'deterrent' effect are often those unable to access even the worst jobs, for whom benefit sanctions are punitive rather than productive. A combination of quality training and 'sheltered' work at real wages can often help them. But unfortunately much of the training offered to unemployed people is poorly designed and delivered, and aimed at too low a level to lift them out of the reach of long-term flexploitation. Unemployed people often aspire to forms of training too long or too advanced to be available within the array of free training schemes provided for jobseekers on benefits. Quality training is a costly but fundamental requirement for all those seeking escape from the lowest levels of the labour market, whether actually out of work or in low-paid or insecure jobs. The increasing involvement of employment agencies and other labour market intermediaries in welfare to work programmes raises issues about their accountability and their control over the careers of captive 'clients'.

Chapter 9

In conclusion, we can seek to define alternatives to workfarism inspired partly by research with unemployed people themselves. They want a less punitive benefit system, with opportunities to retain part of their benefits if they come by part-time or casual work. They are resentful of the very rich, and see a strong case for limiting inequality of incomes. They see supply side economics as inherently anti-worker and anti-unemployed. Ultimately it has to be accepted that the apparent trade-off between job quantity and job quality is a matter of distribution. 'Work-sharing' by reducing working time has a certain appeal, although its implementation without loss of pay confronts the same challenges as any other kind of pay rise. The preservation and extension of the public and non-profit sectors are necessary to generate more jobs without letting wages and conditions fall. A climate must be created for greater investment in collective services, both those that support employment, like childcare, education and training, and those that meet other social needs under-supplied by the market. Ultimately the future of benefits and collective services depend on the wage/profit share-out of output, which is the stuff of the class struggle. The fatalism with which neo-liberal economic theory regards this share-out needs to be questioned. So too does the problematic of 'creating more jobs' when what people really want are income, leisure and a sustainable planet. A different kind of society might move away from the labour *market* and instead share out socially necessary work – but to elaborate on this would be another book.

2

The Welfare State and the Unwaged: Past, Present and Future

Income maintenance is seen by Esping-Andersen (1990) as a means of 'de-commodification' of labour power, sheltering the worker from the pressures of the labour market, and from its tendency to treat human beings as the 'commodity' of a supply of labour. In the fundamental inequality of the labour market, where sellers must sell or starve, unwaged benefits help jobseekers to reject the worst job offers and retain a modicum of bargaining power. The extent of 'de-commodification' is a valuable yardstick by which to assess benefit systems. Its opposite, 're-commodification', sums up the effect of any curtailment of benefit rights, including the imposition of extra conditions for claiming them.

In Esping-Andersen's classic typology of welfare states, the highest 'de-commodification' power is shown for the 'social-democratic' welfare regimes typified by Sweden and Denmark, with high benefits, a large stock of quality jobs in the public sector, high employment rates especially for women and a relatively egalitarian income distribution. Low 'de-commodification' capacity is attributed to the English-speaking countries, the 'neo-liberal' type, with the USA in particular identified by low benefits, high income inequality and extreme vulnerability of workers to unregulated labour market pressures. In between are the 'conservative' or 'corporatist' states, so called because their welfare tradition derives from the nineteenth-century tradition of Bismarck's pioneering social insurance schemes in Germany. This group includes Germany, France, Belgium, the Netherlands and Austria. Social rights, including rights to healthcare, depend largely on individuals' contributions to social insurance funds, and those of their employers. Such systems favour workers with a long contribution record in stable jobs. Youth and people in temporary or part-time jobs are often effectively excluded from insurance benefits because they have not accumulated enough contributions, or in some instances because their employers are exempt. Women with little or no paid work record must generally depend on their husbands' rights.

Some writers have distinguished a separate, south European type with less developed welfare provisions, including Italy, Spain, Portugal and Greece (Guillén and Alvarez, 2002). These countries are characterised by a large informal sector, in which workers have neither social insurance nor regulated employment contracts. Italy, Portugal and Greece also have relatively extensive self-employment, and in Spain almost one-third of all workers are in temporary jobs, struggling to build a sufficient contribution record to benefit from unemployment insurance. Hence the proportion of unemployed receiving benefits is relatively low in these countries (EC, 1998c). Whereas in the north European states, people without unemployment insurance can fall back on social assistance schemes, minimum income guarantees are only just being developed in southern Europe and the family remains the main source of support for the uninsured.[1] In Spain, the expanding minimum income provisions have some workfare obligations attached, as discussed in Chapter 8.

For unemployment benefits, Esping-Andersen's original index of 'de-commodification' capacity (Esping-Andersen, 1990) includes four variables: the standard replacement ratio for a single worker, the qualification conditions in terms of length of contribution period, the number of 'waiting days' before benefit begins, and the percentage of unemployed persons receiving benefit. One might now argue for a different choice of variables. Developments in social protection since 1990 suggest new dimensions of 'de-commodification' and re-commodification, including the extent of benefit conditionality (such as job search and availability for work requirements) and of workfare obligations, as well as features of labour contract regulation. Including these new dimensions introduces an important division within 'social-democratic' welfare regimes, as well as within corporatist ones.

Swedish and Danish practices in benefit administration might be regarded as 'trade union oriented'; formally strict conditionalities are in practice applied with a velvet glove, and decisions about sanctions rest with the claimant's trade union, which administers the unemployment insurance fund. However, the Danish benefit system is gradually changing in a neo-liberal direction, with recent cuts in social assistance benefits and a reduction over the 1990s of the importance of trade union-managed insurance funds in favour of social assistance arrangements run by municipalities, which have always been more strongly conditional. Taking also into account the increasing workfare obligations for social assistance claimants in both countries (see Chapter 8), one can identify a certain degradation in the 'de-commodifying' power of the 'social-democratic' regimes of Sweden and Denmark.

At the other end of the spectrum, the 'neo-liberal' welfare regimes such as the USA and the UK offer much less generous benefits. They are within the gift of the state, rather than managed or even negotiated by trade unions, and thus more vulnerable to the state's use of benefits to manage, control and discipline the unemployed labour reserve. Workfare, widespread in the USA, is exemplified in the UK by some elements of the New Deal programmes for unemployed people. The USA's workfare model has had a profound influence on European labour market programmes in recent years, although workfare and intensified use of benefit systems to maintain labour discipline and reduce wage pressure have appeared to some degree in all regime types. In later chapters, we examine the reasons for these developments and assess their theorisation as the dawn of the 'workfare state'. Workfarism is becoming the typical form of adjustment of labour market policy in the face of global pressures to reduce labour costs and 'flexibilise' the labour market. However, it is not the only possible response to such pressures, as discussed in Chapter 5.

The decline in 'de-commodification' within Europe has taken two different forms. Social insurance funds have tightened conditions about jobseeker behaviour, deliberately offering less shelter from 'bad' job offers than before. Moreover, fewer people can access them, partly because of changes in insurance contribution rules and length of entitlements, partly because of the increasing 'dualism' of the labour market, with a rising share of temporary jobs and unfavourable part-time contracts. 'Atypical' workers are often excluded both from secure full-time jobs and to varying degrees from social insurance. They fall back on social assistance benefits – means-tested, often stigmatising and often subject to workfare requirements. Thus the degradation of social protection is closely linked to the exclusivity of social insurance, which has given rise to a substantial critique of Esping-Andersen's concepts, with feminists arguing that for women to have benefit rights independently of their male partners is a key dimension of any 'de-commodification' analysis, and others asserting the importance of immigration and settlement policy as influences on the labour market status of migrants.[2]

Within the 'corporatist' regimes, marked differences between benefit systems in the 1990s are now diminishing. Until 2000, France and Belgium had much less 'policing' of claimants' job search than Germany. This reflects, to some degree, the greater involvement of unions in managing social security and their greater influence over conditions for benefit entitlement. France and Belgium also permitted extensive co-receipt of benefits and part-time or casual wages; they had high earnings 'disregards', or 'cumul' as it is called in French. 'Cumul' makes 'bad' jobs more acceptable to unemployed people, although as discussed later it may have some negative effects on wages and conditions. All this has changed in France with the introduction of a more neo-liberal benefits regime in 2001, similar to the UK's Jobseeker's Allowance (JSA), pushed through against sharp union opposition. Recent moves to greater 'activation' and job search testing of Belgian claimants are leading in the same direction. In both UK and German systems not only are job search and job acceptance requirements very strict, but sanctions are now applied vigorously. Germany also has a subsidised low-wage sector to absorb unemployed people into full-time work, in the context of an explicit policy emphasis on using the benefits system to reduce wage pressure. With regard to unemployed people, Germany has in effect split from the 'corporatist' group and joined the UK as a 'hard neo-liberal' or 'workfarist' regime.

STATISTICAL PORTRAITS OF SEVEN COUNTRIES

Table 2.1 presents a selection of different statistical indicators about the performance of the seven countries' economies over the period 1991–2001. Where possible, comparisons are made with the EU average and with the USA. Drawn from several different sources, these data are not always available for all countries or for exactly the desired dates. However, they enable us to gain a general picture of developments in the quantity and quality of employment. The indicators are in five groups: employment/unemployment variables; economic growth; job quality and security including the extent of unionisation; inequality; and gender (in)equality. In each column, the country with the best performance is highlighted in bold type, and the worst country is underlined.

Relating these indicators first of all to the welfare regime typology, we see that the UK scores very badly on inequalities (overall and gender), although job security is fairly good and both macro-economic and employment performance are good. The 'social-democratic' welfare regimes both have very good scores on equalities, including

Table 2.1   Statistical portraits of seven countries

		Belgium	Denmark
A	**Employment and unemployment variables**		
A1	Employment rate 2001	59.9	**76.2**
A2	Employment growth p.a. 1991–2001	0.58	0.57
A3	Unemployment rate 2001	6.6	**4.6**
A4	10-year change in unemployment, % points	0.0	−3.8
A5	Long-term unemployment rate 2001	3.0	**0.9**
A6	10-year change in LTU rate, % points	−1.2	−2.0.
A7	Male non-employment rate 2001	<u>30.9</u>	**19.8**
A8	Female non-employment rate 2001	49.5	**28.0.**
B	**General macro-economic variables**		
B1	GDP per capita, average growth p.a. 1991–2001	1.9	1.8
B2	Growth of labour productivity p.a. 1991–2001	1.6	1.9
B3	State spending as % GDP, average 1989–2000, excluding transfer payments	37.0	38.0
C	**Job quality variables**		
C1	Rank order within EU of % in dead-end jobs (1=least)	2	3.
C2	% in temporary jobs	9.0	9.2
C3	10-year change in share of temporary jobs	3.9	**−2.1**
C4	Rank order within EU of % leaving temporary jobs for permanent within one year	5	9.
C5	% with job tenure less than one year	**13.7**	<u>23.2</u>
C6	Union density	69.0	74.0.
D	**General (in)equality indicators**		
D1	Wage dispersion (P90/P10)	2.8	2.8
D2	Gini coefficient, mid to late 1990s	0.230	0.240
D3	% with usual hours over 45	**3.0**	6.0.
D4	Relative employment rate of low-skilled non-EU nationals	0.64	0.75.
E	**Gender equality indicators**		
E1	Female/male earnings ratio	**92.7**	89.6.
E2	Female/male employment rate	0.7	0.9.
E3	Childcare provision	30.0	48.0

Note: bold indicates the best performing country on a particular variable; <u>underlining</u> indicates the worst.
Variable definitions:
Employment rate 2001: % of 15–64-year-olds in employment
Unemployment rate 2001: ILO definition (available for work and seeking work)
Long-term unemployment rate 2001: those seeking work over one year
Non-employment rate: those not in employment as a percentage of all aged 15–64
Dead-end jobs: see Chapter 6 for a description of this concept
Union density: union members as a proportion of all employees
Wage dispersion (P90/P10): ratio of 90th percentile (the boundary between the top 10% of incomes and those below) to the lowest percentile (the boundary between the bottom 10% of income and those above)

Germany	Spain	France	Sweden	UK	EU15	USA	
65.8	56.3	63.1	71.7	71.7	63.9	74.1	A1
0.08	1.48	0.72	−0.56	1.58	1.31	1.00	A2
8.2	12.3	9.8	6.1	5.3	7.4	4.7	A3
2.6	−4.1	0.3	3.0	−3.5	−0.8	−2.1	A4
3.9	5.1	2.9	1.2	1.3	3.3	n.a.	A5
1.6	−2.8	−0.6	1.0	−1.2	0.1	n.a	A6
27.4	29.1	29.7	29.7	21.7	27.0	n.a.	A7
41.2	58.1	43.9	29.6	34.9	45.1	n.a	A8
1.4	2.4	1.4	1.3	1.8	1.7	2.1	B1
n.a.	1.3	1.3	2.4	1.8	n.a.	1.9	B2
28.0	27.0	32.0	39.0	27.0	n.a.	n.a.	B3
9	13	4	n.a.	8	7.5	n.a	C1
12.4	31.7	14.9	13.5	6.8	13.4	n.a.	C2
2.2	−0.6	4.6	5.4	n.a.	n.a.	n.a.	C3
3	13	12	n.a.	4	8	n.a	C4
14.5	20.9	15.9	15.9	19.5	16.4	n.a.	C5
26.0	17.0	10.0	93.0	30.0	n.a.	n.a	C6
3.2	4.0	3.3	2.6	4.5	n.a.	5.6	D1
0.300	0.306	0.290	0.222	0.346	n.a.	0.375	D2
7.0	8.0	8.0	n.a.	30.0	n.a.	n.a	D3
1.02	1.22	0.82	0.63	0.63	0.91	n.a	D4
80.6	85.7	89.2	n.a.	75.7	83.8	n.a	E1
0.8	0.6	0.8	1.0	0.8	0.8	n.a	E2
50.0	3.0	23.0	33.0	2.0	17.0	n.a.	E3

Gini coefficient: a standard measure of inequality, which ranges from 0 (all income equal) to 100 (all income going to the richest 1%); for an explanation see Atkinson (1983)

Relative employment rate of low-skilled non-EU nationals: their employment rate as a ratio to the overall employment rate

Childcare provision: proportion of under-fives for whom there is a publicly funded place

Sources:

EU Economic Statistics Pocket Book, 2000; Employment in Europe, 1998–2002; OECD, 2001b; Visser, 2002 (for union density); Caminda and Goudsward, 2002 (for Gini coefficients); Lodovici, 2000 (for working hours); Rubery, Smith and Fagan, 1999 (for childcare provision)

gender equality. However here the similarity ends; whereas Denmark has high scores on most indicators, Sweden is still struggling to recover from the crisis of the early 1990s, so that employment has fallen and job security is declining sharply. Sweden nonetheless still has a lower unemployment rate and a much higher employment rate than the EU average. Among the 'corporatist' regimes are found one relatively successful state and three with poorer performance. In Belgium, job quality/job security and equality scores are good, and so is macro-economic performance. Unemployment is lower than the EU average and stable over the decade, although the employment rate is low. However, there is high inactivity; among men this is partly due to voluntary early retirement. The gender pay gap is large, despite relatively extensive childcare provision.

The remaining three countries are less successful in most respects. Germany has high and rising unemployment, poor economic growth, high wage dispersion and quite a lot of low pay, although job security is relatively good. Its star performance on childcare provision relates to the early 1990s when numbers of facilities survived from the old East German regime, but many of these have since closed. The German situation is still dominated by the intractable problems of reunification, which are resistant to the measures to reduce labour costs, as discussed in Chapters 5 and 8. France also has poor employment and macro-economic performance, poor and declining job security, high wage dispersion and only middling gender equality. Spain has the highest unemployment in the EU's present 15 countries, although this situation has at least improved considerably over the 1990s, associated with rapid growth of GDP per capita but low productivity growth. Scores for job quality/security and for inequalities are also very poor.

One of the first puzzles of this statistical story is how to account for the star performance of the Danish economy, compared to the continuing employment difficulties in Sweden, which has a similar welfare regime. It is hard to attribute their difference to the extreme flexibility of Danish labour contracts, much admired by the OECD. The high incidence of temporary jobs in Denmark, associated with relative freedom for employers to fire, is not associated with a high incidence of low pay. Moreover, Denmark is the only EU country in which the share of temporary work has fallen during the 1990s, while in Sweden it has been rising faster than in the other six countries portrayed here. Some commentators (discussed in Chapter 8) have attributed Danish labour market performance to the extensive use of active labour market programmes. But Sweden's pioneering development of such programmes from the 1950s onwards did not save it from economic crisis in the early 1990s, and some problems from that period persist while the use of such programmes in Sweden remains very high. Moreover, it is hard to attribute overall economic success to Danish policies, which are applied to, at most, 3 per cent of the labour force – and, moreover, applied precisely because these jobseekers' potential productivity is thought to be low. The differences in employment performance in these two countries are more rooted in their macro-economic performance. Sweden is more heavily exposed to the pressures of globalisation than Denmark; its manufacturing sector has some very large companies, which have outsourced much of their production to lower-cost countries in recent years (Benner and Bundgaard Vad, 2000; John Gray, 1998), while the Danish economy retains a relatively large share of medium-sized firms rooted firmly in the national economy (Etherington, 1998). Sweden is also said to have made some mistakes in macro-economic management in the early 1990s, which contributed to the currency crisis of 1992. It then entered a phase of public sector cutbacks in order to prepare for entry into the European Union, which undermined the historic source of quality jobs for women, crucial in some interpretations for the success of the Swedish model as a whole (Gould, 1999). Denmark, by contrast, continued with a strong state sector albeit risking high taxes becoming a source of discontent.

A second question is whether the neo-liberal model of minimal labour market regulation, with an emphasis on creating jobs at the low-wage margin, worked better (on the limited experience of these countries at this period) than maintaining strong protection of labour rights. In other words, does an expansion of flexploitation encourage employment growth? This issue is addressed more thoroughly in Chapter 7. The Danish set-up is rather exceptional since job insecurity is not associated with low pay, and is compensated by very high unemployment insurance benefits. The UK shows a neo-liberal route to employment success, in terms of low numbers out of work and rapid employment growth – although this 'success' must be qualified by its unusually large share of sick or disabled people, a point to which we return in Chapter 5. However, the UK's flexibilised labour market, established during the Tory years with trade unions deliberately weakened by legal restrictions, has had a considerable cost in terms of inequality, both between upper and lower labour incomes and between women and men. This has persisted under New Labour, which despite some reregulation and new legal provisions concerning trade union recognition, insists on employers having much more freedom than in most EU states, as described in Chapter 6. The poor gender equality scores in the UK reflect an expansion of low-paid part-time jobs usually taken by women, in the face of historically very poor public childcare provision. Since 1998, with childcare tax credits and new part-time state provision for under-fives, this is improving, but full-time childcare is still expensive and in short supply. The low incidence of formally temporary contracts in the UK is deceptive, for reasons to be discussed in Chapter 7. Moreover, with the proportion of people who actually stay in jobs less than one year almost as high as that of Spain, the UK may be in danger of over-flexibilising its labour market. In France, poor job quality/security and high wage inequality have not secured employment growth; some would argue that growth has been held back by the high minimum wage (at 60 per cent of the full-time median one of the highest in Europe[3]). But if there is an argument about 'excessive' labour costs, it can apply to the top of the income ladder too.

Spain has the misfortune to be the European capital of both unemployment and job insecurity. Employment growth has taken place rapidly in Spain in the last decade, but temporary jobs have fallen only slightly as a share of the total. Because of very tight protections on dismissal and redundancy compensation for permanent workers, which were introduced by Franco's government to try to pre-empt pressure for free trade unions, Spain has been under pressure from employers, the OECD and the EU for some years to relax these protections. Some changes have been made, firstly in the mid-1980s to permit temporary contracts, then to permit agency work in 1994, later to reduce slightly the protections of permanent workers. Until 1995, temporary and 'off-the-books' employment soared as a share of the total as employers sought to avoid restrictions on firing. Very high unemployment emerged in the 1980s associated with the decline of traditional farming, restructuring and shrinkage of the manufacturing sector, and rapid growth of the number of young workers and women entering the labour market. The conjuncture of high unemployment and polarisation of jobs between secure contracts and fixed-term or casual ones forced many young people to alternate between temporary jobs and unemployment for long periods. The transition rate from temporary to permanent work is low. In the 1980s, many temporary jobs were 'training contracts', subsidised to give youth a way into work. But by the late 1990s, most temporary jobs did not offer training, and the OECD, in its recent country surveys of Spain, now takes the view that temporary employment has risen too far, prejudicing employee skills development and productivity growth. Flexploitation in the Spanish case appears to be damaging the prospects for full employment recovery.

Working hours are another source of inequality between people and between countries. In the UK an amazing 30 per cent of employees regularly work over 45 hours per week, compared to a mere 3 per cent in Belgium. Not only is the British 'long hours culture' to the detriment of unemployed people, but with more childcare provision, some of the excess hours of UK full-time workers could be taken by mothers who would no doubt improve their career prospects in the process. The notion of work-sharing has been a key element of centralised bargaining between government, employers and trade unions in Belgium about national pay deals and employment policy (Bastian, 1994). It led in the 1980s to a right to paid educational leave, and in 1997 to an offer of reduced social security contributions for employers in companies that negotiated work-sharing measures. Permitted measures included career breaks, job-sharing, overtime reductions, a shorter working week, educational leave, sabbatical leave and subsidised switching to part-time hours especially for older workers.[4] In France, the 'Loi Aubry' of 1999 instituted a gradual reduction of the working week to 35 hours, with compensating subsidies for employers in order not to cut weekly pay. It created up to 400,000 jobs, although with various negative side-effects. Work-sharing measures have a promising future if well-designed, a point to which we return in Chapter 9.

THE ROLE OF WORKERS' ORGANISATIONS IN THE DEVELOPMENT OF SOCIAL PROTECTION

Trade unions, although wary of state intervention undermining the mutual aid schemes of the nineteenth century, which they themselves controlled, sooner or later welcomed national insurance systems as ways in which employers could be obliged to contribute. Prolonged or large-scale unemployment, such as that of the 1870s in the UK, was more than mutualism could cope with. In Denmark, Sweden and Belgium, social insurance was established because of pressure from the trade union movement, and is still administered through trade unions, although in Belgium their involvement is somewhat less 'hands on' than in the other two countries. In Germany, the

UK and later Spain, the state established social insurance as a way of pre-empting the growth of working-class power; consequently its management was kept in government hands. In France, social insurance developed gradually from individual occupational schemes jointly managed by employers and unions. Not till 1967 were these brought together under one administrative umbrella, a joint employer/trade union board known as UNEDIC, which negotiates social insurance arrangements between unions and MEDEF, the French employers' organisation, at national level.

Contributions to unemployment insurance funds are seen by trade unions as an extension of the wage, since both employers and employees pay for them (with varying degrees of state subsidy) conveying the right to refuse an 'unsuitable' job and the collective power to defend labour standards against their erosion under pressure from high unemployment. Where unions are involved in managing social insurance they have tended to place unemployed benefits relatively high on their bargaining agenda in national 'deals' with the employers. Large union federations with accepted power to negotiate over social insurance and other benefits have had a major influence on how the state treats benefit claimants. They have also been influential on the form of rights at work given by law, which are of most interest to the ex-unemployed and others (especially carers) in a weak bargaining position. The most notable example of this is Sweden, where a single trade union federation, working with and through a social-democratic government for most of the period, made striking gains in terms of welfare provision and workers' rights from the 1930s to the mid-1980s. Union pressure secured a reversal of the cuts in Swedish unemployment benefit introduced in 1996. In Denmark, centralised bargaining arrangements have kept unemployed people high up on the agenda, not least because people must be union members to gain access to union-managed unemployment insurance funds, providing a strong motive for them to join and – if unemployed – to remain members. Nonetheless Danish unions have accepted some elements of workfare for youth with little or no work experience as well as for social assistance claimants, as we shall see in Chapter 8. In Belgium, relatively centralised bargaining has led to continual 'trading' of wage restraint against policies for job creation and for working time reduction intended partly for that end; and also to a system of unemployment insurance that until recently had relatively 'slack' conditions, as described in Chapter 5. In France, the benefit reform of 2001 was highly conflictual; negotiations between

MEDEF, the employers' confederation, and the unions broke down for a while over the changes MEDEF demanded, resulting eventually in a weaker version of the reform than the employers had wanted.

Tripartite arrangements for labour market management may help the state to impose wage restraint, sometimes by offering concessions in terms of policies to reduce unemployment or raise benefits; or they may enable a united trade union movement to push through gains. There is a need to distinguish the different political character of 'social pacts' designed to promote wage restraint and other centralised negotiations that help the labour movement to increase its bargaining power, not only over wage levels but over the social wage and the nature of labour market regulation. Centralised collective bargaining is often advocated by those who see 'wage restraint' as a policy goal, as a system that induces 'moderation' of wage demands. This is because it provides a central forum for negotiation under government pressure. It avoids 'leapfrogging' – the process by which workers in a strong bargaining position seek an even larger pay rise than the last percentage figure to hit the news – and substitutes a unified negotiated settlement for a wide range of sectors and situations. The Swedish system exemplified 'solidaristic' wage policies, in which trade unions sought equal pay for equal work across a whole occupational group regardless of employers' differing performance. Standardised wage rates across all employers encouraged expansion by high productivity companies but penalised low productivity companies, leading to higher productivity overall. While by the late 1980s this system had become a vehicle for wage restraint (Stephens, 2001), over most of the 1960s to the 1980s it was a vehicle both for raising both wage growth and the 'social wage'. The employers' organisation eventually felt it was losing from the system, withdrawing from centralised bargaining arrangements in 1990–91.

Even in those continental countries where trade unions are not involved in running social insurance, they expect to be consulted on proposed changes. Examples are the Toledo Pact about pension reform in Spain, in the early 1990s, and the involvement of German union representatives in the Hartz Commission, set up in 2001 to design reforms of unemployed benefits. Agitation outside of partnership or consultation arrangements has also played a key role in France and Spain in recent years. The benefit reforms of 2001–03 in France met with widespread demonstrations from the radical union SUD and from unemployed people's organisations. Spanish trade unions and social movements fought through demonstrations and strikes to reverse the benefit cuts and tighter conditionality, which the government sought to impose in 2002, and secured abandonment of most of the changes proposed.

'Social dialogue' between unions, the state and employers is the European norm; its weakness in the UK a remarkable exception. What is striking is the generalised expectation, in continental Europe, that trade unions are important players in decisions about benefits policy and the management of unemployment, while this expectation is almost absent from the British political landscape. Margaret Thatcher's anti-trade union laws and the exclusion of unions from governance led to their political emasculation; since 1997 little has been done to reverse this. Now that the tripartite or 'corporatist' institutions of the 1970s have passed into oblivion, unions' influence over the social wage is weak and is located in their decaying links with the Labour Party rather than any national negotiating framework. Thus collective representation by the trade union movement on behalf of the unwaged is conspicuous mainly by its absence. However, the damage may have begun before Thatcherism, with the assumption at the heart of the Beveridge system that the state will take care of the unwaged, who are constructed as the mere objects of social policy, people attached to no social 'constituency' that has, or needs to have, a voice.

THE ORIGINS OF THE WELFARE STATE

The interaction between class struggle over social insurance and ruling class strategies is best understood in historical perspective, looking at the interplay of government, trade unions and employers in shaping the systems that existed by the late twentieth century. Social protection developed partly, but only partly, in response to working-class demands. At various stages in the history of welfare states, the ruling class has had its own motives for introducing poor relief, social insurance, public medical services or regulation of labour contracts. The evolution of social protection has been driven, at different times and places, either by the desire to pre-empt revolt and dissent or a need to mould, mobilise, preserve or develop the labour supply. Mingled with these motives is a thread of genuine concern to alleviate the suffering caused by poverty. The line-up of class forces is complex, since the cause of the poor has often been taken up by middle-class reformers, while trade unions have sometimes opposed state intervention for fear it would undermine their own bargaining role or the support systems they had developed for their members.

According to Marxist theories of the welfare state, welfare performs various *functions* for capital. Without endorsing its determinism, this notion is crucial both for an understanding of the early development of social protection, and for an analysis of how capital may seek to remould the welfare state in the era of globalisation. James O'Connor (1973) argued that the capitalist state must perform functions of accumulation and legitimisation. That is, capitalists will sometimes see a 'business case' for welfare, but states will also use it to court votes or head off discontent. The idea of 'legitimisation' in O'Connor's work enables this conceptual framework to embrace the class struggle. However, O'Connor left himself open to criticism for his 'functionalism'. As Mishra (1977) argues, functional 'needs' of the 'system' are confused with demands from particular political groups. Gough (1979) moved away from O'Connor's functionalism by emphasising that the scale of welfare expenditures is the outcome of working-class struggle for a 'social wage'.

O'Connor argues that some social expenditures, such as health and education, increase productivity; today one might include training for unemployed people or other measures to preserve their 'employability'. Others, such as social insurance or child benefits, O'Connor says, reduce the 'reproduction cost' of labour. The second point is more controversial. We discuss in Chapter 3 a widely held view that high social insurance contributions add to labour costs, and in Chapter 5 argue that some transfer payments (such as tax credits) enable the beneficiaries' employers to pay less. It depends who really bears the cost of the benefits. A third function of social spending is 'legitimisation' of the capitalist order by maintaining social harmony and exercising social control. The conditions attached to unwaged benefits have generally had a 'social control' aspect, intended to drive jobseekers into work (Ginsberg, 1978), although their main rationale is to avert social unrest by limiting poverty.

Some key developments of the nineteenth century and earlier can be illustrated from the history of the UK and Germany, the oldest industrial states. In the UK, the desire to impose labour discipline dominated the form of poor relief from the sixteenth century until the Napoleonic wars. Henry VIII's poor laws permitted vagrancy to be punished by enslavement (Fraser, 1973). The aim was to discourage workers from leaving their parish of origin, so that landed estates would not lose their labour supply to the growing towns. Under the

Elizabethan Poor Laws, persons considered 'idle' could be imprisoned and set to work in 'houses of correction'. Workhouses served as a deterrent to remaining without work, and thus as an incentive for labourers to accept whatever wage was offered without much argument (Ginsberg, 1978). By the eighteenth century, workhouses had become widespread and were seen by a number of employers as a source of profit from cheap labour (Linebaugh, 1991). In both ways, they were a precursor of twentieth-century workfare.

Eighteenth-century practice was to limit 'outdoor relief' – the provision of cash allowances outside the workhouse – to those who could not work: for widows, orphans, the sick and aged. However, during the Napoleonic wars, the rise in the price of bread extended acute poverty even to labourers who had work (Bruce, 1961). The Poor Law Guardians in the village of Speenhamland, in Berkshire, broke with tradition and used cash allowances to guarantee a basic subsistence allowance to the poor, whether or not they were working. This system became a widespread model for other areas. Unscrupulous employers took advantage of the public subsidy to their labour costs to freeze or even reduce wages, increasing the system's cost and provoking unrest (Bruce, 1961; Polanyi, 1957). The 1834 Poor Law reform abolished the Speenhamland system as unworkable, and workhouses once more regained their importance as a punitive device to deter idleness and control dependency on public funds (Ginsberg, 1978). However, the workhouse system was not sufficient in periods of mass unemployment, once industrial business cycles became a major force in the economy. Fear of riots then became a factor in the decision, in the 1880s, to introduce relief work outside the workhouse in exchange for assistance (Ginsberg, 1978). It was deliberately low-paid, so as not to become too attractive (Bruce, 1961).

The first state to introduce health insurance (Bismarck's Germany) did so not as a result of mass democratic pressure, but rather in an attempt to pre-empt the growth of working-class organisations (Esping-Andersen, 1990). The German government feared revolution: the Paris Commune of 1870 was too close to home. Sickness and accident insurance was widely supported by German employers in the development of Bismarck's proposals of the 1880s, as long as the cost fell on general taxation or the workers themselves. Hence industrialists initially opposed Bismarck's proposal for an employer contribution to a state scheme. Bismarck's government, however, insisted on employers' contributions; it was important to draw workers away from their own mutual aid societies, which Bismarck saw as an important power base for the workers' movement. Universal social insurance part-financed by employers would take this power base away. Similarly, in the UK, Lloyd George's Liberal government sought to deter the growth of a rival socialist party by taking initial steps to establish the national insurance system (Fraser, 1973). More recently, the Spanish system of social insurance, like Spain's system of labour market regulation, emerged from the Franco government's desire to prevent a resurgence of the workers' movement.

The more far-sighted employers in the nineteenth century were conscious of the need to preserve the working capacity of the labour force; they did not want 'free riders' among their own number. Thus some German employers, prior to Bismarck's insurance initiative, had already introduced their own systems of accident insurance. Generalisation of these systems prevented employers without insurance provisions from undercutting those who had. Likewise, British employers who took advantage of the wage subsidies available through the Speenhamland poor relief system were criticised by others who were thus forced to contribute more to the poor rates. A 'race to the bottom' in terms of labour standards adversely affects productivity and attracts worker resistance; hence UK employers could see a 'business case' for restricting the working day in the 1830s (Fraser, 1973) and for introducing Trade Boards (the predecessors of wages councils) in 1909 to fix minimum rates of pay (Hunter and Robertson, 1969). The movement for the early Factory Acts of the 1830s (Fraser, 1973) was promoted not so much by workers themselves as by certain of the employer class. Thus the concern about 'social dumping' in the EU today has historical precedents.

In Belgium mutual aid schemes developed by workers' organisations in the late nineteenth century provided the springboard for the development of social security. These were also present, but to a lesser extent and with less lasting influence, in France, the UK and Germany. Mutual aid tended not to include lower-paid workers; like any insurance system, it excluded those with high risks. Belgian mutual aid societies negotiated state support from the1880s, when mass unemployment made their work unsustainable without it. French social security developed as a hybrid of a state system modelled on Bismarck's and a number of separate mutual aid schemes for better-paid workers. While these covered sickness and pensions, there was no unemployment insurance until 1958. The present national scheme was set up in 1967 through a partnership between unions and employers' associations (Birks, 1987). Alongside insurance, means-tested social assistance under a number of separate benefits for lone parents and disabled people developed in the 1970s, while a residual poor law also survived, so that an unusually high share of social expenditure was still means-tested in 1980 (Esping-Andersen, 1990). The RMI, from 1988, complemented these separate schemes by providing a general all-purpose non-insurance-based benefit.

In Denmark, the motive force for welfare state development was the labour movement. Danish trade unions demanded, and won, the establishment of a social insurance system in 1901. From the 1980s it was financed entirely from general taxation. In Sweden, comprehensive social insurance and policies to support full employment were developed by the Social Democratic Party, which remained in power continuously from 1932 to 1976.

To sum up, the widespread development of social insurance in western economies over the period from the 1880s to the 1930s was a project that attracted class consensus. The 'business case' for it, supported by governments even when not led by working-class parties, was that it 'bought off' discontent and offloaded some of the costs of existing provision, especially workplace accident insurance, from employers to the state and the workers themselves. Employers had previously had to support some form of poor relief, and national social insurance schemes meant that there were no 'free riders' among the employer class.

During the last quarter of the twentieth century, strong international forces began to affect policy choices of individual national governments. Globalisation threatens to undermine welfare provisions and national labour market policies, making it more difficult, in various ways, for trade unions and working-class parties to defend previous gains. Can we identify a 'baseline' of minimal provision to which welfare systems might fall in the absence of working-class resistance? If welfare is stripped down to the minimum for which there is now a 'business case', what would it look like?

It is no surprise that as social protection has come under various pressures from macro-economic and international forces in recent years, those systems that have a strong labour movement influence embedded in their institutional structures have resisted better than those that have not. The British system of social security has fared particularly badly, perhaps reflecting the relative lack of union influence in British social policy. Germany, where historic union power has been challenged by the reunification crisis, has also seen considerable erosion of benefit rights, while Sweden, still a bastion of trade union strength despite the welfare state crisis of the early 1990s, has stood relatively firm against the threats from fiscal tensions and neo-liberal influences. Benefit systems in France, Denmark and Belgium have all survived better than in the UK. Chapter 5 is the story of that process. But first, we consider how the welfare state has been affected by globalisation and by the development of the European Union.

3

Globalisation, Welfare and Labour

GLOBALISATION – A THREAT TO SOCIAL PROTECTION?

The period since the mid-1970s has seen a much faster expansion of international trade than of output across the OECD. This includes a considerable transfer of industrial production from Europe and the USA to newly industrialising countries (Went, 2000). Assisted by the increased speed of modern transport, companies based in Europe or the USA can now 'outsource' production to the other side of the world without having to keep huge warehouse stocks. The development of telecommunications and electronic data transfer enables operations such as data processing or even call centres to be 'outsourced' as well.

As companies become able to transfer production to any part of the world, they take less interest in the future of the labour force in any particular country. The landowners of Berkshire or the mill-owners of Manchester in the early nineteenth century had an interest in seeing that the community from which they drew their labour force did not starve – or it would not be there next year – and was not moved to rioting, or their property would be at risk. The more far-sighted industrialists in the period of a more nationally rooted capitalism saw some merit in regulation of working hours, to prevent cut-throat competition based on the lengthening of the working day from which all employers would eventually lose through workers' revolt or ill health. Later in the nineteenth and early twentieth centuries, employers across Europe gradually came to accept social security contributions towards workers' sickness and accident insurance, and in Germany several large employers set up their own schemes before the state began to intervene. But the attitude of internationally mobile employers is one of 'regime shopping' – to relocate or subcontract to wherever wages, taxes and social security charges are least. They do not necessarily have a business case for supporting social expenditures for any particular national labour force.

During the 1990s there has been widespread academic debate about the consequences of capitalist globalisation for the welfare state. At issue is the effect of potential 'regime shopping' on labour standards and on ways of financing welfare, and reduced effectiveness of fiscal and monetary policies in the face of greater international money flows. Although the internationalisation of capital, as many Marxists have recognised, started in the late nineteenth century, a distinctive feature of globalisation is the mobility of production. There is also a new 'internationalisation' of policy that supports the accelerated internationalisation of capital, and is fed by company political lobbying. Strange (1997) suggests that globalisation seriously reduces the policy autonomy of the nation state. Supranational organisations – the IMF, the OECD, the World Bank, the WTO and to some extent the European Union – have all gained greater influence over national governments and have promoted policies of deregulation of labour (and other) markets, reduced fiscal and other legal obligations for companies.

Globalisation has generated a more difficult environment in which to maintain the apparent gains, in terms of levels of social protection and worker-friendly full employment policies, of the 'golden age' of Keynesianism in the thirty or so years following the Second World War. According to Went (2000, p. 108), 'advancing globalisation will make its negative effects sharper and sharper ... [with] progressive levelling down of wages, working conditions and social security; ... a greater role for unaccountable international institutions and a further undermining of democracy'. Guy Standing (1999) also emphasises the effects of globalisation on labour standards; the heightened pressure to reduce labour costs and tax burdens in an international arena has eroded wage levels, fringe benefits and job security. John Gray (1998) argues that global markets apply pressure to externalise costs from the company that a well-managed market should internalise, and that the reduced fiscal capacity of the state threatens to make social democracy unworkable.

What we can call, for short, the 'Globalisation Against Social Protection' hypothesis (GASP) has several different parts. In summary, the threats suggested by various different contributors to this debate are as follows:

1. **Higher unemployment**: globalisation involves companies becoming more mobile, and more ready to move plants around or switch their suppliers to take advantage of lower costs abroad. Jobs then become more insecure and the individual risk of becoming unemployed rises (Euzéby and Chapon, 2002). Frequent restructuring of industry leads to generally higher unemployment

rates. The state has to maintain unemployed people, but it is difficult to pass back this cost to employers by raising their social security contributions without reducing their willingness to invest in the country.

2. **Declining job quality**: states will compete with each other to attract investment by having low labour costs; this affects the sustainability of high wage levels, of high employers' contributions to social security funds, of minimum wage regulations, job security and pro-worker regulations about working hours.

3. **Reduced capacity to maintain full employment**: the scale and unpredictability of international capital movements reduces the effectiveness of traditional Keynesian policy instruments. Keynes himself predicted that the internationalisation of finance capital would undermine the ability of national governments to maintain full employment (John Gray, 1998, p. 78). The Maastricht Treaty involves additional constraints on traditional Keynesian policies, to be discussed in Chapter 4. This throws the responsibility for reducing unemployment more on unemployed people themselves. Workfare, other mandatory 'welfare to work' measures and stricter benefit conditions are used to push them to accept low-paid jobs offered by employers on the open market. Whereas Keynesian employment programmes tended to use public funds to create jobs in hard times, those of the globalised era focus on the idea that private employers will hire more people if they can do so cheaply enough.

4. **Reduced capacity to tax capital**: globalisation heightens the risk of countries competing for investment by having low taxes on profits. Governments may raise higher taxes on wages or consumer expenditure to compensate, but voters' limited tolerance of this shift may mean difficulty in financing social expenditure at the same per capita level as before.

Each of these factors is a problem or pressure, but whether they manifest themselves in policy change depends on a political process. Herman Schwartz (2001) rejects fatalistic perspectives on globalisation, and warns us to beware of arguments that 'lack a causal mechanism' (p. 19) or which 'substitute functional necessities for welfare state change or contraction [maintaining that] political actors are driven to retrench the welfare state regardless of preferences'. John Clarke (2001) rejects the crude 'apocalyptic' view of globalisation, which he regards as 'crude economic determinisim'. In his view, there is a need to recognise globalisation as a discourse or an ideology; but it becomes more than just a discourse, because discourses become embedded in the practice of policy-makers.

Globalisation, job loss and job quality

The risk of higher unemployment goes beyond the once-off shift of manufacturing production to newly industrialising countries, which was a feature of the 1980s. The greatest threat posed by globalisation to jobs is not about the shift of industry away from Europe but the change in the way industrial location decisions are made and the advent of a form of capitalism much less attached to particular countries, to their communities and institutions. However, not all European countries are affected by this to the same degree. David Etherington (1998) notes that Denmark has benefited from a relative absence of powerful corporate giants; most of its economy is characterised by medium and small-sized national companies with whom the state and trade unions can negotiate more easily than with multinationals. Sweden, on the other hand, suffered considerable pressure in the late 1980s from a small number of large firms who had come to dominate the export sectors of the economy, employing more people outside Sweden than within the country (Benner and Bundgaard Vad, 2000).

The increasing power of multinational corporations makes local economic landscapes more volatile and jobs more insecure than before. Their ability to decide, at a few months' notice, that they will redistribute their activities between plants in different countries gives these companies much more bargaining power, over trade unions and over governments. John Gray (1998, p. 97) gives an example of how working-class gains in Germany are being eroded by the way in which large companies threaten to take jobs to other countries if concessions are not made. Under pressure that Osram, the electrical manufacturer, would relocate, trade unions agreed to increased flexibility of shift working patterns, jeopardising the short working week that had previously been negotiated. Conversely, employer-friendly labour regulations are rewarded with jobs: Hoover moved back to the UK when John Major refused to sign up to the 'Social Chapter' of the Maastricht Treaty (Garrett, 2000).

More than ever before, jobs come to low-cost people and low-cost locations. Knowing this, government agencies bend over backwards to woo the 'inward investor' or retain the large companies they have on their territory in order to avoid mass unemployment. Offers of road building, low-cost factory sites, training packages for new workers, and regional aid subsidies became common bargaining counters as regional and local governments sought to keep and attract employers in the high-unemployment days of the 1980s. Standing (1999) mentions that in 1997 Volkswagen was offered over £100,000 in subsidies and other benefits for each one of 2,300 jobs created in Germany, and a South Korean company received £30,000 per job to set up a semiconductor plant in Wales. It is not uncommon for large firms to go 'subsidy shopping' to see which area or which country will offer them most. For example, in the early 1990s Ford-Volkswagen was considering Setubal in Portugal together with the UK and Ireland as alternative sites for new production facilities. Each government offered extensive subsidies (in the Portuguese case partly based on European regional aid funds).

Companies involved in globalised production have placed actual or implied pressure on governments and workers to make labour costs cheaper; to accept less secure jobs and working time changes as well as slower wage growth. Globalisation thus induces 'regulatory competition' between states to reduce labour standards. Out of the apparent imperatives of globalisation comes a drive for wage restraint. The OECD, IMF and the EC all advocate policies of containment of wage growth as a way of maintaining competitiveness. 'Flexibilisation' of labour markets, with greater ease for employers to terminate employment contracts or impose non-standard working hours patterns, has also become the orthodox policy prescription in the face of globalisation. As we shall see in Chapter 6, flexibilisation tends to create a stock of second-class jobs with less security, worse conditions and poorer union organisation. Keeping workers docile and labour costs low is a strategy adopted by many countries to attract foreign investment. In more extreme cases, some newly industrialised countries have brutally repressed trade union activity and restricted trade union rights (Standing, 1999, p. 76). This clearly encourages multinationals with a presence in Europe to outsource production to low-cost economies or even to relocate facilities there. European governments have responded to the pressure of this type of competition by seeking to 'deregulate' labour markets – in other words, to reduce some of employers' legal obligations in the interests of gaining or keeping jobs, while tightening regulations on other aspects of employment contracts. It is a complex picture to which we return in Chapter 7.

Globalisation and the decline of Keynesian policies

The 1980s saw the gradual demise of Keynesian macro-economic policy, with its commitment to maintain full employment by management of demand for labour. Governments from the late 1970s onwards found it increasingly difficult to manage the economy through the typical Keynesian 'toolkit' of fiscal and monetary policy. Inflation had a tendency to accelerate; the hike in oil prices from 1973 produced a sequence of price increases and compensatory wage demands. Greater freedom of capital movements led to another problem for the Keynesian policy 'toolkit': with companies free to borrow and invest across frontiers, it became harder for governments or central banks to influence the interest rates at which they did so. In a trade and monetary regime without controls on international capital movements, and with floating or more frequently changed exchange rates, state spending had to be carefully constrained lest a threat of accelerating inflation led to a fall in the value of the currency and to capital flight. Sweden's high state spending led to a crisis of this form in the late 1980s, when fear of devaluation made bond markets increasingly reluctant to lend to a government accused of spending beyond the country's means in a period of recession. Not till the government had devalued and made severe welfare cuts did the markets' confidence in the value of the kroner return.

Gradually the Keynesian 'toolkit' was set aside in favour of 'supply side' economics – the notion that employment will grow if labour is sufficiently attractive to employers in terms of its cost, skill and flexibility. Inflation, in the supply side model, is addressed through management of the money supply, and if controlling inflation leads to higher unemployment, this must be addressed through the supply side of the labour market. Whereas traditional Keynesian policy – and indeed Keynes himself – took it for granted that real wages would hardly ever fall, because of political and trade union resistance, supply side economics envisages that 'wage flexibility' may be needed. By the early 1990s, this view was enshrined as current orthodoxy in documents of the OECD, which reflects the consensus view of western governments on the style of economic management to be adopted. Labour market flexibilisation, as we shall see in the next chapter, became a major economic policy goal of EU member states. Keynesianism in one country was always difficult, but globalisation made it more so (Esping-Andersen, 1996b, pp. 256–7). This is a particularly serious consequence of globalisation for unemployed people, because it impedes the use of public investment to reduce unemployment while sustaining wage levels. Instead it drives the state towards 'supply side' policies for curing unemployment, which essentially operate by using the 'reserve army of labour' to hold down wages until the labour market clears.

If globalisation has impeded Keynesian policies, so also has the chosen form of European integration; but other forms could have been chosen. The Maastricht convergence criteria, with limits on state borrowing and government debt, and determination of interest rates left to the European Central Bank, more or less amount to a self-denying ordinance against Keynesian macro-economic policy.[1] This, if nothing else, drives European governments towards supply side solutions and the flexibilisation of labour markets. The convergence criteria are currently (November 2003) being breached by two of the EU's largest economies, France and Germany, and political pressure may build to change them. Keynesian policies should in fact be made easier by European integration were it not for a commitment to neo-liberalism. There is no reason why deficit financing should not be used on a European scale, taking advantage of the euro's now established role as a world currency. But deficit financing is not the only casualty of the self-denying ordinance; Maastricht also sets limits on the growth of government spending, even if tax-financed. It thus forces member states to forgo one of the key policies in the Swedish success story of the 1980s: a large state service sector, creating quality jobs especially for women and providing support for them to stay in paid work through their childrearing years. This contributed to a very high employment rate and low wage inequality.

Most EU member states have found it difficult to meet the Maastricht requirement that government debt should not be more than 60 per cent of GDP. While it is a widespread view that the Maastricht ceiling may have been set unreasonably low, there are no simple criteria for setting any particular ceiling – the 'prudent' level of debt depends partly on tolerance of inflation, partly on interest rates and the way government borrowing affects the cost of loans to the private sector, and partly on the financial markets' confidence in the state's ability to service and repay the debt.

Globalisation, taxes and social expenditure

Were the changes in benefits systems seen in the 1990s simply due to budget constraints? Higher unemployment in the last two decades certainly involved a larger bill for benefits and reinsertion programmes, with a slower rise in tax revenues to meet it. But unemployment contributed rather less to rising state costs than the growing ratio of retired people to those of working age, while both were more than offset by the fall in the number of children needing education. Table 3.1 shows that during the period 1970–93, the proportion of children in the OECD countries' population fell by 12.3 percentage points, while the proportion of elderly rose by 3.2 points and of non-employed persons aged 15–64 by 1.2 points. However, it is frequently argued that the capacity of welfare states to raise taxes in order to meet new needs was limited by the changed environment of globalisation. High spending on healthcare, pensions and other benefits involves higher taxes on wages and salaries (encouraging political resistance or large wage demands); or it needs higher taxes on capital, including employers' social security charges. These responses affect profits, with the risk that capital will go elsewhere.

Table 3.1   Trends in dependency ratios

	Dependent age groups as % of population of working age							Non-employed persons as % of all aged 15–64	
	Under-15s and over-64s			Over-64s only		Under-15s only			
	1960	1970	1992–3	1970	1992–3	1970	1993	1970	1993
Germany	47.5	57.1	45.7	20.7	21.9	36.4	23.8	30.9	34.0
France	61.3	60.5	52.6	20.7	22.0	39.8	30.6	33.9	41.0
UK	54.0	59.1	54.0	20.7	24.3	38.4	29.7	29.2	32.9
Belgium	55.0	52.4	50.3	21.3	23.0	31.1	27.3	39.2	43.1
Denmark	55.8	55.2	48.2	19.0	23.0	36.2	25.2	25.6	26.1
Spain	55.1	60.0	47.3	15.2	21.1	44.8	26.2	38.9	54.3
Sweden	51.8	52.7	56.9	20.9	21.2	31.8	35.7	26.8	28.8
OECD average	59.5	59.7	50.6	17.0	20.2	42.7	30.4	33.9	35.1

Source: adapted from OECD (2001b), p. 16 and OECD (1998), p. 37

Reduced capacity to tax and spend

The last point of the 'GASP' hypothesis, concerning reduced capacity to tax and spend on the welfare state, can be tested by looking at trends in four key variables: social expenditures; total government expenditure; social security taxes; and public debt.

Trends in social expenditures

If there is a tendency for welfare states to reduce their social expenditure in order for national economies to compete on labour costs, one would expect these expenditures to converge over time, probably towards a lower level, although some states with low labour costs might have a chance to improve their provisions. Alber and Standing (2000) considered trends in social expenditure for all the countries in the world with available data for 1980 and 1992, 38 in all. Introducing a large number of countries, including several developing countries, enabled them to control for the fact that social spending as a proportion of GDP generally rises with GDP in the long term. Between 1980 and 1992 the average ratio of social spending to GDP in these 38 countries rose. Overall, the countries became more different in this key ratio rather than more alike. However, the group of wealthy European countries with the world's highest welfare expenditures in 1980 did show a slowing up of the rate of growth of these expenditures; by 1992 they came closer to the 'trend line' expected for their GDP levels. This group included Denmark, the Netherlands, France, Belgium, West Germany, Austria and Luxembourg. Sweden remained the world's highest welfare spender (in relation to GDP), and actually raised its ratio from 1980 to 1992 (but this may be misleading, since there were severe cuts just after Alber and Standing's data series stop). Finland had only an average ratio in 1980, but became the world's second highest by 1992. The UK remained close to the average at both dates. Among the high-income countries with much lower social spending than expected in relation to their GDP levels, the USA, Canada, Australia, Japan and Switzerland remained among the world's lowest at both dates, while New Zealand moved closer to the 'trend line'.

These trends do suggest some pressure from some factor, possibly globalisation, on the highest social spenders, especially where benefits are financed from social security taxes. But several other factors also affect the trends being discussed here, including the level of unemployment, and changes in the economic growth rate. GDP growth tends to slow up when unemployment is high, leading to increased welfare costs in relation to GDP. Moreover, another and more up-to-date source shows that within the EU, the twelve countries that were members in 1980 show a large increase in social expenditure *per capita* between 1980 and 1997 (Guillén and Alvarez, 2002, p. 71).

Total government expenditure

Looking at trends in *total* government expenditure – and over the period up to 2000 – globalisation pressures do not seem to have provided a justification for cutting expenditures on unemployment.

Government expenditure as a share of GDP rose in almost all OECD countries over the period 1973–2000 as a whole; although most cut back slightly in the 1990s, this was partly owing to lower interest rates on government debt. Total social benefits as a proportion of GDP also rose over the whole period, although in the 1990s only they did fall in three countries (Belgium, the Netherlands and Spain).[2] The main reason for this was the rise in the elderly population, hence higher pension expenditure despite some attempts to restrict access to early retirement. The reduction of benefit entitlements for unemployed people in many European states, which will be described in Chapter 5, has been mostly the result of policy choices. Falling unemployment from the mid-1990s was associated with falling benefit payments per unemployed person, but this took place within the context of rising public expenditure overall.

Social security taxes

The effect of tax burdens on the race between countries to retain employment should not be exaggerated; they are only one of several cost factors that companies take into account in their investment decisions. However, employers' social security contributions, which impact directly and very obviously on labour costs, do appear to be an issue in a 'globalised' environment; it is said that they have contributed to the relatively slow growth of employment in Europe compared to the USA (Esping-Andersen, 1996b). Consequently one would expect a tendency over time for high social security taxes to be reduced in response to international pressures. A few countries did reduce employers' contributions – but substantial reductions occurred in only six out of 22 countries for which the OECD provides data for 1983–94.[3] These were Belgium, Denmark, Finland, the Netherlands, Norway and Sweden. Only in Sweden was the sharp reduction in employer contribution levels associated with major cuts in welfare expenditures; but some of these cuts were restored later in the 1990s.

However, it does seem to be true that where social security taxes are high, the quality of jobs suffers. Employers take advantage of concessions for part-time or temporary staff and self-employed subcontractors, creating a series of second-class jobs with lower non-wage costs but no insurance rights, which often fall to the lot of young people and women. High social security taxes, combined with at least partial exemptions for 'atypical' jobs, encourage employers to create a two-tier labour market. It is the full-time, permanent jobs, with their high associated burden of non-wage costs, that are most at risk from international competitive pressures. Some corporatist welfare states have especially high social security taxes for employers – an average of 34.8 per cent on top of wages in Belgium, 46 per cent in France and 19.4 per cent in Germany, compared to just over 10 per cent in the UK and zero in Denmark, where much of the benefits bill is financed from general taxation.[4]

Government debt

There is little evidence of convergence between welfare states to a lower 'norm' of the level of social spending owing to international pressures (Paul Pierson, 2001). Public expenditure as a whole continues to rise, and governments have room for choice between benefits, public services and other expenditures. Government borrowing has increased, but since there is no clear defence of any particular limit to the scale of public debt, this can be used either as an argument that cuts are now necessary or that the welfare state has managed to survive and can continue to do so.

However, the rising trend of social expenditures generates political tension around the acceptable levels of government borrowing and taxation, as well as budget priorities. Government expenditure across the OECD rose faster than the tax take throughout the period 1970–94,[5] resulting in rising levels of public debt.[6] In the view of the EC, rising costs of social protection during the 1990s show that entitlements and demands on resources are becoming too large, threatening to become an inflationary force. Governments are enjoined to contain and avoid them by, for example, active labour market measures to reduce unemployment. The main constraint imposed on social protection budgets by international competitive pressures concerns social security taxes, which directly affect labour costs. However, the Danish example shows how high levels of benefits can be financed largely from other taxes. In general, the case that globalisation forces the state to reduce social spending is weak, given considerable international variations in the ratio of social spending to GDP.

Theories of fiscal crisis

Several writers in the globalisation debate take up the issue of fiscal crisis, pointing out that while globalisation may make it worse, the problem is a long-standing one, which emerges from several nationally based causes (Christopher Pierson, 1991; Paul Pierson, 2001; Scharpf and Schmidt, 2000). There is a widespread perception that the 'welfare state' form of capitalism entered a crisis phase from the 1970s onwards. Concern about this antedates the globalisation debate, which did not emerge in academic literature until the early 1990s.

From the late 1960s, there were signs that demands on the welfare state were becoming too great for its capacity to raise funds. Thus the 'fiscal crisis of the welfare state' had as much internal as international causes. Marxist analyses of this crisis (O'Connor, 1973; Gough, 1979) focused on the falling rate of profit. They drew attention to the conflict between rising demands for the services and transfers that form the 'social wage' and the narrowing margin of surplus value that could be demanded from employers to pay for it. During the 1970s the average rate of profit fell in most European countries. According to the 'fiscal crisis' argument, this gave governments less scope for raising taxes on profits to finance welfare services or benefits. At the same time, voters showed dissatisfaction with high rates of income tax. In the strong bargaining conditions that still prevailed in the late 1970s, any increase of taxes on employees could possibly have been passed on as wage demands, leading back to the profit problem.

The same theme was taken up from a non-Marxist standpoint by Ramesh Mishra (1984). Social trends of the 1970s raised fears that without enormous tax rises, welfare budgets would be unable to expand to meet all the demands placed upon them. There were rising expectations about the extent and quality of public services, as well as a larger number of unemployed and elderly. More mothers were entering the labour force, leading to rising demand for childcare provision. Rising divorce rates in most European countries created many more lone parents, in need of benefits, childcare or both. However, by the late 1980s theories of crisis had taken back stage in the literature of comparative social policy (Christopher Pierson, 1991); somehow, the welfare state carried on albeit with reduced provision in several fields. 'Fight the cuts' was a constant battle-cry of the left in Tory Britain, from 1979 to 1997. Similar struggles also occurred in several other European countries as well. For example the mid-1990s saw massive protests about pension provision in Germany (Taylor-Gooby, 2001), France and Italy and about cuts or tougher conditions in unemployment benefits in France, Spain, Belgium and Sweden.

Provision for an ageing society has recently been the focus of new concerns about welfare state finance. Population ageing is expected to add an average of 3.9 per cent of GDP to the cost of pensions and a further 1.7 per cent of GDP to the cost of healthcare in OECD countries between 2000 and 2030 (Paul Pierson, 2001). However, the increased ratio of elderly to workers was offset in several European countries during the 1970s to 1990s by a fall in the ratio of children to working age people, as shown in Table 3.1. The 'ageing society' threatens the finances of the welfare state less in the short term than in the long term, when birth rates and the child-dependant ratio will have stabilised at a lower level, but life expectancy will continue to rise.

Forms of adjustment to globalisation based on the 'Third Way' are sometimes advocated as solutions to the pressures it imposes on welfare states (Ferrera and Rhodes, 2000). Given 'adjustment', 'recasting' or 'recalibration' of social protection, it is argued, the European social model can survive and is surviving. However, the proposed forms of 'adjustment' in fact contain severe losses for the working class, especially for unemployed workers; 'obligations' for unemployed people to accept compulsory activation programmes; pricing people into work; and deregulation of part-time and temporary work.

Mary Daly (2001) characterises the various challenges to the welfare state arising from globalisation and internally generated fiscal tensions as 'pressure points', which influence or constrain traditional policies and institutions but will not necessarily lead to their collapse. The hypothesis of fiscal crisis, particularly in the Marxist version, is flawed, because the supposed constraints are rather poorly defined. What sets the floor to the rate of profit that capital finds acceptable – other than that of alternative places to invest, which leaves us with no real answer about the floor to its international level? What sets the ceiling to workers' tolerance of tax levels, which in any case is highly variable over the period since 1945? What, in any case, determines the state's budget priorities – given that defence for example, in a few cases rivals the scale of social security spending? Fiscal tension or pressure is a more appropriate concept than 'crisis', because it conveys the idea of a policy conflict or dilemma without any apocalyptic associations.

THE SCHUMPETERIAN WORKFARE STATE

The theory of the Schumpeterian Workfare State (SWS for short) is an interesting attempt to combine an analysis of globalisation pressures on the welfare state with the Marxist analysis of its internal contradictions drawn from Gough and O'Connor. Jessop (1993) argues that the observed patterns of development in western capitalism since the 1940s can be encapsulated in the ideal type of the Keynesian Welfare National State (KWNS), which evolves into another ideal type, the Schumpeterian Workfare Post-national Regime (SWPR). The KWNS was associated with the Fordist period of capitalist development, in which mass industrial production under relatively stable market conditions facilitated the growth of strong trade unions in manufacturing and steady growth of wages, which in turn helped to maintain markets for consumer goods. In the KWNS, management of macro-economic demand was feasible, and high public spending benefited capital by maintaining a high level of demand for national production. Social protection was based on citizenship rights and secured high levels of mass consumption, in turn providing a good market for nationally based businesses.

In Jessop's view, globalisation was not the only pressure on the KWNS. There were also political and social forces: a growing resistance of voters to high taxation, the intensified industrial conflict that followed the oil price hike of the early 1970s, and a desire for a choice of alternatives to state welfare provision. These combined pressures, but primarily the economic crisis of the KWNS, led to its evolution into a new policy constellation, the SWPR. This is 'Schumpeterian' because it promotes the competitiveness of the national economy through innovation and flexibility, notably flexibility in the labour market through 'supply side' policies. 'Workfare', because, as an adjunct to this supply side approach, welfare benefits are recast in a regime that emphasises the obligations of citizens to be self-sufficient through the labour market, adapting themselves to employers' demands. Post-national, because economic policy is driven by the need for international competitiveness in a globalised investment field, and supranational institutions such as the EU, OECD and IMF assume a larger role than before. The two ideal types of KWNS and SWPR do not necessarily exist in pure form, Jessop argues – features of one may be found mixed with those of the other – but what is important as a broad observation is the tendency for the KWNS to evolve towards the SWPR. The notion that capitalism 'needs' this evolution is not so different from the 'necessity' expressed in OECD and EC documents for social protection to be modified in a workfarist direction to serve the needs of the economy.

The theory of the transition from KWNS to SWPR seems to be especially prone to the charge of functionalism.[7] It is hard to find the agents or actors who make it happen, either in Jessop's account or in Jones and Peck's (1995) more specific analysis of the workfare state and labour market policies. However, in later writing Peck takes care to emphasise the process of 'political mediation' between labour market developments and the introduction of workfare (Peck, 2001, p. 35) and that workfare is a political choice rather than an inevitability (p. 80). It is certainly true that several features of the SWS – the change in treatment of unemployed people, and the tendency to privatisation of some welfare functions including delivery of 'welfare to work' policies – are becoming widespread in capitalist economies. But this may have as much to do with the dissemination of these policies through supranational institutions and other channels of spreading the neo-liberal message, as because they are the only appropriate policies for the post-Fordist or globalisation era.

Jessop (1993, 1994) cannot entirely escape a charge of determinism. While taking care to distance himself from any illusion that the trajectory of the capitalist economy provides a complete explanation for social policy forms, he does not say under what conditions Keynesianism might have survived or been replaced by something different. Thus, in practice, the notion of the SWPR leads one to assume that the observed patterns of development are the only ones that could have taken place within a capitalist environment.

CAN THE PRESSURES OF GLOBALISATION BE AVOIDED?

Neo-liberal policies may appear to be a 'necessary' response to globalisation whereas in fact their spread is an ideological phenomenon. However, where the neo-liberal response is adopted, there may be pressure on other countries to do likewise; Schwartz (2001) argues that there is an epidemic of labour market deregulation spreading from the USA, which drags other countries into deregulation also in order to compete with it. Counterposed to this process would be the alternative possibility of setting minimum global labour standards, just as British (and other) capitalists have at various times accepted measures such as the Factory Acts, minimum wage regulation and the European Working Time Directive as an alternative to competition based on falling labour standards. This might be one of several elements of a solution to the problems of the KWNS, which demand the development of a whole battery of new policy instruments. Jessop's and Peck's accounts of those problems are not in dispute; but what is questionable is the *inevitability* of the transition to the 'workfare state'. If we assume a shortage of full-time secure jobs – one result of globalisation – and a very limited role for the state in providing or promoting employment, it may be true that unemployed people have to take what the market gives them – and be bullied to do so. But this particular solution is not universal – France, for example, used extensive public funding of local authorities and non-profit organisations to create jobs during the 1990s, and only very recently moved towards a stricter benefit regime.

The notion that benefit systems, public services or labour standards 'must' be scaled down, or modified, in order for the national economy to retain jobs in a globalised environment invites some fundamental questions. How much of the cost of welfare can be shifted on to expenditure taxes, or personal wealth taxes, or on to temporary borrowing? This depends on political and institutional factors; there is no clear set of threshold levels that cannot be passed. How large a tax burden or how low an average rate of return can capital tolerate? There is an absence of criterion values, either in practice or in theory. As Will Hutton (2002) argues, there is considerable variation between western economies in what constitutes an 'adequate' rate of profit, what determines that and over what time horizon it is considered to be adequate. The UK and USA are unusual in that stock markets place considerable emphasis on maximising short-term shareholder value. Where a larger share of production is in the hands of small and medium-size enterprises whose shares are not publicly traded, as in Denmark and to some extent in Germany, there is less pressure to maximise short-term profit and less pressure to obtain similar short-term returns as in other sectors or other countries. In short, there are policy variables and locally variable features of capitalism that can in principle be used to modify market pressure to equalise profit rates with those of capital elsewhere. The evidence for fiscal tension and other 'globalisation pressures' on welfare provision or wage levels must be viewed in this light.

Many writers take the view that globalisation is as much a set of policies as of market processes – and that other policies could have been chosen to manage capitalism. For short, we can call this the Possibility of Other Policies hypothesis (POP). Some commentators distinguish between neo-liberal globalisation – the actually existing form, which is heavily dominated by free-market processes 'managed' in the interests of giant companies – and other potentially possible forms of globalisation. Bob Deacon (2001) argues that the choice was made in the 1980s for a neo-liberal form of globalisation in which policy-makers 'assumed, mistakenly, that globally unregulated markets would maximise welfare'. An alternative might have been, and could still be, social-democratic policies at international level. Deacon suggests that global governance institutions could raise global revenues to facilitate global redistribution, oversee a set of global social regulations to ensure that economic activity served a social purpose and empower citizens to demand social rights that were inscribed in international agreements.

Guy Standing (1999) also argues that alternative policy responses are possible; he proposes the twin policy objectives of income security through a universal guaranteed income, and upholding established labour standards – the opposite of the supply side focus of neo-liberalism that is enshrined in the policy prescriptions of the OECD and the IMF. Such policies, he believes, could reduce the risk of a 'race to the bottom' in terms of labour standards, facilitated by repression of trade unions and reduction of workers' rights. The realisation of Standing's vision no doubt depends on breaking one of the vicious circles of globalisation: it weakens trade unions, but their power is required to turn around the decline in labour standards.

In so far as the KWNS was more worker-friendly than the SWPR, and provided a vehicle for a large public sector, strong trade union power and better treatment of the unwaged, its demise marks a real loss for the workers' movement and the advent of a more difficult era in which to make headway. Could the Keynesian project be revived, if the Maastricht straitjacket was set aside? Possibly, though the gains to the working class would remain limited by the legacy of the recent past. Robert Went (2000) believes that neo-liberal policies have left lasting damage. Privatisation and other institutional changes have shifted power away from the working class, making it more difficult to win back the gains of the Keynesian period. In the UK, the anti-trade union laws of the Thatcher period dealt the power of the labour movement a massive blow from which it has not so far recovered, although the 1999 Employment Relations Act led to rerecognitions in some workplaces, and the resurgence of a more militant and politicised trade unionism in 2002–03 suggest that change may be in sight. Likewise, privatisation and subcontracting in the public sector have created huge vested interests against any reversal of that process. Privatisation, in so far as it reduces the scale of the state sector and the quality of jobs in 'public' services, is a barrier to the development of quality full employment based on the public sector, the model that Sweden pursued so successfully from the late 1940s to the 1980s. But if alternative policies to neo-liberalism would now be more difficult, they are not impossible. POP, reasserting that policies are made by people and not by the 'invisible hand' of the market, is a necessary counterweight to the functionalism of some 'regulation school' interpretations of welfare state change. Between economic pressures and the policies lies a mosaic of institutions and political actors.

THE BASELINE: HOW FAR MIGHT SOCIAL PROTECTION BE ERODED OR LABOUR STANDARDS BE ALLOWED TO FALL?

To the extent that globalisation does produce pressures for welfare retrenchment, how far is it likely to go before employers themselves say enough is enough, and no further cuts would be in our interests?

There are good reasons why globalisation can be expected to impact much more on the management of the labour market – the policy area extending from unemployed benefits and 'welfare to work' through to regulation of employment contracts – rather more than on other transfer payments or state services. This is because 'footloose' companies, or those considering outsourcing abroad, or those engaged in keen price competition with overseas producers, are all much more likely to pressurise government to help them reduce labour costs than they are to concern themselves about state spending on social investment functions. They may welcome good services for health, education or childcare if it helps them improve productivity or spend less on company fringe benefits – or if, in the current vogue for privatisation, it provides new opportunities for profit. On labour standards, employers want some limitation of a race to the bottom, which would bring them into conflict with unions and eventually with governments. EU directives on working time and other labour rights, health and safety issues are all designed to prevent 'social dumping' – in other words, to create a level playing field for competition between employers and between national economies. Employers can agree to some regulation of this kind, in the same way as employers in the early nineteenth century agreed to limitations on working hours and on child labour. However, the protracted and difficult negotiations in the EU's 'social dialogue' process show what a gap exists between management and unions on certain issues, such as the regulation of agency work.

Employers, least of all in a globalising world, have much less motive for supporting benefits for the unwaged than for supporting 'social investment' in services that will help to raise productivity. Policy towards unemployed people is thus much more in the front line of globalisation pressures, and less protected by institutional 'stickiness', than other aspects of the welfare state. Reductions in expenditure on benefits per unemployed person have been widespread in the 1990s, as detailed in Chapter 5. Cost pressures seem to be a minor factor in the transformation of benefit systems, which have been most marked in states with relatively low unemployment. Just as Schwartz (2001) refers to an 'epidemic of deregulation', there appears also to be an epidemic of workfarism in several European states, actively supported by employers' organisations who have no interest in financing the unwaged and every interest in mobilising them as a low-cost labour supply.

Peck and Jones (2001, p. 45) have raised the question of the 'baseline' in relation to provision for unemployed people. They ask, what would be the minimum level to which support for them might fall? The answer would be something like the more extreme workfare regimes in the USA: the provision of work in return for a minimum subsistence allowance, rather than 'passive' benefit. A reversion, in other words, to the principle of the workhouse, but without incarceration in an institution. But they point out that the neo-liberal state faces a dilemma about the high cost of workfare schemes. Thus, policies that induce unemployed people to take low-paid jobs in the open labour market are likely to be chosen as more cost-effective – as shown by recent developments in the UK and Germany, described in Chapter 8.

To sum up, the pressures of globalisation impact heavily on labour markets and labour market policy, although their contribution to the overall fiscal problems of the welfare state is much more marginal. There is pressure to deregulate labour contracts and restrain wage growth, because of intensified international competition on the basis of labour costs. At the same time as globalisation has been the final death blow to the perhaps already moribund model of Keynesianism in single national economies, EU policies, as we shall see in Chapter 4, have not so far realised the potential for using public investment as an expansionary and stabilising force at Europe-wide level. The result has been the widespread acceptance of supply side policies, which essentially throw the burden of macro-economic adjustment on to workers and unemployed people. Both supranational governance and employers' lobbies have been strong advocates of the functional necessity of these policies. However, that necessity is as much in doubt as the 'necessity' of low wages and high profits; income distribution always has been an issue for negotiation, but what is new is the scale and complexity of the negotiating arena. Deacon (2001) argues that if neo-liberal solutions to the problems of the welfare state are widespread, it is because of the prevalence of a particular ideology, embedded in the policy prescriptions of the OECD and the EU, rather than because they are the only possible solutions.

4

The Role of the European Union

The European Union is essentially a project of economic integration rather than political federalism. This has limited the role of EU institutions in the development of social policies in the member states, although that role has been substantial, especially from the early 1990s. The limitation is not just a question of 'subsidiarity' – that is, leaving it up to the member states to pursue their own policies unless integration requires some form of policy coordination. Rather, the objective of a single European *market* gives primacy, in the labour field, to mobilising a labour supply for firms operating in the integrated market. Those concerned to push forward a social agenda within European institutions have had to justify it by reference to the need for minimum social protection standards to avoid competition through 'social dumping', and for 'social cohesion' to underpin legitimation of the single market. In the 1950s, some member states feared that opening their economies to more competition would drive down their labour standards towards those of lower-cost countries; but in practice wages and living standards grew rapidly until the late 1970s. Recession then revived concerns about social dumping, leading to a series of directives on working conditions, health and safety and equality between workers with different forms of labour contracts.

In the late 1980s, French and Belgian social democrats put forward a vision of a 'Social Europe' alongside the project of economic integration. This vision encompassed improvements in employee rights and important advances in social rights for women and for parents. It attracted strong support from trade unions. The pressure for a 'social dimension' led to the Social Charter on workers' rights of 1989 and a series of EU labour directives. But under pressure from employers' lobbying and from the Tory government in the UK, the Social Charter was not incorporated into the Maastricht Treaty of 1992. There followed a period of compromise evident in the Delors White Paper (EC, 1993)[1] and the White Paper on Social Policy (EC, 1994).[2] Later in the 1990s, EU economic and social policies took an increasingly neo-liberal direction, structured by the particular policy framework adopted for the European Monetary Union. Although trade unions and unemployed people's movements hoped that the Employment Chapter of the Amsterdam Treaty in 1997 would generate a collective commitment by member states to job creation, in fact what it produced was a coordinated commitment to supply side employment policies, with the emphasis on 'employability' and 'active labour market measures'. In its attempts to coordinate member states' policies to combat unemployment, the European Commission has advocated 'reform' of social protection, accepting the neo-liberal view that a trade-off exists between job security and employment growth, and between the 'decommodifying' character of benefits and the rate at which unemployed people move into jobs. Thus European institutions in the post-Maastricht era have played a significant role in the flexibilisation of labour markets and in shifting benefit systems for the unwaged in a workfarist direction.

Employers' interests have been given progressively more primacy as EU policies have developed in the late 1990s. Since the end of the Delors period, when 'Social Europe' assumed a certain prominence, the objectives of improving living and working conditions have been largely subsumed into the drive to increase employment through supply side policies. The Lisbon European Council in 2000 gave increased attention to the need for policies to combat social exclusion, but with an emphasis on 'inclusion' through work and a tacit acceptance of workfarism. The Maastricht convergence criteria deliberately prioritised control of inflation as the main macro-economic policy goal of the EU in the run-up to the creation of the Eurozone. The restraint of government expenditure and government borrowing have driven member states away from creating jobs through public investment towards neo-liberal employment policies, that is restraint of labour costs and pushing unemployed people into available jobs, whatever their quality. However, some change of direction is apparent in the concern with 'job quality' since the Lisbon European Council in 2000, with an attempt by the Commission to find ways of reconciling 'flexibility' with job security and opportunities for training. A divide seems to be emerging on labour regulation between the French, Swedish and Belgian leaderships on the one hand, seeking to promote a 'Social Europe' agenda, and the British, Spanish and Italian leaderships on the other, favouring harsher policies towards unemployed people and trade unions.

'SOCIAL EUROPE' – A FADING VISION?

In the 1950s the EU's precursor, the European Coal and Steel Community, emphasised the goal of improving living standards and working conditions. The Treaty of Paris of 1951, which set up the ECSC, expressed a faith in the free market route to prosperity. Unlike the successor institutions of the European Economic Community, it defined policies of fair competition between companies and between countries partly in terms of the wages paid. The High Authority of the ECSC had powers to fine firms that used low pay to undercut their competitors (Geyer, 2000, p. 22). The Treaty of Rome, which established the EEC (then of only six countries) in 1957, envisaged coordinated social policies. This was a demand of the French government, fearing competition from Germany, which at that time had less well-developed welfare and labour rights. Under Articles 117–18 of the Rome Treaty, the EEC was given responsibility for promoting developments of employment law, social security, vocational training, and health and safety at work, through an upward harmonisation towards the best of the conditions in the individual member states. The first Social Action Programme of 1974 made several proposals in these fields and achieved some important measures to secure equal treatment between women and men (Hantrais, 1995; see also Table 4.2 below). It initiated the 'social dialogue' on labour law and workers' representation between the European Trade Union Confederation (ETUC, founded in 1974) and the employers' grouping, UNICE.[3] By 1978 these contacts had ceased, but Jacques Delors, shortly after becoming President of the European Commission in 1985, attempted to revive the social dialogue. It was seen as a way of overcoming the objections by some member states, especially the UK, to Commission initiatives on social policy. The Commission would refer issues to UNICE and the ETUC for consultation, and if employers and trade unions together agreed on a measure, the European Council could decide by majority vote to make it legally binding, while entrusting detailed implementation of social measures to the ETUC and UNICE. The employers' groups were at first reluctant to agree to this process, but by 1991 agreed that negotiated measures were better than imposed ones (Geyer, 2000, p. 100).

In 1986 a further stage of European integration was agreed through the Single European Act, which envisaged a single European market free of all restrictions on cross-border trade and investment by 1992. This raised fresh fears of 'social dumping', especially by

Table 4.1   A chronology of policy developments in European integration 1951–97

	Treaties	Key social policy developments	Accession of new members and other events
1951	Treaty of Paris, establishing the European Coal and Steel Community		
1957	Treaty of Rome, establishing the European Economic Community of initially six states		
1974		Social Action Programme	Accession of the UK, Ireland and Denmark
1981			Accession of Greece
1986			Accession of Spain and Portugal
1994			Accession of Sweden, Finland and Austria
1975		Establishment of European Structural Funds	
1979		Social Action Programme	
1985			Jacques Delors became President of European Commission (until 1995)
1986	Single European Act		
1989		European Social Charter	
1992	Maastricht Treaty (Treaty of European Union) – came into force 1993		
1993		'Delors' White Paper, 'Growth, Competitiveness and Employment'	
1993		Green Paper on social policy	
1994		White Paper on Social Policy	
1995		Social Action Programme 1995–97	
1997	Amsterdam Treaty (June) and the 'Employment Chapter'		Election of New Labour government in UK and end of UK 'opt-out' from Social Protocol ('Social Chapter') of Maastricht Treaty

the French who saw their high social insurance contributions as essential to underwriting social rights. A new vision emerged of a 'social dimension' to the integration process. The socialist French President, François Mitterrand, began in 1981 to define 'l'éspace sociale' in which the EU would develop a Europe-level dialogue between unions and employers, and cooperation in the development of social protection.

Angered by the strongly neo-liberal approach of the UK's Thatcher government, opposing forces within the EU began to press for a 'Social Charter' of workers' rights. This was first proposed by Alan Hansenne, then the Belgian Employment Minister, in 1987. Pushed by Jacques Delors, President of the European Commission from 1985 to 1995, and by the ETUC, it found expression in a Commission working paper, 'The Social Dimension of the Internal Market', in 1988. The Community Charter of the Fundamental Social Rights of Workers, adopted in 1989, committed member states to securing workers' freedom of movement within the EU, fair remuneration, adequate income out of work, equal treatment for women and men, the right to strike and other basic social rights. It sought a maximum limit on working time, and improvement of conditions in part-time and temporary employment. The Community Charter had no force of law; it was merely a declaration of desiderata by member states (Hantrais, 1995, p. 9).

The Maastricht Treaty of 1992, which established the European Monetary Union, tagged on a separate agreement on social policy, the Social Protocol of the Maastricht Treaty (a.k.a. the 'Social Chapter'). This device was chosen so that the UK, strongly resisting the Social Charter under the Tories, could agree to the treaty but 'opt out' of the social provisions. The UK government blocked implementation of social measures, which required universal agreement by member states, but it could not block measures to improve workers' health and safety, which could be adopted by majority voting under the Single European Act 1986 (Article 118a), for example the Working Time Directive of 1993. Only after New Labour's election in 1997 did the British government accept the 'Social Chapter' and its associated measures.

The 'Social Chapter' proposed an enhanced role for the 'social dialogue', replicating at European level the 'corporatist' arrangements for involvement in social protection policy that are common in most member states, the UK excepted. These often include centralised negotiation about these issues between employers, trade unions and the state. Delors initiated, through the 'social dialogue' process, an extended range of social measures under the 'Social Chapter'. From this developed several important directives on labour standards, which were adopted during the 1990s (see Table 4.2).

Delors and his allies also secured an enlargement of the EU's 'structural funds' to bolster social expenditure in the poorest regions. This often gave these regions a degree of autonomy from their central government, and the opportunity for welfare to work policies to be influenced by local administrations or NGOs, sometimes more on the side of unemployed people than the central authorities. Many innovative local programmes to create jobs through the non-market sector, or to provide valuable local experiments in training and job rotation, have been supported by the Structural Funds (ERGO 1, 1992; ERGO 2, 1996).

However, the Maastricht Treaty also represented a victory for neo-liberal economic policies. Member states agreed to very tight control of inflation, of interest rates and of government borrowing, with budget deficits limited to 3 per cent of GDP and public debt to 60 per cent of GDP. A loss of several million jobs was forecast from the deflationary effects of moving towards the single currency (Holland, 1998). Several member states had to shrink their public sector to comply with this tight macro-economic stance, which threatened the level of employment. In 1998 France, Germany, Italy, Spain and Sweden all exceeded the limit on public debt. Cutbacks in public spending meant the death knell for Keynesian employment policies, already in retreat under the pressures described in the previous chapter. Member states' capacity to spend their way out of recession, or to allow an expansion of private credit to revive employment, became severely limited. Will Hutton (2002, p. 255) points out that while rapid employment growth in the UK and the USA in the 1990s was financed by a consumer boom, fed by credit expansion, France and Germany could not do this, nor compensate for lack of private spending by increasing public spending, because of Maastricht obligations.

At the period of the Maastricht Treaty, European integration appeared to the British trade union movement to present two contradictory faces: on one hand a movement towards a platform of broadly trade union-friendly labour regulation, which stood in contradiction to the deregulating policies of the Tories (and which the UK's Tory government tried to block at EU level); on the other hand limits on government spending and borrowing in the run-up to the

Table 4.2   Selected key EU labour directives

Name	Date	Content
Directive on equal pay	1975	Equal pay between women and men
Directive on equality at work between women and men	1976	Equal treatment with regard to access to employment, vocational training and promotion, and working conditions
Directive on Pregnancy	1992	Right to 14 weeks' maternity leave at 80% of normal salary
Directive on Working Time	1993	Limit of 48 hours to working week; right to four weeks' paid holiday per year
Directive on Young People at Work	1994	Prohibits child labour (i.e. by persons under school-leaving age) with a few exceptions for limited part-time work and work experience; special provisions concerning safety, working time and rest periods for workers under 18
Directive on European Works Councils	1994	Requires establishment of works councils in companies operating in at least two member states and having over 1,000 workers
Directive on 'posted workers'	1996	Right of workers sent by their employers to work in a different member state to have the same minimum rates of pay and working conditions as others in the state where they are actually working
Directive on Parental Leave	1996	Right to parental leave (unpaid) for a minimum of three months, following the birth or adoption of a child
Directive on equality for part-time workers	1997	Right of part-time workers to equal pay and working conditions with comparable full-time workers
Directive on Fixed Term Work	1999	Right of workers on fixed term contracts to have equal pay and conditions with comparable permanent workers
Directive on racial equality	2000	Requires equal treatment between persons regardless of racial or ethnic origin
Directive on Agency Work	Still in draft 2003	Right of agency workers to have equal pay and conditions with comparable workers of the company to which the agency hires them out

European Monetary Union that were antagonistic to workers' interests. These two contradictory faces were recognised in TUC debates of this period, and reflected in the fact that while the TUC endorsed EMU, the union UNISON opposed it (Strange, 1997). One face was an essentially capitalist vision of an integrated market; as Ramon Duran (1997, 2000) puts it, the objective was and is to create the 'Europe of Capital'. The other was 'Social Europe', an attempt to place the 'social dialogue' centre stage, with a commitment of European institutions to improvements of workers' rights and of the position of women. What really lay at the heart of this contradiction?

The history of European integration reflects the changing nature of capital and the capitalist state since the 1950s. At the beginning, the European Coal and Steel Community reflected concern with improving living standards, planned adjustment to industrial restructuring within a Keynesian framework, and avoidance of social dumping by states with less advanced social protection. It could be described as a class-consensus project with little to offend social democrats. The European Economic Community from the Treaty of Rome through to the 1980s sought to improve the rate of economic growth through a customs union, gradually enhanced with additional measures; workers' living standards could improve, but mainly through 'trickle-down'. Gradually, the EEC could be expected to, and did, assist companies to produce on a transnational scale, thus increasing their bargaining power over labour – a benefit for capital spotted at an early stage by De Gaulle (Bonefeld, 2002, p. 128). However, it was a customs union grafted on to a gradually decaying Keynesian/corporatist socio-economic model, in which both 'social dialogue' and strong state intervention had been considered normal. From Maastricht onwards, however, the attempt to limit the state sector, and to throw the burden of labour market adjustment on to workers and unemployed people, has shifted the balance of power and wealth much more in favour of capital. Left critics of the European integration project in the 1990s see it as a vehicle for capital, especially transnational capital, to create supranational power structures that are deliberately intended to promote corporate agendas and to bypass national democratic processes (Bonefeld, 2002; Mathers, 1999; Duran, 1997, 2000). According to Bonefeld, the EU helps capital to realise several of the benefits of economic federalism recognised by the right-wing economist Hayek. It helps to defend capitalist structures against the possibility of further working-class gains; it reduces national interference with the operations of capital in favour of minimal state interference designed merely to secure a 'level playing field' between companies operating in different locations. To secure all of these benefits, it passes a range of economic policy decisions to a supranational level where they are relatively free from voter and working-class influence (Bonefeld, 2002, p. 124; Balanyá et al., 2000, pp. 20, 62, 93). Likewise Aaronovitch and Grahl (1997, p. 182) commented that national governments are to some extent using Maastricht as an alibi for their own projects to establish more restrictive welfare regimes, to intensify market disciplines and to favour particular social strata. Only such motives can explain the tax reductions which, in many cases, accompany expenditure cuts and make the achievements of Maastricht public finance targets more difficult.

The very idea of a single currency for 13,[4] perhaps eventually 25 countries, passes over the key policy decision about how much cash the central bank should issue to a supranational level, taking it away from member states. Within the Eurozone, the European Central Bank is entrusted with the task of determining, quite independently of political interference, interest rates and the money supply (in so far as any central bank really can control it, leaving aside some issues about Eurodollars and the stability of credit multipliers). An individual country within the Eurozone cannot decide to increase its money supply to boost demand, nor devalue its currency to assist export sales. Both these were frequently used policy instruments in the old Keynesian toolkit, although the second obviously gains jobs for one country at the expense of jobs in competing countries. Printing money is likely to accelerate inflation, but in moderation this is sometimes preferable to high unemployment; outside of the Eurozone, an individual country retains the choice (Godley, 1997). The challenge may be to change the Eurozone's rules, allowing more flexibility for credit expansion and relaxation of government spending constraints when needed. With Germany and France both in trouble by 2003 for excessive government spending, some relaxation of the Maastricht criteria is at last finding a degree of political support.

THE DELORS ERA

The two faces of the Maastricht Treaty – an economic policy package that placed considerable pressure on workers and jobseekers, and a compensatory 'Social Chapter' – are reflected in two key EU policy documents of the early 1990s, which provide a crucial starting point for understanding the original concept of the European 'social model' and how EU policies have shifted in the subsequent decade. The Delors White Paper on Employment (Growth, Competitiveness and Employment, 1993) (DWP) and the White Paper on Social Policy (1994) (WPSP) both reflect the contradiction between class interests at the heart of the EU policy process. They both attempt a fence-sitting compromise between employers' and unions' agendas. In the view of Norman Ginsberg (1978), the Delors 1993 paper 'concedes much ground to neo-liberalism, but attempts to combine it with elements of Keynesianism' (p. 23). Likewise, Bob Deacon (2001, p. 70) regards the Social Policy White Paper as 'a juggling act' in which the Commission 'wished to support social protection policies; but only insofar as these policies were adapted to the perceived requirements of increased global economic competition'.

The DWP began with an implied attack on certain positions within the European labour movement. It highlighted in the preface the things the EU should not do about unemployment: spend its way out of recession at the cost of higher inflation later; or indulge in protectionism against its avowed objective to encourage growth in poorer countries, or go for reduction in working time and job sharing that would lead to a loss of output, or to a 'drastic cut in wages'. It advocated 'an economy characterised by solidarity' – between workers and unemployed, between generations, between women and men, between rich and poor regions, and in 'the fight against social exclusion'. Productivity gains should be used to invest in more jobs. The issue of (re)distribution between capital and labour was thus avoided.

The DWP diagnosed the causes of the European unemployment problem. Firstly, competition from ' southern' countries meant the EU needed to reposition itself in the international division of labour, developing higher skills to grow new, mainly knowledge-based and information technology-based sectors. Secondly, there was not enough growth in services because of the high cost of unskilled labour, due partly to high social security contributions and insufficient flexibility in terms of employers' ability to hire temporary or part-time labour. Thirdly, social protection had to be 'updated' by spending more on active relative to passive measures. However, there is nothing overtly workfarist about the way this is put:

> the unemployed should be offered, according to how long they have been unemployed, first training leading to meaningful qualifications, then the possibility of working, possibly in the public sector, for a number of months … *this too is a question of social dialogue in which the unemployed should themselves be involved.* [my italics]

There was a clear call for job creation with public money, giving examples of needed public services that would take on unemployed people: home helps, childcare, services for children and youth, home security, local shops, leisure and cultural facilities, housing renovation, public transport, environmental improvement and recycling, energy-saving equipment (p. 20).

The DWP argued that some workers had too much protection against dismissal or redundancy, which deterred employers from hiring because of the high costs of downsizing their payroll later. But it recognised that 'attempts to reduce levels of job protection in order to introduce more flexibility into labour markets have often led to the growth of two-tier labour markets'. It cautioned against 'wholesale labour market deregulation', noting that competition from the south and the difficulties following the oil price shocks have led some member states down this road. But the DWP argued that it risks creating wider inequality, and weakening the position of those who are already disadvantaged in the labour market. Better to reduce high social security contributions, which discourage employers from creating more jobs.

To encourage employment growth DWP recommended wage restraint (rises no more than productivity gains); more employment-friendly tax systems; and increasing the number of jobs for a given level of output. But it argued against legislating for a shorter working week, preferring negotiation at company level, or facilitating career breaks, sabbaticals and job rotation schemes. However, 'an adjustment of working time accompanied by tax incentives would make it possible to increase employment, use equipment more intensively (longer opening) and meet a demand (more practical opening hours, longer free time)' (p. 155). It also recommended that employers should vary hours rather than payroll numbers to deal with cyclical variation in labour requirements – but stopped short of recommending a short-time compensation subsidy, which would encourage this.

The European Commission's White Paper on Social Policy of 1994 reflected the tensions between the different social forces who put forward comments on the proposals in the green paper; essentially, the class conflicts within member states. WPSP's vision of the European social model included high labour standards (ch. 3, p. 29), democracy and individual rights, free collective bargaining, the market economy, equality of opportunity for all and social welfare and solidarity (p. 9). It noted Article 2 of the 1986 Treaty: 'the community shall have as its task ... to promote ... the raising of the standard of living and quality of life and economic and social cohesion and solidarity among Member States'. But Chapter 3, on encouraging high labour standards as part of a competitive Europe, recognised the tension between competitiveness and labour standards and says (p. 31, para. 11):

> on the one hand, there are those who argue that excessively high labour standards result in costs which blunt the competitive edge of companies .... On the other hand, many believe that productivity is the key to competitiveness and that high labour standards have always been an integral part of the competitive formula ... there is no clear consensus on this point.

Later on (p. 19, para. 12), the text identified a consensus among member states that

> greater labour market efficiency and long-run competitiveness is to be sought, not through a dilution of the European model of social protection, but through the adaptation, rationalisation and simplification of regulations, so as to establish a better balance between social protection, competitiveness and employment creation.

This implied that both the move towards greater flexibility of labour contracts and the shift towards active rather than passive benefits (recommended in para. 13) was a mere matter of 'adaptation' that did not 'dilute' the European model. The question of the quality of jobs was sidestepped; WPSP went back a lot on the green paper of a year earlier, which was concerned about both casualisation and the intensification of work. However, the green paper itself had avoided any proposal on this; in effect it recognised flexploitation but chosen to ignore it.

Like the DWP, the WPSP advocated 'reform' of social protection: benefits should shift from poverty avoidance to active labour market programmes. But its tone was apologetic, as if reflecting a fear that social protection was being sidelined in internal market plans. Elsewhere, in its second chapter, the WPSP emphasised investment in training and suggested job rotation to combine continuing training of employees with job training of unemployed persons. But training and employment are not the only solutions to poverty. The WPSP echoed the concerns of the EU Poverty Programme of the early 1990s, which launched experimental projects to address community development, poor housing, access to medical care and services for children as well as long-term unemployment. Social exclusion was seen as multi-dimensional – linked to 'housing, education, health, discrimination, citizenship and integration in the local community' as well as to employment and income (WPSP, ch. 6). Thus 'the provision of new jobs alone – even in substantial numbers – will not lead to the elimination of social exclusion' (p. 49).

In their emphasis on 'reform' of benefit systems towards 'active measures', and their assumption of an immutable trade-off between between job growth and labour flexibility or labour costs and the growth of jobs, both the DWP and WPSP echoed the neo-liberal positions expressed in OECD policy papers of the early 1990s. At the same time the Delors White Paper showed a clear vision of a 'baseline' of labour standards and minimum income maintenance, which the policy framework of the EU is expected to preserve. Downward pressure on labour standards was resisted; the solution in the DWP was thought to be investment by both employers and governments in building the skills of the workforce, to develop a high-skills economy and higher productivity. It also advocated public investment (modernisation of infrastructures such as transport and telecoms). Catch-22 was that this invoked the need for major public spending, when the paper recognised that rising social expenditure was – and still is – a source of budgetary strain. The DWP also recommended reducing non-wage labour costs, by shifting taxes from labour to other factors of production. This implied higher indirect taxes – affecting living costs. The DWP identified the service sector as the main source of future employment growth, suggesting a range of public services that were not – and still are not – being provided on a scale adequate to meet social needs, but that could provide more jobs. It argued that their absence was owing to market failure; that is, they cost more to provide than potential customers are willing or able to pay. This implied a need to subsidise these services – again, a problem for raising sufficient tax revenue. But the paper failed to put forward the essential policy proposal needed to make the others happen: that of special taxes on very high incomes, or on wealth or financial transactions – forms of taxes that do not affect labour costs or the incentive to invest.

Some of the more progressive proposals in the DWP were about reducing working time. Although rejecting legislation for a shorter working week to promote work-sharing – since enacted in France in 1999 – it did advocate other work-sharing measures. Likewise the

Green Paper on Social Policy of 1993 advocated work-sharing, but WPSP merely makes a brief reference to job rotation. Work-sharing has an important place in the employment policies of certain countries, not only the 35-hour week in France (discussed in Chapter 9) but also the very successful job rotation scheme in Denmark. But apart from the Working Time Directive[5] and measures to make voluntary part-time working available to parents and carers, these policies have not been actively promoted at European level.

Neither the DWP nor WPSP discussed the issue of whether participation in active labour market measures should be compulsory. Nor did they consider the possibility that such measures may directly or indirectly lead to deterioration of wages and conditions of people in marginal jobs. The dynamics of workfarist policies as they affect the labour market in general, as described in later chapters of this book, were not considered. If these two key documents focused on 'supply side' solutions to unemployment – the twin projects of flexibilisation of labour and mobilisation of unemployed people as a 'flexible' labour force – they also had a strong element of Keynesianism. That was to disappear in the run-up to the foundation of the euro as the single currency.

AMSTERDAM AND AFTER

The Treaty of Amsterdam in 1997, which paved the way for the Eurozone, appeared also to be a step forward for European social policy. The 'social protocol' of the Maastricht Treaty became part of the Amsterdam Treaty, with provisions for a wider range of social measures to be enacted by a form of majority voting instead of universal agreement of member states. Sweden and the Netherlands successfully pushed for the introduction of an 'Employment Chapter' in the treaty, committing the EU to developing policies against unemployment. The treaty committed member states to drawing up annual Action Plans for Employment (Gill *et al.* 1999). In November 1997, the Luxembourg summit initiated the annual Employment Guidelines, which steer this process under four main headings or 'pillars': employability (of youth and the unemployed); entrepreneurship (to facilitate new business formation); adaptability (of employment contract arrangements, working time patterns and training systems, to promote labour flexibility); and equal opportunities (for women, migrants, ethnic minorities and people with disabilities). Each state then reports to the Commission on what it has achieved through its Action Plan, and (since 1999) the Commission may make non-binding recommendations to any state about future policies relating to the Employment Guidelines. This 'open coordination' method of policy-making (later also used for policies to combat social exclusion) involves no legally binding obligations. Nonetheless, the Employment Guidelines have had considerable influence over the formation of employment policy in member states.

The Amsterdam Treaty was heavily influenced by employers' lobbying. While the left was promoting 'Social Europe', large employers were gathering for battle. In 1983, the Swedish management of Volvo led a number of other industrialists from transnational companies to found the European Round Table (ERT), as a big business lobbying group (Balanyá *et al.*, 2000). It became strongly represented in the Competitiveness Advisory Group set up by Jacques Santer, the European Commission President who succeeded Delors, in 1995. Having acquired an 'official' institutional status, the ERT was in a strong position to push the interests of its membership. It also became prominent in UNICE, the employers' grouping charged with responsibility for 'social dialogue' with trade unions. The ERT's reports are strongly reflected in the content and even the detailed language of the Maastricht Treaty (Balanyá *et al.*, 2000, p. 19).

The ETUC, together with left politicians, had lobbied for the Employment Chapter of the Amsterdam Treaty, and called for a demonstration at the Luxembourg summit. Thousands of trade unionists and supporters of unemployed people's movements gathered to demand job creation. What they got was the European Employment Strategy, which aimed to reduce unemployment by making jobseekers more 'employable' through active labour market programmes and by making it easier for employers to hire labour on the terms they wanted. Member states were also enjoined to 'reduce the tax burden on labour', a goal taken up in several National Action Plans in the form of tax credit policies and reductions in employers' social security contributions. The ETUC described Amsterdam as 'a minimalist solution to the dilemma facing European labour markets', and regretted that employment policy had not been given the same priority as monetary policy. Keynesian dissenting voices throughout the late 1990s came from France, with a proposal for a central investment fund to create jobs, and Sweden, proposing full employment as a goal and as the guiding principle of economic policy (Barnard and Deakin, 1999, p. 362).

In 1998, the Employment Guidelines introduced targets for active labour market programmes. At least 20 per cent of unemployed people were to be 'offered training or any similar measure'. The ETUC supported this target,[6] although the Euromarches highlighted the risk that it would in practice encourage the spread of workfare. Each member state was also enjoined to 're-focus its tax and benefit system and provide incentives for unemployed or inactive people to seek and take up work or measures to enhance their employability and for employers to create new jobs'. The post-Luxembourg Employment Strategy was consistent with the general thrust of EU macro-economic policy in the phase of establishing the single market: to rely on supply side policies to increase employment. In line with the Delors White Paper, the EU adopted the project of flexibilisation of labour markets as a central theme (Barnard and Deakin, 1999). Under the 'adaptability' pillar, the 1998 Employment Guidelines enjoined member states to 'seek to introduce more adaptable types of contracts, whilst providing adequate levels of security'. A sentence was added to the subsequent annual Employment Guidelines in 1999 and 2000 that subtly redefined what might be regarded as 'adequate': 'those working under contracts of this kind should at the same time enjoy adequate security and higher occupational status, *compatible with the needs of business'* [my italics].

Employment policy was developed through successive summit meetings after 1997 (Table 4.3). For the first time in the history of the EU, these meetings began to attract major attention from citizens through a series of 'counter-summits' and demonstrations. Trade unions, left parties and NGOs including unemployed people's organisations mobilised thousands to demand social justice, seen not only in terms of job creation but the quality of life and the environment, and the rights of marginalised groups: the unwaged, casual workers, refugees, asylum seekers and illegal migrants. The Euromarch movement, born in 1997, opposed workfare and benefit sanctions, demanding income guarantees for unemployed people and 'real' jobs to meet the aspirations not only of the jobless but of the 'precarious' workers forced into part-time or casual work for lack of anything better (Mathers, 1999). In these mobilisations, the struggle against the 'Europe of Capital' merged with a more general disquiet about the process of capitalist globalisation and its effect both on workers' conditions and the welfare state.

At Cologne in 1999, the newly elected Social Democrat government in Germany attempted to strengthen the role of the social dialogue,

Table 4.3   Key meetings of the European Council 1997–2002

Date	Event	Policy decisions
1997 (November)	Luxembourg summit	Employment strategy agreed with process of National Action Plans for Employment
1998 (June)	Cardiff summit	Emphasis on achieving market integration
1999 (June)	Cologne summit	European employment 'pact', attempting to give a greater role to 'social dialogue' between employers and unions
2000 (March)	Lisbon summit	Targets set for increasing employment rates by 2010; commitment to establish new policies on social inclusion
2000 (Dec)	Nice summit	Declaration to support the European Charter of Fundamental Rights; commitment to produce National Action Plans on social inclusion. Agreement to enlarge the EU to the east
2001 (March)	Stockholm summit	Intermediate targets set for the Lisbon goals and indicators agreed to monitor progress in economic and social policy
2002 (March)	Barcelona summit	Targets set for childcare provision and for increasing the retirement age

through a European Employment Pact between member states, the ETUC and UNICE. The pact agreed to coordinate macro-economic policy, employment policy, social security reform and wage bargaining in a process involving the social partners as well as governments and the Commission. The 'Cologne process' as it has become known involves attempting to use the 'social dialogue' to reconcile pressures on the labour market with the Eurozone's macro-economic policy. This followed a series of national pacts or partnerships between employers, unions and government in the late 1990s (Gill *et al.*, 1999). Typically these pacts had traded concessions, with outcomes reflecting a variable balance of class forces. For example, regional and sectoral pacts in Germany in 1998 obtained job security for the 'core' workforce against lower payroll numbers and/or lower rates of pay for temporary workers. In Spain, a national agreement in 1998 traded flexibility of working hours in exchange for more job security and funds for job creation. Several regional pacts in Spain involved subsidies to create jobs, as well as conversion of some temporary jobs into permanent ones. The idea of the European Employment Pact was to encourage national and regional level negotiations of this kind under the umbrella of the European Pact. Within a 'social dialogue' framework of this kind, concessions about job security or lower wage rates for trainees and unemployed people re-entering work could be made by unions voluntarily and subject to specified conditions. However, the deflationary stance on macro-economic policies and employers' continuing pressure for more 'flexible' (in reality, insecure) employment contracts, as well as for tax cuts and contraction of early retirement schemes, intensified employer–union conflict. Swedish talks on a social pact had already broken down in 1998 over the issue of tax cuts for upper income groups with few concessions to offset this. Employers there, as in Germany, sought flexibilisation and deregulation of labour contracts. In 1999–2000, talks between the 'social partners' broke down in Denmark, France, Finland, Spain and some parts of Germany (Gold *et al.*, 2000).

From the Lisbon European Council (March 2000) employment and social policy took on a strikingly two-sided character. One side was very clearly neo-liberal, moving away from the Cologne 'social dialogue' approach towards hard targets for raising labour supply, without specifying any demand side measures to achieve them. On the other hand there was a new concern with social exclusion – leading to a whole new policy process about the unwaged – and a concern with job quality, reflected most clearly in the Stockholm European Council (2001). In tune with the labour supply targets, the new policies on social exclusion were heavily focused on the notion that 'the best safeguard against poverty and social exclusion is a job'.[7] This view endorses the emphasis of the Employment Guidelines on 'active' benefits policies and active labour market programmes. It fails to recognise the possibility that these policies may actually worsen job quality and intensify the well-known problem of the benefits trap. In Chapters 5 and 6, we return to this problematic interaction of benefits policies, job quality and work incentives.

Social inclusion – into what jobs and how?

The Nice summit, in December 2000, fleshed out the Lisbon proposals for action on social exclusion, leading to the 'open coordination method' biannual national action plans on 'inclusion'. The purpose of the National Action Plans on Inclusion ('NAPs/incl', as they have become known) is to 'exchange good practice and mutual learning'. Each plan responds to four objectives set by the Commission: to facilitate participation in employment and access by all to resources, rights, goods and services; to prevent the risks of exclusion; to help the most vulnerable; and to 'mobilise all relevant bodies' to combat social exclusion. The Commission's summary of the NAPs/incl and comments on them (EC, 2002c) highlighted the problem of insecure and low-paid employment, especially for youth, women and the unskilled,[8] and affecting especially those without the right skills for the 'knowledge economy', or living in areas of declining traditional industries. All the national plans focused on work as a solution to poverty, but the problem of job quality was addressed mainly through 'making work pay' policies – various forms of in-work benefits or wage subsidies. Rarely was job quality seen as the responsibility of employers – with the limited exception of UK and Irish minimum wage legislation. Although the Commission identifies as best practice those active labour market policies that are 'supportive and developmental and not punitive' (p. 35), there is no recognition of the risk that workfare and excessively strict benefit conditions drive jobseekers into the worst jobs and make it easier for employers to recruit on bad terms. The European Anti-Poverty Network, representing national NGOs working with and for unemployed people, has been closely involved in consultation with the Commission about the NAPs/incl, and in general positive about the NAPs initiative. But it is critical of the emphasis on active labour market policy and of 'a conservative approach to social welfare that focuses on responsibilities of people facing poverty and exclusion, rather than their rights'.[9]

The conclusions of the Lisbon meeting did enjoin member states to 'mainstream the promotion of inclusion in employment, education and training, health and housing policies' and develop measures to assist 'minority groups, children, elderly people and people with disabilities'.[10] But for most people of working age, the solution to poverty was seen to be acquiring more skills to compete more effectively for jobs in the 'knowledge-based economy', for which they should be provided with more education and training. As discussed in Chapter 5 and 8, this raises questions about access to training: who should pay for training for precarious workers, since in practice employers rarely do? Training programmes for the unwaged are often limited to basic 'employability' level; job search obligations and workfare requirements may actually impede unemployed people from pursuing higher-level courses even if they are affordable.

The Lisbon European Council purported to offer a commitment to a Europe that is different from the USA, committed to social inclusion and 'greater social cohesion' through creating 'more and better jobs' through the 'knowledge-based economy'. In fact, according to Will Hutton (2002, p. 304), the commitments of the Lisbon summit 'come straight from the canons of American conservatism and the Washington consensus.[11] Social inclusion ... is an invocation of the importance of jobs in relieving all social ills – jobs whose growth is arrested, Lisbon says, by ... measures which support worker incomes and inhibit mobility and job search.'

Mobilising more labour

The Lisbon meeting set a target to increase the employment rate in the EU from 61 to 70 per cent by 2010, and from 51 to 60 per cent for women over the same period. Significantly, the target was set in terms of the proportion of people aged 16–64 who are working, rather than the proportion of people working among those who actually want jobs. Member states can increase the employment rate by reducing benefit dependency among lone parents and people with disabilities – but while many of these want to work, some do not and historically have been considered as legitimately in need of long-term benefit support. To have chosen the unemployment rate as a target would have failed to do justice to the many people who want to work but do not meet the standard international definition of being unemployed.[12] To have chosen the 'want work rate' – measurable in the standard Labour Force Survey, carried out in all member states, by the question 'would you like to have a job?' – might reasonably have raised taxpayers' eyebrows. But to set employment rate targets without any regard for the 'want work' rate implies a distinctly pro-employer stance; the objective appears to be to mobilise a large, low-cost labour supply especially from women and from workers on the margin of disability or retirement, ensuring competition among jobseekers to keep wages down. In the view of Barnard and Deakin (1999),

> in the context of the Luxembourg guidelines on employment policy, equal opportunities has been embraced as a means of raising the employment rate. This raises the question of whether, in future, the equality principle will serve a human rights function, or merely serve to buttress a policy aimed at the creation of employment opportunities. (p. 371)

On the other hand, the EU's policies on gender equality have unquestionably been successful in making women more equal and their labour more expensive – through the Part Time Work Directive, and provisions for equal treatment at work, maternity and parental leave.

To some degree these provisions are consistent with a policy of trying to raise the overall employment rate of the population, although the treatment of lone parents in social assistance regimes provides a point of tension at which that policy may be taken too far.

Member states can also work towards the employment target by making it more difficult for older workers to retire early, or even by raising the standard retirement age. From Stockholm onwards, prevention of early retirement assumed a major place in the employment strategy. The Stockholm summit set a target of 50 per cent employment rate for people aged 55–64 by 2010, compared to an actual rate of 40.6 per cent for this age group in 2002.[13] This has been associated with tighter rules about access to state pension schemes in several countries, to avoid early retirement becoming an escape route from unemployment. At Barcelona, in March 2002, the European Council decided to aim for an increase of around five years in the effective retirement age by 2010, to contain the rising cost of pension provision in member states. Later retirement, like increasing the employment rate of women, requires demand side policies to secure enough quality jobs; otherwise it just increases competition between workers and results in lower wages. Later retirement would be compatible with a fall in working hours for everyone, or a higher tax take being recycled as public investment. There are lessons here from the Scandinavian tradition of having a large public sector that generates jobs for women (and some men) in the provision of services for families, in particular childcare and daycare for the elderly. In effect, this makes use of the Keynesian principle of the 'balanced budget multiplier' to use high taxes as an engine of employment creation.

Job quality – a new objective

'Quality of work' is now enshrined in the European Social Agenda 2002–05, agreed at the Nice European Council (December 2000). The Stockholm meeting of the council (2001) asked for it to be made a future dimension of the Employment Guidelines. Several dimensions were identified for measurable improvements in job quality, including the working environment, health and safety, gender equality, work–life balance, opportunities for training, employee involvement in decision-making, diversity in terms of age, ethnicity and (dis)ability. Technical work began on defining indicators of each dimension for inclusion in subsequent Employment Guidelines, and the proposed indicators also include job satisfaction, the proportion of temporary and part-time workers who accept such contracts by choice, and productivity.[14] Significantly, however, the extent of wage inequality is not included. In fact the Broad Economic Policy Guidelines[15] of 2003 seem to run contrary to the policies on job quality. They call for lower wages at the bottom of the ladder, to permit greater hiring of the unemployed; low-skilled jobseekers or those in poor regions 'find themselves priced out of jobs' (para. 2.2(i)), implying a need for more training or 'to allow wages to better reflect productivity' (that is, to fall). Governments were urged to 'tackle impediments to wage flexibility' (Euro area recommendations, point 2). Also criticised are 'inflexible labour market regulations, protecting established employees but making it riskier for firms to take on new staff' (para. 2.2(i)). In this same document, the Commission made a lengthy and detailed series of recommendations to individual member states about their employment and social protection policies. Belgium is criticised for 'wage compression'; Germany should reduce regulated minimum wage levels for low-skilled workers, new job entrants and disadvantaged regions, and 'enforce the conditionality of benefits upon active job search'. Spain should 'encourage a reform of wage setting in order to better reflect geographical differentials in productivity and economic circumstances'. Surprisingly in the light of the Stockholm summit, only Spain is asked to improve the quality of jobs, by addressing the divide between those with permanent jobs and those who move constantly between temporary jobs and unemployment.

Better jobs, according to the Lisbon summit, could be achieved through training and education to raise productivity. But, for precarious workers, higher productivity is not necessarily a guarantee of job security. Moreover, the gains from higher productivity may raise profits, rather than earnings, unless workers and jobseekers have greater bargaining power. Both flexibilisation of labour markets and workfarist benefit systems, embedded in the current EU policy framework, actually reduce their bargaining power and threaten to undermine the role of trade unions, which is at the heart of the European social model of labour regulation, a problem we shall examine in more detail in Chapter 7.

The Nice summit adopted the European Charter of Fundamental Rights. Expanding on the 1989 Charter of the Fundamental Rights of Workers, this document set out not only provisions on workers' rights, but also sections on basic freedoms, citizenship and justice, and it included an important prohibition on discrimination, whether based on race, religion, age, sexual orientation or gender.[16] However, its provisions on job security and on the right to strike fell short of trade union expectations. Drafting of the text was entrusted in 1999 to a commission that consulted with employers, trade unions and NGOs. But once the draft charter had been published, certain amendments were accepted at the suggestion of the UK government, egged on by the Confederation of British Industry, while others proposed by the ETUC were rejected. These pro-employer amendments watered down the proposed protection against unfair dismissal. It would apply 'in accordance with Community law and national law and practice', thus ensuring that workers had no more rights than they had anyway under national law, and that the charter could not be used, for example, to challenge the ability of UK employers to dismiss, without giving any reason, workers who had been less than one year in post. Moreover, the right to strike would apply 'at the appropriate levels' rather than 'at all levels'. Trade unions were disappointed; the charter would fail to protect them from any future national plan to undermine or suspend existing rights to strike. The charter was not given legal force at the Nice meeting, much to the disappointment of the ETUC and the NGOs. However, it is proposed to incorporate it into the new European constitution of the 25 states in 2004.

CONCLUSION

One reading of EU policy developments since the early 1990s is that the single European market can become a successful 'balancing act' between workers' and employers' interests, fulfilling the vision of Delors and other centre-left leaders such as Jospin and Schröder. In this view, the slow progress of policy developments to address rights at work, unemployment and social exclusion is owing to institutional factors: the difficulties of policy coordination, disagreements between employers and trade unions in the 'social dialogue' process, and the reluctance of member states to relinquish sovereignty on social issues – especially in the case of the lengthy British 'opt-out' from the Maastricht 'Social Chapter'. Some commentators (for example Begg and Berghman, 2002) see the 'open coordination' process as a major step forward, reducing institutional obstacles to EU social policy.

A second interpretation is that the macro-economic policies laid down at Maastricht have provided both pressure and excuses for neo-liberal labour market policies. In the view of the ILO,

Western Europe's increased unemployment and recession of the early 1990s may have been caused by the steep rise in real interest rates that came with stringent monetary policies and by budgetary and wage restraint – largely associated with the requirements of monetary union and employment policies geared to cutting labour costs.[17]

The Maastricht convergence criteria severely impeded 'demand side' solutions to unemployment, leading member states and the EU policy process to place great pressure on unemployed people and precarious workers to adjust to the labour market, rather than expanding and shaping the labour market to help the people. But the single market and currency – even though a fundamentally capitalist project – did not have to be done the Maastricht way. Limits on government spending and borrowing were set too tight; but this could have been different and could still be changed (Hutton, 2002; Godley, 1997; Abraham, 1999). Even some employers regret the restrictive monetary and fiscal policies adopted in the early years of the single European market. Moreover, some governments struggle to keep state spending and borrowing within the limits, especially Germany and France who may press for relaxation of the budget rules.[18] On this score they would find support from the IMF, whose report in September 2003 'warned that an over-rigid application of Europe's fiscal rulebook could push the eurozone deeper into trouble'.[19] However, the report also criticised European governments for expensive welfare states and rigid labour markets. While some critics of the Maastricht framework see its abandonment as a precondition of a more Keynesian, more social-democratic form of capitalism, employers and the supranational gurus of neo-liberalism would prefer that opportunity to be used for corporate tax cuts.

A third interpretation of the single European market is that it is inherently resistant to this kind of change, because of the power relations involved and because it serves the purpose of large companies who lobby supranational institutions for the policies they want. Balanyá *et al.* (2000) present a slightly conspiratorial version of this view, emphasising the extraordinary influence of company lobbyists on EU policy developments. Social dialogue is at risk of being dominated by the superior lobbying resources of the employers' side, as shown by the extensive power and influence of the employers' grouping, the European Round Table. Bonefeld (2002) emphasises instead the structural importance of the EU as a way of removing economic and social policy decisions from democratic control. Not all governments find this to their advantage – for example, the Thatcher/ Major governments opposed the supranational 'impositions' of the Maastricht 'social chapter'. But more generally, the EU economic policy framework provides an apparent neo-liberal imperative that the capitalist state can use as a bargaining counter against workers' representatives; competitiveness of the national economy must essentially be sought by methods that make labour cheaper, and shrink the public sector.

The truth may lie somewhere between the second and the third interpretations. Thus to suggest a radical reformulation of EU social and employment policy is neither utopian nor does it idealise the Keynesian form of capitalism in the way that perhaps underpins some of the arguments against the 'Maastricht straitjacket'. A rethink must start by asserting that Europe is, or should be, a people rather than a market, and that labour is not a commodity. Rather than maximising the supply of labour, the primary aim of policy should be to empower people to obtain better living and working conditions. In the case of the unwaged and of precarious workers, this invokes the need to protect them, and help them to protect themselves, against market forces – the process that Esping-Andersen (1990) identifies as 'de-commodification'. The 'work first' approach of the 'employability' guideline and to some extent even of the National Action Plans on Social Inclusion is antagonistic to 'de-commodification'. 'De-commodification' would rather imply a focus on rights to income and services. This is the perspective of unemployed people themselves, whose views and experiences are reported in later chapters of this book; their needs, rather than those of employers, should inform the design of benefits policy.

A minimum agenda for reform of EU social and employment policy might have four elements:

- slackening of restrictions on public spending and borrowing, and a commitment to use public spending as an engine for expansion of state services and the social economy, financed by taxes on the wealthy and on environmentally damaging activities. This would also entail a halt to privatisation, which reduces the share of employment under the control of non-market forces and emasculates the capacity of the state to act as employer of last resort;

- a minimum income standard for unwaged benefits, at least defined as a proportion of each average national wage level;
- minimum targets for collective service provision, along the lines of the targets to improve childcare provision, which were agreed at the Barcelona summit of March 2002.[20] Action on poverty and the rights of the unwaged must go beyond minimum income guarantees to include rights to education and training, medical treatment, housing, cultural activity, opportunities for social contact and geographical mobility. These are essentially collective services, which require public finance;
- an upward harmonisation of labour standards in terms of wage levels and rights to job security. This will become more and more necessary as new and poorer countries join the EU, providing a reserve of low-cost workers whom employers will be ready to exploit.

The question of EU labour regulation is addressed further in Chapter 7. The existing directives do not address minimum standards across member states, except in a small range of areas – such as working hours, paid leave, parental and maternity leave. Others are about equality between different kinds of workers within countries, rather than equality between countries; they are provisions to make 'flexible' work acceptable rather than to achieve upward harmonisation across countries. A part-time worker can claim equal pay with a comparable full-time worker in the same country, but if the lowest wage of full-time workers is still one of the lowest in the EU (as in the UK) that may not be much comfort, or much protection against 'social dumping' for better-paid workers elsewhere. Moreover, none of the EU directives effectively provide a right to job security. In 1994 the ETUC and European Parliament wanted EU legislation for protection against individual dismissal,[21] but the Nice charter leaves such protection to existing national law. Privatisation, frequent relocation of plants, the shift towards 'throwaway labour' – all continue to undermine job security in most member states, as we shall see in Chapters 6 and 7. They also undermine trade union power, but EU law has not guaranteed a right to trade union recognition or to protection for strikers against employer action short of dismissal.

With the 'poverty trap' and insecure employment a major dimension of debates on social protection, it is crucial that the employment dimension of 'inclusion' should not be equated with getting a job of any kind. If employment is to be a solution, we must ask, what kind of job? The poor wages and conditions of jobs accessible to unemployed people were among the most important grievances of benefit claimants in all the four countries investigated in the Minima Sociaux research.

5
Benefits Enforcing Work

There is a Europe-wide tendency towards a 're-commodification' of labour through tightening of the conditions for claiming unemployed benefits. All seven countries studied here have increased the conditionality of benefit in the last ten years (Lodovici, 2000). That is, the range of job offers that must be accepted gets wider; pressure to accept low-paid or temporary work is increased. Job search is being more closely monitored, and more claimants are obliged to take training not of their own choosing or to join workfare schemes (described in Chapter 8). This intensification of jobseeker obligations is presented as a shift towards 'active' benefits (European Commission, DGV 1998c, 1999), a goal that has been enshrined in the 'employability' pillar of the EU's Employment Guidelines since 1998. Reduced access to benefits for the unwaged is motivated by the view that 'over-generous' allowances lead to people remaining dependent on them longer than necessary. Through its Jobs Study of 1994 and survey reports on individual countries, the OECD has provided political and theoretical driving forces for the transformation of income maintenance into 'welfare to work' policy.

Unemployment insurance is becoming less a social right to compensation for job loss (which unemployed people often feel they have paid for through contributions) and more a payment for job-seeking – reflected in the UK title of the benefit from 1996, 'Jobseeker's Allowance' and in its French translation, 'Allocation de retour à l'emploi'. This transformation can be traced only partly to cost pressures on social insurance funds; in 1993, the cost of pensions was over 70 per cent of social transfers in the EU, compared to less than 10 per cent for unemployed people.[1] Moreover, the new placement, training and workfare programmes are themselves costly. Rather, the changing treatment of unemployed people is due more to a deliberate policy choice. 'Supply side' policies focus on getting them into the jobs the market offers, rather than using the state to create jobs of last resort.

The erosion of benefit rights and tighter conditions about seeking and accepting jobs is a response to change in the labour market, although it also feeds that change, as we shall see in Chapter 8.

In the UK and Germany the margin of wages over any reasonable level of benefits is falling as the lowest wages fail to keep up with the economy as a whole. Low-paid jobs have grown faster than those in the middle third of the pay ladder in the UK, Denmark and Belgium during 1993–2001 (OECD, 2003a, pp. 41–2). Most EU countries – especially France and Sweden – have seen a rising share of temporary and part-time work in recent years. This rise has been even more apparent in the 'stock' of vacancies that confronts unemployed people than in actual jobs. Since low-paid, temporary or part-time vacancies offer poor incentives, the result is a rise in the ratio of unfilled vacancies to unemployed jobseekers.[2] The 'stick' of tighter benefit conditions is increasingly used to push the dole queue into them. 'Workfare state' theorists such as Peck and Theodore (2000b) write of the trend to an increasingly 'workfarist' benefit system, in which tightening of benefit conditions serves the same functions as workfare itself – that is, driving unemployed people into low-paid or insecure jobs that they would rather reject.

Policy-makers face a challenge: how to induce unemployed people to take much less attractive jobs than the ones they held in the past. At least four solutions have been tried. Tightening benefit conditions is perhaps the most widespread; others are:

- reducing the level of benefits: Germany, the UK and Denmark have done this in the last decade, as described later. The Swedish government tried in 1996, but was forced by trade union pressure to reverse its decision;
- shortening the maximum duration of insurance-based benefit: this cuts some people off because they fail to pass the means test for the last-resort social assistance benefits; the UK, Denmark, and Belgium have done this;
- wage supplements such as tax credits: this type of policy often described as 'making work pay'. It is clearly helpful, but has some negative effects, discussed later. The UK introduced Family Credit in 1988. Tax credits replaced Family Credit in 1999, with higher wage supplements for low-paid parents, and in 2003 they were extended to workers without children. France, Germany and Belgium also introduced tax credits in 2000–01.

The alteration of benefit conditions is one way in which the state manipulates and mobilises the 'reserve army' of labour. Only those who are actively searching for work and 'employable' will serve the economic function of the labour reserve in the capitalist economy, to reduce pressure for wage increases and for better conditions. The shift to 'workfarist' benefits prioritises this economic function of the unemployed reserve and pushes protection from poverty into second place. Supply side orthodoxy holds that less wage pressure will lead to more jobs. In the view of Richard Layard:

> new jobs are created when the effective supply of labour increases ... if the labour supply increases and the number of jobs does not, inflation starts to fall ... which in turn increases employment. (Layard, 1998, p. 26)

In Layard's interpretation the 'effective' supply of labour will increase as the unemployed become more 'available' through more active job search and reduced wage expectations, and as participants in active labour market programmes become 'employable' through training and work experience. Such policies do appear to reduce long-term unemployment, largely through pricing jobseekers into low-paid or insecure work. However, they have a cost – to wage earners in general through keeping down wage levels, and to the taxpayer, through making it easier for employers to hire short-term workers who are maintained by the 'dole' between jobs.

INTERNATIONAL DIFFERENCES IN BENEFIT ENTITLEMENTS

Among the seven countries studied here there are wide differences in insurance-based benefit levels; Denmark and Sweden stand out as having the highest replacement rates of earnings for unemployed people, and the UK the lowest. The UK system is flat rate, while all the others are earnings-related. The first column of Table 5.1 shows entitlements to insurance-based benefit, as a percentage of earnings, for those who could claim it. The highest replacement ratios in Denmark and Sweden apply only up to a certain wage level. Effective replacement rates in all countries may vary between men and women, and in Germany with family status. The last two columns of Table 5.1 show average entitlements to national benefit schemes for all unemployed people, including those not covered by insurance.[3] They are lower and reflect differences in the coverage and duration of benefit entitlements as well as the replacement rate. Thus the difference between Sweden and Denmark in these columns reflects the much longer duration of insurance benefit in Denmark.

Jobseekers usually have access to means-tested social assistance when their insurance entitlement is used up. In most cases social assistance is qualitatively different from social insurance and may involve being placed under some kind of social work supervision through a 'reintegration contract' (France, Belgium, Spain) or an 'activation plan' (Denmark, Sweden). Increasingly, activation or reintegration contracts involve workfare obligations, discussed in Chapter 8.

Table 5.1   Replacement rates, duration and coverage of unemployment insurance benefits 1991–95

	1	*2*	*3*	*4*	
	Replacement rates for over-25s, unemployed for three months	*Maximum duration of unemployment benefit, years*	*Coverage rate of unemployment benefits*	*Benefit rates before tax as % of previous pre-tax earnings (OECD synthetic indicator)*	
	1993	*1995*	*1995*	*1991*	*1995*
Belgium	45–50%	indefinite	82	42.3	41.6
Denmark	65–80%	5.0	84	51.9	70.3
France	65–70%	5.0	45	37.2	37.5
Germany	45–65%	0.5–3.5	75	28.1	26.4
Spain	50–60%	2.0	32	33.5	31.7
Sweden	80%	1.2	n.a.	29.4	27.3
UK	25%	1.0	64	17.5	18.1

Sources and notes:
Column 1: Eurostat data for average entitlements of all claimants over 25, insured and unemployed for three months (from EC (1998c), pp. 97–8)
Column 2: adapted from Lodovici (2000), p. 61. The figure for Sweden includes a period of mandatory participation in a labour market programme; for Germany, duration depends on age and status
Columns 3 and 4: OECD's synthetic indicator of the generosity of benefit systems, based on combining replacement rates for claimants in a wide range of different situations regarding family, length of unemployment and level of previous earnings; OECD database. Note that these figures exclude entitlements to regional and municipal social assistance schemes, but include national schemes for people who have exhausted insurance rights

Coverage of insurance benefits – the proportion of unemployed entitled to claim – is affected by the duration of entitlements and also by the extent of temporary jobs. In Spain, the prevalence of short-term jobs, especially for youth, meant barely a third of unemployed people were covered by insurance benefits in 1995, compared to a European average of around two-thirds (European Commission, 1998c, p. 97). This is especially harsh in view of under-developed social assistance provisions. Gradually, during the 1990s, the regions of the

Spanish state have developed 'minimum income' schemes, led by the Basque country and Catalunya. In Catalunya, the grants have been highly discretionary and linked to training and other 'reintegration contract' obligations sometimes amounting to workfare. In 2000, a national reintegration income scheme was introduced for uninsured unemployed aged over 44 who have dependants. This is conditional on taking part in activation of some kind.

The gap in replacement rates between the highest and the lowest countries narrows considerably when one looks at the combined entitlements of particular kinds of household to unemployment insurance and other benefits such as social assistance, housing allowances and family benefits. The OECD calculates these entitlements as a percentage of a 'reference' wage equal to two-thirds of average net earnings (Table 5.2). Single people in the UK do much better on this comparison, because Housing Benefit is included. The effect of the UK's 1996 reforms is seen in the fall in replacement rates during the late 1990s. The OECD argues[4] that there is a slight upward drift in maximum benefit entitlements in the late 1990s. However, many people get less than the maximum because of means-testing.

Table 5.2   Benefits from all sources as a percentage of a low wage 1995–99

| | Benefits from all sources as percentage of two-thirds average post-tax earnings | | | |
| | Couple with two children | | Single person | |
	1995	1999	1995	1999
Belgium	76	79	86	85
Denmark	95	95	90	89
France	87	82	85	78
Germany	76	75	73	67
Spain	73	76	70	76
Sweden	85	90	78	82
UK	80	54	75	66

Source: OECD (1996b), Annex, Table 5.2; and OECD web site http://www.oecd.org, accessed 15.8.03
Note: figures are for legal entitlements at the beginning of an unemployment spell, assuming rent is a constant percentage of income in all cases.

CHANGES IN BENEFIT RATES, DURATION AND ACCESS CONDITIONS

Over a longer period, a useful indicator of changes in benefit generosity is expenditure on unemployment benefits per unemployed person measured as a percentage of per capita GDP. This is presented in Table 5.3, which shows a decline in spending per unemployed person between 1980 and 1993. This was partly owing to longer, more frequent spells of unemployment, so that fewer claimants had full insurance records, and partly to cuts in duration of entitlements or stricter contribution requirements. No later data are available in such detail, but according to the European Commission average expenditure on benefits per unemployed person fell during the 1990s in the EU as a whole, largely owing to the second factor.[5] However, it did not do so in all countries. The falls in Belgium, Denmark, Germany, Spain, France, the UK and Greece contrasted with a stable level in Sweden and Austria, and a rise in benefits per jobseeker in the Netherlands, Ireland, Portugal and Finland. These data reflect the changing composition of the unemployed as well as changes in entitlement rules.

Table 5.3   Expenditure on unemployment benefits per unemployed person, as a percentage of GDP per capita

	1980	1990	1993
Belgium	65.3	59.6	48.2
Denmark	88.0	61.3	61.8
France	38.6	33.2	36.1
Germany (West)	58.7	36.0	45.0
Spain	79.6	52.5	73.7
Sweden	n.a.	n.a.	n.a.
UK	48.1	29.8	34.9

Source: EC (1998c)

There is evidence that the longer the maximum duration of benefit entitlements, or the higher the ratio of benefits to average earnings (the 'replacement rate') the higher is unemployment (OECD, 1994; Esping-Andersen, 2000a, pp. 109–10; OECD, 2003a). From this derives a common OECD recommendation to individual countries that benefit entitlements should be curtailed.

The proportion of jobseekers able to receive insurance-based benefits fell in Germany, Denmark, Belgium, Sweden and France during the 1990s, largely due to rule changes, throwing more people on to means-tested benefits.[6] In the UK the number entitled to insurance benefit fell dramatically when its duration was halved from twelve months to six in 1996. France, however, raised benefits for some categories of long-term unemployed people as a concession alongside the tighter benefit conditions introduced in 2001. Back in 1988, the RMI (Revenu Minimum d'Insertion) was introduced to compensate for the low and falling coverage of unemployment insurance. Youth remained outside this system; almost half a million people under 25 without dependant children cannot claim the RMI, so that a 'basic income' for everyone has become a popular demand among unemployed people's movements in France. A similar demand has developed in Spain.

The main changes in rules concerning duration and level of unemployment insurance are illustrated in Table 5.4. In Germany, Spain, Sweden and for youth in the UK, insurance-based benefits have been reduced in the 1990s. But France in 2001 improved benefits for certain groups. In Denmark and Germany, benefits for long-term unemployed have also been cut. Several countries introduced tougher conditions about contribution records and about the maximum length of claim, throwing more claimants on to means-tested social assistance schemes, which often also have workfare obligations – described in detail in Chapter 8.

Access to income maintenance has also been reduced in some countries for other unwaged groups. The 'reserve army of labour' has fluid boundaries, which can be shifted by changes in the design of the benefits system. It potentially includes lone parents, a growing element of the unwaged population in many European countries. In continental Europe, lone parents have generally been required to seek work as a condition of receiving benefits when their children are quite young; the UK, allowing them to remain full-time carers until the youngest child is 16, is unusual (Gough, 1997). Requiring lone parents to have a Job Centre Plus interview about their prospects of work brings UK policies more into line with the rest of the EU. In 2001–02 compulsory interviews gradually began to be introduced for both lone parents and people with disabilities. Previously their only contact with the employment service had been if they chose to take up the voluntary 'New Deal' programmes for these categories. Now all claimants of income maintenance benefits, unless very seriously disabled or with very young babies, must attend interviews to examine their prospects of returning to the labour market. The intention is to offer advice rather than pressure to seek work. To encourage economically inactive women to enter the labour market, the UK also now requires the partners of unemployed claimants to make themselves 'available for work' in certain cases.

The boundary between active jobseekers and other unwaged is also influenced by the ways in which people can transfer to early

Table 5.4   Changes in income maintenance benefits (rates and availability) since 1990

Belgium	1996	Level of insurance benefit reduced and waiting period lengthened
Denmark	1994–99	Duration of 'passive' unemployment insurance rights (i.e., before claimants are obliged to join an active labour market programme) reduced gradually from seven years to one year. Minimum contribution record increased from 26 weeks to 52
	2002	Cut in social assistance rates
France	2001	'Degressivity' feature ended, so that benefit no longer falls as claim lengthens
	2002	Longer waiting period for those with redundancy pay; increased contribution requirement for unemployed over 55
	2003	Duration of ASS (Allocation Specifique de Solidarité), the benefit claimed by those whose insurance rights have run out, restricted to two years
Germany	1994	Small reduction in unemployment insurance rates and unemployment assistance rates (by 1% of former earnings for those with children, otherwise by 3% of former earnings). Redundancy pay to be taken from benefit entitlement. Lower benefits for asylum seekers. Sickness benefit also reduced
	2003	Further benefit cuts announced in October
Spain	1992	Benefit rates cut from 80% of former earnings to 70% for first six months of unemployment, and from 70% to 60% after that. Minimum contribution record raised from six months to twelve
	2000	Nationwide minimum income scheme introduced for older unemployed with dependants, but with obligation to join reintegration programmes
Sweden	1993	Minimum contribution record raised (and again in late 1990s). Benefit rates cut from 90% of former earnings to 80%
	1995–97	Benefit rates cut from 80% of former earnings to 75%, then restored to former level
	1999	Cash ceiling on maximum unemployment benefit raised, allowing more people to claim the maximum 80% rate
UK	1995	Tougher medical tests for access to disability-related benefits (giving exemption from the duty to seek work)
	1996	Duration of insurance benefit reduced from twelve months to six months
	1998	Benefit rates reduced for under-25s. Housing Benefit maxima restricted. One Parent Benefit abolished, meaning lower income for certain lone parents

Sources: EC (1998c), www.eiro.eurofound.ie

retirement provisions or incapacity benefit. International differences in the proportions of 'disabled' and 'retired' probably reflect differences in benefit systems more than health status (EC, 1998c; Kvist, 1998). In the UK, an unusually high proportion of men of working age are not working because of sickness or disability (Alcock *et al.*, 2003, pp. 31, 159). This observation concerns how people describe themselves in the Labour Force Survey; but it is also true that claims for *incapacity benefit* are correlated with local unemployment rates. Incapacity benefit in the UK may provide an 'escape route' for older men in poor health who cannot find another suitable job and, in a more flexible state pension system, would be permitted to retire. In Denmark, Sweden, Germany, Spain and Belgium, people in their fifties can access their state pension early at a reduced rate, although such rights are gradually being curtailed to persuade people to work longer and preserve the financial viability of pension systems in the face of an ageing population.

CONDITIONALITY: FORMS

Five key features of benefit systems influence claimants' jobseeking behaviour:

(1) job search requirements: what people must do to demonstrate adequate commitment to finding work;
(2) 'availability for work' rules: what jobs must be accepted, or may be refused (also known as the 'job refusal' test or 'job acceptance' condition);
(3) rules on how voluntary quits affect benefit eligibility (also known as the 'job departure test');
(4) the extent and severity of sanctions for breaking the rules;
(5) the extent of 'earnings disregards', or permitted co-receipt of benefits and earnings; in Francophone countries this is known as 'cumul'.

We now examine how these features work and attempt a cross-national overview of how they have changed during the 1990s

Job search conditions

A requirement for intensive job search is thought to be crucial for reducing unemployment. In the early 1990s it was shown that the UK's 'Restart' interviews, questioning claimants about their job search strategy and persuading them to consider particular vacancies or accept training, tended to reduce unemployment duration (White and Lakey, 1992). This approach is intensified in the New Deal personal adviser system. The idea of a job search contract setting out what a person will do to seek work entered UK practice in 1989, with the 'back to work plan'. From 1996, this developed into the 'Jobseeker's Agreement', in which claimants must agree what steps they will take to seek work and show what they have done every two weeks. Action plans similar to the Jobseeker's Agreement were recommended by the OECD's Jobs Study in 1994. After their introduction in Germany in 1996, the use of sanctions rose sharply (Adema, Gray and Kahl, 2001).

Influenced perhaps by the apparent success of the UK model in cutting unemployment during the 1990s, France and Spain also developed proposals in 2001–02, for UK-style 'back to work' plans and frequent compulsory interviews. In Belgium, a new initiative in 2000/01 put more resources into systematic interviewing and monitoring of claimants.[7] To their opponents, these measures signal a curtailment of claimants' freedom to refuse unsuitable jobs. As described in Chapter 2, there was fierce opposition in France from unions and social movements of the unemployed. In Spain, similar reform proposals were eventually withdrawn after protests, as described later.[8]

How compulsory interviews and sanctions are used in practice depends on staff resources and on whether there are enough jobs and programme places to offer. In times and regions of high unemployment, even the best-resourced employment service in Europe, the Swedish one, has had difficulty applying job search and job refusal conditions. Both in the UK and Germany, the Minima Sociaux interviews suggested that the strictness with which availability for work rules are applied varied between individuals – and in the UK also between areas. In line with other studies of UK unemployed (Finn and Blackmore, 1998), jobseekers found their interviews sometimes bullying, sometimes lax.

'Availability for work' conditions

'Availability for work' conditions define the types of job offer that claimants must accept. They vary widely; in Sweden, Spain, Denmark and at the beginning of Belgian claims, a suitable job is defined in relation to qualifications and experience. Later in Belgian insurance claims, it is defined by reference to benefit levels and thus bears some relationship to previous earnings. In Germany, jobseekers in their first six months of unemployment can refuse jobs offering less than a certain percentage of their previous earnings. After that, they must accept any wage at least equal to their benefit entitlement. Certain categories of jobseekers can be required to accept almost any job;

this applies to German and Belgian claimants of social assistance and to most people in the UK who have been out of work over three months.[9]

'Availability for work' conditions also affect permission to study or do voluntary work. UK rules limit study or voluntary work to a maximum number of hours per week, usually 16. Both in the Minima Sociaux fieldwork and in Finn and Blackmore's survey (1998), this occasioned many arguments with Job Centre officials about what was permitted. In France and Belgium, recent tightening of benefit conditions implies more difficulty for claimants studying outside official reinsertion programmes.

Rules on voluntary quits

Most benefit systems penalise people who leave a job voluntarily, with the exception of Denmark where an unemployment insurance claim can be resumed within a month. In the UK, benefits may be denied for up to six months following a voluntary quit or an 'own fault' sacking; in Belgium for up to a year and in Spain indefinitely (OECD, 2000, p. 135). In practice this makes claimants fear to take a job if they are not sure about its suitability or whether they will be fairly treated. They can be trapped in a job that turns out badly by the fear of several months without benefits. France and Germany have slightly less severe rules on this point.

Sanctions

Of the seven countries considered here, the UK uses sanctions most frequently. In 1997–98 they affected over 10 per cent of JSA claimants, compared to just over 4 per cent in Belgium or Denmark. Since a summary of the rules was last published by the OECD,[10] relating to 1997, sanctions appear to have become more frequent, perhaps continuing the trend reported by Adema *et al.* (2001). They probably affect far more now than the 1.1 per cent reported by the OECD. Sanctions were a major issue for German informants in the Minima Sociaux project (Lévy et al., 2000a), who felt heavy pressure to take low-paid jobs and workfare placements. Several insurance claimants had appealed against sanctions imposed for refusal to pursue a job opportunity that they felt was too low-paid. Social assistance claimants who refuse a job may have their benefit cut by 25 per cent; repeated 'offences' can lead, in extreme cases, to no benefits at all except for the claimant's dependant children (Adema *et al.*, 2001). Conflicts between officials and claimants have recently developed over the increasingly frequent sanctions and strict availability for work conditions (which the Schröder government has made even tougher in 2002–03). In several areas trade unions and unemployed people's associations were meeting with employment office managers to try to resolve such conflicts. In France, only 5 per cent of those leaving registered unemployment in 1999 lost unemployment benefits because of sanctions (Lévy *et al.*, 2000b). Sanctions for claimants of the RMI are very rare, a mere 0.03 per cent of cases in 1999 (Enjolras *et al.*, 2001). Sanctioned persons can sometimes keep part of their benefit, or even claim social assistance, but not in the UK where 'hardship payments' (usually 60 per cent of normal entitlements, and not available for some single people) are the only possibility. However, indefinite exclusion from insurance benefit is possible in the other countries in extreme cases, while many instances of sanctions imposed in the UK are only two to four weeks, and the maximum is six months.

Does the use of sanctions induce people to find jobs faster? According to studies in the Netherlands, yes, it does (OECD, 2000, p. 140). But they can only do so if there are vacancies and if employers will accept them. For some jobseekers, the problem is not their lack of effort but that employers continually reject them. Thus the effect of sanctions, or the fear of sanctions, on the most disadvantaged – ex-prisoners, people with fragile mental health, people at risk of racial discrimination – may be just to add to their problems, rather than chase them into jobs that they cannot get. For this reason Handler (2003) questions the usefulness of sanctions imposed by American welfare caseworkers, in particular for the 'hard to help'. While almost all unemployment insurance systems have always had some powers of benefit suspension to use against 'free riders', their extensive use may interfere with the process of advising claimants, who may be afraid to discuss job search problems frankly if they think the caseworker is looking for reasons to stop their benefit.

In Denmark and Sweden, sanctions practice and the overall tone of officials' treatment appears very different from that in the other countries, at least for insured unemployed. When Danish employment service staff may recommend to the unemployment insurance funds that someone should be sanctioned for refusing to accept a certain job or 'activation' offer, it is up to the trade union officials in charge of a fund to decide whether to impose a sanction. They have little financial incentive to do so, since the funds are mainly financed by central government (OECD, 1995b, p. 123). Although since 1994 the Danish Employment Service has a right to challenge a fund for refusing to impose a sanction, in practice this may not often happen. In 1995–96, the Danish government became suspicious that the fund administrators were too lenient with people who turned down jobs and set up a special unit to monitor this issue (OECD, 2000, p. 141).[11] The 'activation' regime for insurance claimants and social assistance claimants was unified in 2002, opening the door to harmonising the sanctions regime and taking it beyond trade union influence. At the same time the government set up a non-union unemployment insurance fund, which people may join as an alternative to the union ones; it was dissuaded by union pressure from a plan to scrap the existing union-administered funds.

Surprisingly in view of Sweden's reputation for strict benefit rules, only 0.4 per cent of insured unemployed were sanctioned in 1993; no more recent information seems available. Weak enforcement of apparently strict rules seems to have occurred partly because high unemployment stretched the resources of the employment service, and partly because trade union-run insurance funds questioned officials' decisions. The OECD referred to 'reluctance among unemployment insurance funds to punish their members' but also suspected that the public employment service itself did not want to impose severe sanctions on claimants.[12] A later OECD report comments that 'while the formal eligibility and availability criteria were more stringent than in most other countries, their enforcement was weak' (OECD, 2001a, p. 60). In 1999, sanctions were reduced in order to encourage their more frequent use.[13]

'Cumul' or earnings disregards

Both France and Belgium, in the late 1990s, had particularly extensive facilities for legally doing casual or part-time work alongside benefit – the practice known as 'cumul' (co-receipt) of benefits and wages. This permits many claimants to combine benefits with a low part-time wage, take a few days' casual work without losing benefit, or 'top up' wages earned within labour market programmes. Around one in six of all registered unemployed in Belgium in 1999 were involved in part-time work of some kind, or registered for occasional casual jobs under workfare arrangements (Ballal and Bouquin, 2000). Part-time work combined with a part-time benefit claim is also extensive in Sweden, and is criticised by the OECD as a loophole in the system of 'activation', which is supposed to draw people back into full-time work.[14] German, Danish and Spanish arrangements allow part-time work to be combined with benefits to some degree, but without attracting such extensive use of 'cumul' as in France or Belgium. The UK, however, has a very low limit of disregarded earnings. Since 1996, part-time claims for insurance-based benefit are no longer possible.

'Cumul' helps jobseekers to avoid the risk of sanctions, by making it easier to take low quality jobs voluntarily. It helps the large number who can only find part-time work. Claimants can also gain or maintain work experience without having to make the (often difficult) decision to rely entirely on a low wage. But there is a widespread impression that 'cumul' permits employers to fill low-paid or short-hours jobs more easily.[15] In particular, 'cumul' may make it easier to fill short-term agency jobs through which employers casualise their workforce. In France, 215,000 unemployed in 1999 were registered with non-profit temporary help agencies for erratic short assignments (Lévy *et al.*, 2000b), an arrangement encouraged by 'cumul' and suspected of substituting for regular jobs.

New arrangements in France and Belgium are likely to restrict 'cumul'. The French government is currently considering changing the RMI to an RMA (Revenu Minimum d'Activité), which would require those who can work to accept a part-time workfare placement and not to take any other job unless they cease claiming altogether. Belgium has also introduced new workfare obligations for claimants of the former 'minimex' (now renamed the Revenu Minimum d'Intégration Sociale) and is trying to discourage 'cumul', instead drawing people into full-time work through tax credits.

CONDITIONALITY: TRENDS IN THE SEVEN COUNTRIES

We now consider, country by country, the shift towards greater conditionality since the early 1990s. In Scandinavia and in the UK, this has been a gradual process. In France and Belgium, conditionalities in 1999–2000 (at the time of the Minima Sociaux fieldwork) were generally weaker and much less strictly applied than in the neo-liberal regimes. However, they have since been considerably tightened. Germany, confronted with an intractable post-reunification unemployment crisis, embarked on a series of benefit changes and cuts in 2003–04, which are still in development at the time of writing.

Denmark

Prior to 1994, the 'activation' regime required claimants to attend review interviews, analogous to the Restart interview in the UK, at three monthly intervals. After three months, they had a compulsory job search course lasting one or two weeks. After two and a half years, they were entitled to a public sector job offer at normal wages, lasting up to nine months, which qualified them for a new claim on unemployment insurance if needed.[16]

Danish labour market reforms in 1994 abolished this 'requalification' option, so that benefits are now strictly time-limited. Successively stricter time limits on 'passive' benefit receipt were introduced till in 1999, people over 25 had to join an active labour market programme after one year (Madsen, 2003, p. 76). Mandatory active labour market programmes (ALMPs) for youth had already been introduced in the early 1990s. In 1997, the Social Assistance Act strengthened the duties of social assistance claimants to take part in ALMPs, which no longer requalify them for new insurance rights. If they refuse, they lose 20 per cent of their social assistance.

Since 1995, job acceptance rules in Denmark have been tightened; claimants must accept any type of work they could manage to do with minimal training (European Commission, 1998c, p. 102). In practice, many low-paid jobs advertised by employers through Job Centres are rarely proposed to jobseekers because they would get less than benefits, so that the maximum rate of unemployment benefit acts as an informal wage floor (OECD, 1995).

The Liberal-Conservative government elected in 2001 introduced, a year later, reforms that may gradually change this situation. Social assistance has been cut; for singles to 40 per cent less than the maximum rate of unemployment insurance benefit, and for couples to 20 per cent less, to induce people to take low-paid jobs.[17] There will be more emphasis on finding people 'real' jobs rather than training or ALMP jobs in the non-profit sector.

Sweden

The immediate effect of the jobs crisis of the early 1990s was to weaken conditionality; in the mid-1980s, about 4 per cent of unemployment insurance claims were questioned by the public employment service for alleged breach of labour market conditions, but by 1993, the PES had few vacancies available to test jobseekers' intentions, and the proportion of claims questioned fell to 0.4 per cent (OECD, 1995b, p. 64). People suspected of inadequate job search may be challenged to accept a programme place sooner than usual, and may be sanctioned if they refuse. The sanction for refusing a job offer or a place on an ALMP is a one-month benefit suspension; or in severe cases suspension of all benefits till the person has done 20 days' work. In 1999 the 'job refusal test' was tightened; claimants had to accept a wider range of occupations and a wider geographical radius of search. In the 1980s, jobseekers had a right to be offered a job at normal wages, or a training programme, when their insurance benefit ran out. As the job guarantee became more difficult to meet, this right was gradually replaced by a duty to join municipal workfare schemes, as described in Chapter 8.

However, Swedish unions have so far resisted erosion of benefit rights, even achieving an increase in the maximum UI amount in 2001. Until 2002, it was still possible to requalify for a new insurance record by taking part in ALMPs, including training schemes – a provision the OECD attacked as an unduly long extension of the benefit entitlement. This right has now been abolished; to rebuild a contribution record for insurance-based benefit, Swedish jobseekers must get a normal job rather than just join a programme.

UK

The tightening of benefit conditions in the UK took place in many stages, going back to the introduction of the Restart Programme of compulsory 'counselling' interviews in 1986 (Finn, 1995; Jones, 1996). In 1989 the penalty for refusing a 'suitable' job was lengthened from 13 weeks' benefit loss to 26 (Finn, 1995), and a condition was introduced that any full-time job must be accepted after the end of the claimant's 'permitted period' to search for his or her normal occupation, usually 13 weeks. Enforcement of this was made stronger by the introduction of the Jobseeker's Agreement in 1996,[18] through which the claimant must agree with an adviser the minimum acceptable wage from the start of a claim, the range of jobs that is acceptable, and the steps that will be taken to find work. Also in 1996, benefit levels for youths aged 18–24 were substantially reduced.

The transformation of Unemployment Benefit into Jobseeker's Allowance (JSA) in 1996 marked new conditions and sanctions powers. Claimants without children can now be denied even hardship payments for the first two weeks of benefit suspension. Previously, only one-week Restart courses had been compulsory; but under JSA, for the first time, claimants could be sanctioned for refusing to comply with a 'jobseeker's direction' to join any training programme. This set up the framework for the compulsory Project Work in 1996–97 and the New Deal from 1998, described in Chapter 8. Sanctions for various reasons had almost doubled in 1995/96, to an astonishing 300,000 or 14 per cent of unemployed claimants (Murray, 1996); but surprisingly, after JSA was introduced, the number fell back to only 65,849 (5.5 per cent) in 1998/99. The compulsory New Deal programmes occasioned a further rise in the use of sanctions, reaching at least a fifth of all youth participants (*Working Brief*, August 1999, p. 12; Bryson *et al.*, 2000). The sanctions rules on the New Deal have been tightened over time.

Germany

Job acceptance rules for German jobseekers are complex and have become considerably stricter in the 1990s. Formerly, insurance claimants could restrict their search to occupations similar to what they had done before, but since 1994 this is no longer permitted. Hence, for some claimants interviewed by Martin Gueck (Lévy *et al.*, 2000b), occupational downgrading following job loss was a major issue. In 2001, the Job-Aqtiv Act introduced a formal 'jobseekers' agreement', which was criticised by trade unions for placing more pressure on unemployed people to accept lower-paid jobs.[19] Jobseekers were obliged to widen the geographical area of search, and single people can even be obliged to move to different regions – a response to the more severe unemployment in the East compared to the West. Stricter conditionality has had a major effect on the numbers unemployed[20] – but only by enforcing the acceptance of lower wages in some sectors and locations, as detailed later.

The OECD, in a recent report on Germany (OECD, 2003b), suggests that 'social assistance benefits should be cut substantially for recipients who are able to work but reject job offers'. It also opposes the exemption from job search requirements of unemployed who are over 58, which is 'a form of early retirement'. Following the Hartz Commission on benefit reform, the Schröder government seems to be taking the OECD's advice. There will be cuts in benefit rates for the long-term unemployed in 2004.[21] There are plans to make benefit rules still tougher with the amalgamation of 'unemployment assistance' (the lower rate of earnings-related benefit received in 2003 and earlier for one year after insurance entitlement runs out) and social assistance into a single regime with very tight job acceptance conditions.[22]

Spain

The Spanish government's proposals to change the benefit system in 2002 met with huge opposition. Compared to the UK or Germany, the conditionalities to be imposed seemed mild: a 'suitable job' was to be defined as one similar to any job the applicant had previously held for at least six months, and reduced social security taxes were offered to anyone who accepted lower pay.[23] But the proposals envisaged a 'back to work plan' system similar to the French PARE and the British Jobseeker's Agreement – signalling a move towards much more monitoring of job search. Phasing out of the 'subsidio agraria', the special – almost unconditional – rural social assistance for agricultural workers who could only find work for part of the year – caused outrage; its purpose was apparently to induce these unemployed to seek work in the cities, thereby depressing wages there and displacing migrant workers. In the presence of such a highly casualised and dualised labour market, the anxieties of Spanish trade unions and social movements can easily be understood. Several other provisions of this large and complex reform ran contrary to union demands. After a general strike and huge street demonstrations, the government backed down.

France

Until the advent of the PARE programme (Plan d'Aide au Retour à l'Emploi) in 2001, the French system had relatively lax job search and job acceptance requirements. There was little definition of the conditions under which someone could be sanctioned for refusal to accept a certain job. In any case the capacity of many ANPE offices to test 'availability for work' is limited by the small number of jobs they have to offer; sometimes referral to training schemes is used instead.

Insurance-based benefits can be withdrawn for up to four months for voluntarily leaving a job, or two to three months for failure to seek work. About 5 per cent of those leaving registered unemployment – and probably a smaller percentage of the unemployed 'stock'- lost benefits because of sanctions in 1999. Some sanctioned individuals may later succeed in claiming RMI.

Beneficiaries of the RMI (Revenu Minimum d'Insertion) can be obliged to sign a 'contrat d'insertion' or 'insertion contract'. Around one-third of contracts include a requirement to seek work and 18 per cent to undertake training. In fact only 40 per cent of RMI beneficiaries actually have a contract, possibly because around half are said to have health problems (Lévy *et al.*, 2000a). Although sanctions for breaches of RMI contracts are very rare, French unemployed people's organisations reported an increase in sanctions and surveillance of job search in 1999–2000, for claimants both of RMI and other unemployed benefits. However, the impact of any pressure to accept a low-quality job is softened considerably by 'cumul'. French jobseekers who accept part-time jobs can claim insurance-based benefit for part of the week; on RMI, their allowance is unaffected until their current three-month award runs out, and they can continue a partial RMI claim for several months after that. However, if and when the RMI becomes the RMA, 'cumul' will cease except for insurance claimants.

Belgium

A new sanctions rule was introduced in 1996 on the recommendation of the OECD, which felt that conditions in Belgium were too lax. Claimants can be struck off insurance benefit altogether when the duration of their claim reaches 1.5 times the regional average.[24] More recent changes have focused on the social assistance regime, formerly the 'minimex' but in 2002 renamed the 'Revenu Minimum d'Intégration Sociale'. Job search requirements for the 'minimex' in some areas were barely enforced at all in 1999–2000, although others used the facility under national rules to impose a 'contrat d'intégration sociale'.[25] Such contracts had potential workfare obligations for claimants under 25 and for low-skilled unemployed over 46. Since October 2002, all claimants of the 'revenu minimum d'intégration' are in principle required to accept any available job if fit for work, including placements on workfare programmes.

THE EFFECTS OF CONDITIONALITY

Strict conditionality of benefits is widely held to 'work' in getting jobseekers to accept jobs beneath their desired level, reducing unemployment and reducing wage pressure (OECD, 1994, 2000). Indeed, the unemployed people interviewed in the UK and Germany for the Minima Sociaux study complained forcefully of how the labour market conditions and the threat of sanctions put pressure on them to leave the dole quickly, even where this meant accepting very poor wages or conditions. Not so in France or Belgium, where at the time of the fieldwork, job acceptance conditions were much milder. French and Belgian jobseekers had better incentives to take very low pay or risk a temporary job, since they could do so and still keep part of their benefit.

Perhaps not surprisingly, increased conditionality and greater threat of sanctions leads people to drift from registered unemployment into other forms of benefit claim. The early Restart interviews in the UK led to a significant rise in men's invalidity benefit claims, which more than doubled between 1981 and 1996 (Alcock *et al.*, 2003, pp. 65, 112). Through stricter medical tests introduced when the old 'invalidity benefit' became 'incapacity benefit' in 1995, the UK government attempted to block an 'escape route' that was even encouraged by Restart counsellors in the previous few years, in their attempt to reduce the unemployed register. Since 2001, all but the most severely disabled must attend Jobcentre Plus interviews about their prospects of returning to the labour market. Those receiving sickness or disability benefits are a rising group in many EU countries, provoking several governments to tighten eligibility criteria.[26] In Denmark, the rate of flow from unemployment into 'disabled' benefit status has increased since passive benefits were curtailed in 1994 (Madsen, 2003, pp. 91–3). However, the Danish government's response has been to focus on the employers, encouraging them to hire and retain older workers and those with health problems.[27]

In the UK, the proportion of the working age population claiming benefits as disabled or sick[28] is strongly correlated with the local unemployment rate (Alcock *et al.*, 2003, pp. 114–16). They infer that take-up of incapacity benefit depends not only on medical status, but on the local labour market. It could also be related to variations in the response of people with health problems to the changing obligations of unemployed claimants. Those with limited capacity may have particular difficulty in labour markets where there is little choice for anyone, and face rejection by employers when there are plenty of fitter candidates available.[29] If their health status is on the margin of fitness for work, they may attempt to claim incapacity benefit rather than suffer continued rejection and the risk of very low wages. Martin Gueck's research in Germany (Lévy *et al.*, 2001a) found that older unemployed interviewed in Germany were anxious about whether they could cope with physically heavy work, which the employment service often challenges claimants to take, like crop picking or street sweeping.

In the context of an explicit objective that people should leave benefit dependency as soon as possible, at whatever wage, counselling and 'action plans' present a double-edged sword. British claimants see both positive and negative aspects in the intensified job search and placement process associated with the introductory phase of the New Deal, the 'Gateway'. It provides personal attention, which most participants welcome; but also pressure to accept low pay. However the 'Jobseeker's Agreement' is regarded rather as a blunt instrument for beating down the minimum wage or length of contract they will accept. French unemployed groups have criticised the PARE programme for a formulaic approach to the individual jobseeker's needs. What purports to be an individualised response all too easily becomes a client-processing machine subordinated to employment service performance targets. There is, however, a need for good counselling, and some German jobseekers praised their national vocational guidance service. The Swedish employment service, with an unusually high ratio of staff to jobseekers, offers a lot of help to find a job that corresponds to the claimant's qualifications and experience, including generous training facilities and assistance with relocation. Historically this has been part of a policy model strongly influenced by trade union concerns. Torfing (1999) argues that the 'action plans' used in Denmark are highly valued by jobseekers, because they emphasise 'empowerment rather than control and punishment' and are usually the gateway to some form of skills training.

THE JOBS WE WOULD RATHER NOT SEEK: STORIES FROM THE FRONT LINE

The Minima Sociaux fieldwork found that claimants in the UK and Germany felt under considerable pressure from the benefit rules to accept lower-paid and less-skilled jobs than the ones they were looking for. However, their ambitions seemed not unreasonable; most specified a 'reservation wage' consistent with normal rates for low-paid jobs in their local labour market. Low pay was seen in terms of fairness, dignity and reward for effort, not just the relationship of wages to benefits. In Germany, informants were incensed by the government's expectation that they should accept the special low-wage jobs set up for unemployed people through wage subsidy schemes, in which pay may be set as much as 20 per cent lower than collectively agreed rates. Over three-quarters of the 119 claimants who had been offered a vacancy by the German employment service said that the wage was typically 'too low' or considerably below the union rate (Lévy et al., 2001a). Many felt considerable difficulty about replacing their pre-unemployment wage, and were concerned that going on to a lower wage affected the amount of earnings-related benefit they would get in the future. Nonetheless almost half of them gave a 'reservation wage' towards the bottom of the pay ladder for the economic sector in which they sought work.

The context of this is the huge pressure of unemployment on the wage-fixing process in Germany during the 1990s. Rates of less than DM10 per hour were found at the lower end of the pay scales in no less than 43 sector collective agreements by 2000 (Lévy et al., 2000b). Many collective agreements now permit specially low rates for people leaving unemployment, reflecting the unions' acceptance of a neo-liberal fatalism concerning the 'trade-off' between wage rates and jobs. Some employers have left the employers' associations with whom unions make sector-wide collective agreements, so that the bottom is dropping out of the bargaining-based minimum wage system, and unemployed people feel the coldest blast of this process. The downward wage mobility when unemployed people return to work no doubt results partly from these growing inequalities; but some unemployed people who had moved into low-paid work attributed their income loss to the stricter conditionality of the benefit system.

However, low pay was not the only problem. Martin Gueck (Lévy et al., 2001b, p. 228) mentions 'the fear of leaving the relative safety of a regular flow of benefits for the uncertainty of a job that may prove too demanding in terms of the required qualifications, or the required fitness'. This goes particularly for the older jobseekers. Although 39 per cent said that the jobs offered had skill requirements that were 'too demanding' or 'too high', suggesting that some had a real 'employability' problem. However, 43 per cent said the skills involved were low or too low; many felt they were at risk of occupational downgrading. Over 80 per cent said that the last job offered to them had been temporary or short-term, and 71 per cent said the hours proposed were 'too flexible', 'very flexible' or 'poor'. This reflected a disproportionate share of jobs with variable or part-time hours among the jobs offered to unemployed people, compared to the labour market as a whole.

Turning to the UK, according to one official evaluation of the New Deal, one-third of those passing through the New Deal 'Gateway' experience pressure to apply for unsuitable work (Hales and Collins, 1999). Such was also the experience of many New Deal participants in Chesterfield, interviewed for the Minima Sociaux project (Gray, 2001). A later survey in the Chesterfield area found that 'young people, through New Deal in particular, were steered towards low paid work with neither prospects nor appropriate training for advancement'.[30] Moreover, almost one in seven of those on JSA had joined training programmes at least partly because they felt pressurised to do so by Job Centre staff.

A conversation with New Deal youth in Bradford illustrates the gap between their own ideas of a suitable job offer and those of their Job Centre advisers (see Box 5.1; names are fictitious, as elsewhere in this and subsequent chapters).

Box 5.1 What's a reasonable wage to expect?

AG: *So do you find the Job Centre (in Bradford) expecting you to go for lower-paid work because you've been out of work a long time?*

Mary: *I told them that I wanted £200 a week.*[31]

Alan: *They looked at me funny when I said that! Even when I told them £180 they looked at me funny.*

Martin: *They said if you're prepared to claim on £35 a week ...*

Jamie: *But that's without getting your hands dirty!*

Martin: *... Then surely you'll be happy with £50 a week, but you're doing a full day's work, aren't you?*

AG: *So are the Job Centre right, that you could get a job if you were prepared to work for a low enough wage?*

Jamie: *You could but you wouldn't be able to survive on it, not really ... with food, bills, rent ... if you got £100 you'd be left with about £10 for yourself.*

Martin: *It would be no more than you get signing on!*

Jamie: *It would be like, say goodbye to your social life ...*

The powerlessness of the jobseeker on benefits may be aggravated by the way in which employers and Job Centres work together. This is illustrated by the story of a jobseeker in Norwich. He describes 'blanket coverage', a system in which the firm says it will accept virtually anyone the Job Centre can send, regardless of qualifications or characteristics:

> ... the wages are so low, but basically if you don't take the job, you'll lose your benefit ... turn it down, you get a six-month suspension ... the one I went for at XYZ Books was office staff. They had two jobs, but then they said, there's 16 places at £4.25 an hour, and then there was 300 places at £3.60 an hour. The £3.60 were operatives, basically. You walk around, it's like a grand factory, you walk 27 miles a day, putting the books on a trolley and that ... you went to the interviews, and I knew that all the jobs went to the very first one that they had. They said, 'I'm afraid that all of you

have come for the office staff … we've only got the operatives, so you'll have to start on the operatives.'

Thus this man had gone to be interviewed for an office job, and ended up feeling he dare not turn down a warehouse job at the minimum wage.

In Belgium (Lévy *et al.*, 2001a), the interviews revealed a frequent process of downgrading from secure manual or driving jobs, which older workers had held in the past, to less skilled jobs or smaller, more insecure workplaces as industrial restructuring reduced and fragmented the sectors people had relied on. The older unemployed have a certain idea of their own value, derived from their skills and experience. In relation to this, the salary offered may be quite unacceptable:

I went to see someone, it was for a wage of 33,000 francs. For someone like me, who'd already had 70,000 francs, 33,000 and for more than 8 hours per day, I couldn't live on that. So I walked out of that workshop straight away.

A similar process was revealed in France (Lévy *et al.* 2001b). French jobseekers described most of ANPE's offerings as 'non-jobs': temporary part-time contracts on job creation schemes, or agency assignments, often merely a couple of days here and there (Lévy, *et al.*, 2001a, 2001b). As in Germany, some people who wanted training were offered none, while others who did not were pushed to take it.

A group of seven women, once skilled and well-paid garment workers, redundant from a large factory near Lille, had reconciled themselves to expecting a new job at no more than the minimum wage. Only 35 out of 541 employees who lost their jobs from this factory had found another over a year later. At best, if they found work, it was to be downgraded from the largest and best-paying garment manufacturer of the area to take temporary and part-time work with smaller firms; because of their middle age (40s and 50s) and relative lack of education they were not offered retraining. They wanted to leave behind the industry that had failed them, to try something different, but all their advisers suggested was the same occupation at lower pay and farther from home. The women accused employers of deliberately splitting up full-time posts into two or three part-time ones to get more wage subsidies for hiring people like them – a charge later supported by French government research.

The French fieldwork also highlighted transport and relocation difficulties. ANPE[32] sometimes offered vacancies that were at least 50 km away. One woman expressed an interest in hotel work, and found herself being pressed to consider a vacancy in the Pyrenees, leaving behind her husband and her nine-year-old daughter. Some areas have very little public transport, especially to serve evening or night workers. Both in rural France and in the far-flung suburbs of large cities such as Marseilles, ANPE staff thought few people would get work without a car, even though municipalities and SNCF offer large discounts on fares for unemployed people. Here there is a clear case for bringing work to the workers, but instead there is increasing pressure on jobseekers in France, Germany, Britain and Spain to accept long journeys to work, and in Germany those without children must even be willing to move home.

Temporary, seasonal and agency work

Low pay was not the only problem; another was temporary, dead-end work, in which the jobseeker would confront the dole again in a few months. Temporary jobs were not seen as a stepping stone to permanent work; several people in all four countries had already had and lost them. Some people in the UK said they had felt pressure from Job Centres to take temporary work; 'the job may be only for a few weeks, but you go for it anyway, because the Job Centre says so'. However, one Job Centre manager stated that 'we would not force people into temporary work'. Job Centre staff said they would occasionally advise a claimant to seek an interview for a temporary job if there seemed no other solution, but they would prefer that people achieved long-term jobs rather than see them come back again and again. Although in principle a temporary job cannot be refused after a jobseeker's 'permitted period'[33] has expired, officials have discretion about how the rules are applied.

Agency work was perceived to be a last resort, in which the jobseeker has no control over hours, location, or length of contract. In the UK voluntary quits attracts a penalty of up to six months without benefit.[34] This rule naturally creates a pressure to stay in work, even if the job turns out to be unsuitable or exploitative. Together with the vulnerability of agency workers to sacking, the rule on voluntary quits makes it hard to challenge an employer on breaches of labour regulations. The story of a young woman from Lowestoft sums up these pressures, illustrating why the cold and gruesome tasks of the 'chicken factory', referred to as the worst job by several informants, had perhaps replaced the workhouse in the iconography of unemployment:

> I worked at a chicken factory with an agency, in H ... [village], and I stuck it out for six weeks , then I quit. ... I found it absolutely soul-destroying! ... you are standing eight to twelve hours, standing, with a knife, and even if you haven't got problems with your joints, it's going to start, you have to sign a contract saying that you will get this. I stayed for six weeks and then I quit. I didn't bother going to the Job Centre, I could not be bothered, even though I didn't have any money saved up, could not be bothered to go through the whole thing again. So after one week I found some work, with an agency in Norwich, ... to start work in another factory. Anyway I did three day-shifts, and the next day we were supposed to go in, we were supposed to get picked up from the station at 4 o'clock in the morning. The lift didn't come in, and I was phoning up, and phoning up subsequent days, and just nothing. And after being promised work over the Bank Holiday, part for double time, part time and a half, not only did we not get the extra work but there was nothing, no contact, nothing. So in the end, when I went down to the Job Centre ... . I guess it worked out in my favour, because I had been laid off, I wasn't referring to [the first factory] where I had left voluntarily, but I had to wait nearly six weeks from signing on until I could get any money.

MAKING WORK PAY?

If the 'sticks' of benefit conditionality bear harshly on unwaged people seeking a good job rather than just the first one available, what about the alternative 'carrot' of supplements to low wages? The OECD has advocated wage supplements as an incentive to accept low-paid jobs (OECD, 1997a). These may take the form of tax credits, other in-work benefits such as high housing or family allowances, or reductions in social security charges for the low-paid. Faced with the poverty trap, over four-fifths of British claimants interviewed for the Minima Sociaux project in summer 1999 thought that higher in-work benefits would help them. Hopefully the tax credit developments in the UK have done so; they began in November 1999. But three-quarters of interviewees agreed with the statement that 'even if you can get in-work benefits to top up your wage, what matters is being paid a fair rate for the job'.

In-work benefits raise several problems. First of all, they are very costly – the Danish government rejected wage supplements in the early 1990s for this reason (Torfing, 1999), and the UK government's bill for tax credits in 2002 was around £6.6 billion.[35] Why should employers not raise wages instead? Tax credits are provided as much to the employees of a highly profitable national supermarket firm as to those of the struggling corner shop, to workers in multinational fast food chains as well as marginally profitable organic farms. Since large companies have often squeezed productivity as high as it will go, would they really shed workers if obliged to pay more? Despite initial fears that the National Minimum Wage in the UK might lead to job loss, such effects have in fact been minimal.[36] The government now has a vested interest in pushing the minimum wage still higher, to save tax credit payments. Time will tell if the further 7 per cent increase being considered in 2004 will be the last big jump for a while, or if inequalities will continue to be compressed. Additional tax reliefs for small companies, conditional on target pay rises being awarded to low-wage workers, would save the large sums now being spent on subsidising labour costs for firms that could afford to pay more.

Secondly, there are some forms of disincentive to work that in-work benefits do not reach. The Minima Sociaux research revealed high housing costs – especially mortgages – high travel to work costs, and maintenance payments to a divorced partner, as difficulties of this kind. Tax credits are an important way of helping lone parents, who are 56 per cent of all beneficiary households. But, in a society where over 70 per cent of the population are home owners, divorce comes to owners and tenants alike. Several lone parents were afraid of losing their homes if they went to work on the wages they could get, even with help from in-work benefits.[37] Getting a job meant losing that part of Income Support or Income-based JSA that provides means-tested help with mortgage interest.[38] Housing Benefit for tenants presents another 'benefits trap'. Some of the most excluded people live in homeless hostels where the rent is too high to qualify for in-work Housing Benefit, so they 'cannot afford' to work. Low-paid people essentially need low-cost public services – cheap public transport, low-cost childcare and low-rent housing in which the subsidies go to construction and maintenance rather than as a means-tested allowance to the tenant.

A third problem with various forms of wage supplement is that they risk actually encouraging low pay. Arguing that tax credits and other wage supplements may repeat the errors of the nineteenth-century

Poor Law, critics have pointed to the possibility of a 'Speenhamland effect': employers may freeze or even reduce wages in low-paid jobs because the supplement makes it easier for them to recruit at very low wage levels. This has been argued in relation to UK tax credits (Kitson *et al.*, 2000; Wilkinson, 2001) as well as in relation to the tax credits introduced in France in 2001,[39] where debate has focused on the risk of encouraging lower or frozen wages (Clerc, 2001; Concialdi, 2001). Some evidence of a Speenhamland effect was found in an evaluation of the UK's Earnings Top-Up Pilot, which suggested that in-work benefits make it easier for employers to recruit to low-waged jobs (Marsh *et al.*, 1999).

In Germany, a form of tax credit, the 'Mainzer Model', went nationwide in 2001 after an experimental phase.[40] It offers a subsidy to employees' social insurance contributions in low-waged jobs, tapering as the wage rises. There is a workfare aspect, since unemployed people must accept the jobs involved if one is offered. Concern has been expressed that if offering an earnings top-up induces more people to accept low-paid jobs, wages in the 'Mainzer Model' jobs could fall further, leading to a re-emergence of the benefits trap the 'top-up' is designed to resolve.[41] Interviewees in the Minima Sociaux project feared employers would use the Mainzer model to sack higher-paid workers in favour of subsidised ones. Although the subsidised wages must be at least the collectively agreed minimum, they thought employers would refuse future wage demands because of the earnings top-up arrangement.

Similar effects are attributed to a wider range of wage supplement arrangements in France and Belgium, including 'cumul' of casual wages and benefit payments (Ballal and Bouquin, 2000). 'Cumul' is a form of wage supplement for the precarious worker. Combining benefits and wages may exacerbate existing pressure for low pay and casualisation in the labour market as a whole (Lévy *et al.*, 2000b); for example, 'cumul' in France facilitates agency work, as mentioned earlier. There are concerns that this supply of super-flexible subsidised labour may encourage a proliferation of part-time casual jobs offered by builders and other small firms, possibly at the expense of longer-term jobs with more regular hours. While unemployed people clearly want and welcome opportunities for casual earnings, any work they do for employers (as distinct from households) needs to be integrated into an effective regulatory framework to ensure fair conditions for temporary and agency workers. The low disregard level for casual earnings is a bone of contention for UK claimants; 74 per cent of the Minima Sociaux sample wanted a more relaxed regime in this respect, and several previous studies confirm their concerns.[42] To bring disregards more into line with the continental systems would help people take part-time and temporary jobs, but how to reconcile conflicting objectives in this area is a major challenge for the future of European benefit systems.

AN UNCONDITIONAL BASIC INCOME?

An unconditional basic income has been a key demand of the Euromarches, as a response to the increasing conditionality of benefits (Mathers, 1999). Unemployed people's movements have seen this demand as a way both of surviving employment precarity and of resisting it, of opening up the choice to refuse unattractive jobs. Their view finds support from a long line of writers to advocate a guaranteed basic income or 'citizenship income' as a solution to poverty in the flexible labour market. For example, Guy Standing (1999) argues that it would strengthen the hand of workers resisting poor conditions, since they would have an alternative to work without workfarist conditions (p. 367). It would also provide an unconditional income for those engaged in unpaid work, as full-time parents, carers or volunteers. However, he warns that a citizenship income 'must not be understood as a panacea. It is only part of a redistributive strategy that would be consistent with globalisation and flexible product and labour markets' (p. 355).

The demand for an unconditional basic income has a curious capacity to be all things to all people, supported by a wide range of opposing political tendencies for different reasons (Gray, 1988, 1993). For some advocates on the right, it is seen as a way of 'pricing people into work' or encouraging a supply of flexible, partly paid labour to meet employers' demands for just-in-time casual workers. In this view, it would encourage creation of low-paid and temporary jobs; but there is some naivety in thinking these would be additional to, rather than instead of, existing full-time or permanent jobs. Whether basic income would become, like the Speenhamland system, the taxpayer's gift to bad employers, or alternatively the friend of jobseekers holding out for better jobs, would depend a good deal on its level. People might just about live on a high basic income, refusing unattractive jobs; but would be driven to supplement a low one. Most scenarios for introducing a basic income envisage its introduction by stages, gradually replacing other forms of income transfer including (in most proposals) social security benefits. On this basis, it might do harm to wages and conditions before it would do any good. Moreover, there is a curious alliance between those who advocate basic income as an improvement to a still-capitalist welfare state, and those who see it as the essence of post-capitalist income distribution, divorcing income from wage labour. Standing borrows awkwardly from the latter vision when he endorses Tony Atkinson's proposal for a 'participation income guarantee' (Standing, 1999, p. 366; Atkinson, 1995). But a universal duty to perform some kind of community work, to go with a universal right to basic income, would be dangerously close to universalising workfare, at least in the present political context. The Euromarches, on the other hand, envisage basic income as the antithesis of workfare. Moreover, for some of their supporters, basic income is associated with André Gorz's (1985) vision of the end of wage labour, in which work becomes a collective social duty and income a share of collective wealth.

WANTED: A 'DE-COMMODIFYING' BENEFITS SYSTEM

For the present, taking capitalism as 'given', the problem is a different one: what kinds of benefit arrangement can best improve the bargaining power of the unwaged – or indeed give them any – against bad employers? Certainly the re-commodification of labour through workfarist benefits systems reduces their bargaining power, compared to the less conditional systems of the 1980s.

When unemployed people assess their national benefits systems, their criteria are couched not merely in terms of benefit levels, but in terms of how far the system allows them to make choices that are driven by their personal ambitions, rather than the pressure from the market to adapt those ambitions to employers' demands. Clearly they are seeking 'de-commodification'. The 're-commodifying', 'workfarist' or 'work first' systems aim to get claimants out of unemployment as fast as possible. The ideal type of a 'de-commodifying' system would permit each person an 'optimum' search time, determined by his or her individual history and prospects. The optimal search is long enough to maximise prospects of getting whatever the individual regards as a best replacement for the job s/he lost; or, for youth with no experience, long enough to maximise career prospects. Beyond a certain duration of unemployment, the risk of decaying skills and of employer discrimination against the long-term unemployed sets in, so clearly at that point the individual must lower his or her sights or risk worse prospects. The 'ideal' de-commodifying counselling process would help each person identify the limits of the optimal search time and maximise his or her chances of finding a good job within that time, sometimes by retraining. This is a highly individual issue, not compatible with rigid rules about a 'permitted' period to search for a job as good as the last. Safeguards against abuse of the benefits system would be more readily accepted if the government was committed to providing quality jobs for all who need them, rather than expecting unemployed people to accept the burden of keeping labour costs low for the national economy.

Reversing the new conditionalities of the 1990s would certainly make unemployed people less vulnerable to bad employers; but it would not provide them with decent jobs. To do that, we have to fix the jobs rather than the benefits system. The next two chapters examine the dimensions of the 'bad jobs' problem and what can be done about it.

6

Flexploitation and the Unemployed

The concern with job quality, which as we saw in Chapter 4 has begun to appear on the EU employment policy agenda, responds partly to a declining share of full-time permanent jobs in European labour markets. Part-time jobs rose from 12.7 per cent of total EU employment in 1985 to 17.9 per cent in 2001; fixed-term contracts went up from 8.4 per cent in 1985 to 13.4 per cent in 2001.[1] Altogether full-time jobs on 'open-ended' contracts fell from 78.9 per cent of the total to 68.7 per cent. The last 20 years have seen a decline in reasonably paid, full-time, secure jobs for lower-skilled people.

This chapter analyses the reasons for this trend, linking it to the rise in the ratio of vacancies to unemployed people, already mentioned in Chapter 5. There are some jobs available for the unemployed, but they are not always acceptable jobs – at least not for long. As job quality declines, unemployed people often get the lowest-paid and least secure work. European Commission research provides one source of evidence on job quality and the work unemployed people get. The Minima Sociaux fieldwork also provides several stories from the 'front line', from four countries and in particular from the author's own fieldwork in the UK. Such stories show that if unemployed people turn jobs down, it is not just because they are being 'fussy'. Reluctance is often based on actual experience of bad jobs they lost – or found untenable – in the past, in their history of the revolving door between unsatisfactory work and having none. If we are looking for solutions, raising the ratio of wages to benefits is not enough. Jobseekers have other concerns too: dirty or dangerous work, lack of control over working hours, job insecurity and the fear of not being able to regain their benefits if they lose their wage. Insecurity appeared in the European Community Household Panel Survey (ECHP) for 1997–98 as one of the main reasons for a lack of job satisfaction, together with low pay, and a lack of responsibility or career development opportunity.

FLEXIBILITY AND FLEXPLOITATION

The 'flexibilisation' of the labour market has been accompanied by a major increase of job insecurity and of under-employment in the form of involuntary part-time working. 'Flexible' jobs are often the worst paid, and flexibilisation is being used by employers both to reduce the amount of labour time they pay for, and to minimise effective hourly rates. Hence flexibility becomes 'flexploitation', which especially affects jobs taken by the unwaged, who are under most pressure to accept poor conditions and are least likely to be unionised.

EC researchers have developed a fourfold classification of jobs.[2] Least desirable are the 'dead-end' jobs, with no contract security, no supervisory role and no employer-provided training. These amount to 8 per cent of the European total, and 3 per cent are both dead-end and 'low-paid' (i.e. under 75 per cent of median hourly earnings for the country concerned).[3] Next are the 17 per cent of all jobs that are low-paid but offer at least a permanent contract or training. A further 37 per cent of jobs are described as 'reasonable quality', with pay at least 75 per cent of the hourly national median and either job security or training. 'Good' jobs are the 38 per cent offering all three desiderata. The description of 'flexploitation' applies most to the 'dead-end' jobs – but it should also include some of the 'low-paid' category, which is third in the quality ranking.

Table 6.1   Differences in job quality: those leaving unemployment compared to others

| | Transitions out of unemployment: | | | Whole workforce: |
	% into high-quality jobs	% into low-quality jobs	Ratio of low-quality jobs to high-quality jobs for those leaving unemployment	Ratio of low-quality jobs to high-quality jobs for the whole workforce
France	3	18	6.0	0.25
Portugal	6	27	4.5	0.42
Greece	7	28	4.0	0.64
Spain	7	23	3.3	0.63
Italy	7	12	1.7	0.27
Austria	13	18	1.4	0.64
Netherlands	8	11	1.4	0.19
Germany	12	16	1.3	0.30
UK	15	17	1.1	0.29
Ireland	10	11	1.1	0.43
Belgium	9	6	0.7	0.21
Denmark	22	11	0.5	0.24

Source: adapted from EC (2001a), p. 75; EC (2002b), p. 93, based on European Community Household Panel, 1997–98. Definitions of 'high' and 'low' quality: see text.

Note: the first two columns add up to all those leaving unemployment over twelve months, per 100 unemployed at the beginning of the period.

We look first at international differences in job quality, presented in the last column of Table 6.1.[4] These differences reflect productivity, labour market regulation, the pressure of the unemployed labour reserve and the extent of trade union power, interacting in complex ways. Space prevents a full account of these factors here, although some are discussed in the next chapter. Table 6.1 shows that:

- The Netherlands, which has taken special measures to try to combine contract flexibility with job security,[5] gives workers the lowest risk of a low-quality job compared to a high-quality one;
- Belgium and Denmark have the next lowest ratios of low-quality to high-quality jobs among the twelve countries for which data are available. Both of these countries are relatively highly unionised;
- The highest share of low-quality jobs is in Greece, where agricultural employment is over 18 per cent of the total, compared to 4 per cent in the EU as a whole. Sector comparisons show that agricultural work is most likely to be of low quality across the EU; large also is the share of low-quality employment in hotels and restaurants;
- The risk of a low-quality job in Spain is almost as high as in Greece. Temporary work is unusually common in Spain – around a third of all jobs.

Low-quality jobs (dead-end or low-paid) are as common across Europe in industry as in services – farm work aside, the differences are within sectors rather than between sectors. Among part-time workers, 14 per cent have 'dead-end' jobs, rising to 26 per cent for 'involuntary' part-timers. Jobs for less than 15 hours per week are especially likely to be of low quality (three out of four are). Over 16 per cent of 'involuntary' part-time workers are unemployed a year later, compared to only 3 per cent of full time workers and 2.2 per cent of voluntary part-timers.

Table 6.1 also shows, in the third column, that unemployed people have a far higher risk of low-quality jobs than the average for the workforce in their country. The first two columns show that only in Belgium, Denmark and Austria did more unemployed people enter high-quality than low-quality jobs – and even there, their risk of low-quality jobs is much higher than the workforce as a whole. In France the ratio of low quality to high-quality jobs among work obtained by unemployed people is very high, as is the difference between the chances of getting a good job for the ex-unemployed compared to other workers. In Germany, the UK, Ireland and the Netherlands unemployed people were slightly more likely to enter low-quality than high-quality jobs.

Gregg, Knight and Wadsworth (1999) note that weekly wage rates for those entering a job from unemployment are much lower than the wage rates for all jobs. This reflects three factors: the skill and experience mix of unemployed people, lower hourly wage rates for the same kinds of work as established workers do, and the fact that many of the jobs obtained by unemployed people are temporary or part-time.

Unfortunately, unemployed people do not always move on to better jobs. Other data presented by the European Commission[6] show that an unemployed person has on average a 17 per cent chance of being in a dead-end or low-paid job a year later, and only an 8 per cent chance of moving into a 'high-quality' job (taking the 'reasonable quality' and 'good' categories together). Of all those in low-quality jobs, 12.5 per cent are unemployed a year later – five times the proportion of those in high quality jobs who move into unemployment.[7] Around half of those in dead-end jobs are still in dead-end or low-paid jobs a year later. From all low-quality jobs there is only a 29 per cent chance of progressing to a 'high-quality' job. A more hopeful finding is that during the late 1990s, exits from dead-end jobs into permanent work became slightly more common, and exits from temporary work into unemployment became slightly less common.

British evidence illustrates considerable evidence of being trapped on low levels of earnings for long periods. Over a five-year period, 22 per cent of men in the bottom 10 per cent of the earnings distribution remain there while 30 per cent increase their income, but only one-third of those progress to the fourth decile or above (Dickens, 1999). For women, there is only slightly greater mobility. Stewart (1999), using data from the British Household Panel Study, confirms this general picture of low earnings mobility for the low-paid and a relatively high risk that they will lose their jobs.

Although there is a sense in which a temporary job is better than no job, jobseekers will only gain from casualisation of employment if temporary jobs are extra jobs, rather than replacing permanent ones. Even if deregulation of labour markets achieves extra jobs, this may be at the expense of an *overall* decline in security and working conditions. The employers' pressure for deregulation arises precisely because they often use casualisation to weaken trade union strength and pressurise workers into doing more for less. In the words of a docks shop steward who spoke to TUC researchers, 'Agency workers are used as cheap labour and a visible threat to permanent employees' job security' (TUC, 2001, p. 41).

THE FALL IN JOB QUALITY

Europe's recovery from the recession of the 1980s left a trail of closures in manufacturing, shipbuilding and mining, and a loss of relatively secure, reasonably paid jobs for experienced male manual workers. Recovery was focused on the service sector and on new industrial sectors such as electronics, with a consequent shake-up in the location of job opportunities and skill requirements. During the 1990s jobs tended to polarise on the one hand towards low-paid and insecure work, often associated with low-skilled service employment, and on the other highly paid career positions, usually requiring high levels of education and associated with the new 'knowledge economy'. Service employment often paid less for manual or routine tasks than the lost manufacturing jobs had done. Temporary and part-time hirings are extensively used in the growing service sector because it cannot 'stockpile' its product; workers are needed in the same time-patterns as the customers, whose number fluctuates over the day, the week, the seasons and the business cycle.

However, the shift towards services was not the only reason why the 1980s and 1990s saw inadequate growth of full-time, secure jobs in most parts of the EU. Employers' quest for flexibility in hiring labour resulted from new strategies to reduce costs within all sectors. Fixed-term and agency contracts have spread in the public (or ex-public) sector, where downsizing and privatisation often lead employers to avoid long-term payroll commitments. Manufacturing firms turned to new sources of labour supply such as part-time, often non-unionised women, and to casualisation, including agency labour.[8] Sometimes this can be attributed to the competitive pressures arising from globalisation, but highly profitable manufacturing firms are also casualising their workforce. According to an employment agency manager in Norwich, interviewed in autumn 1999, 'the food industry is turning to agencies throughout the country'. One major food-processing employer in a nearby town replaced a large share of its workforce with cheaper agency workers in 2000–01, despite a considerable rise in profits.

Flexibilisation is sometimes said to be mainly 'supply-led', reflecting women's demand for part-time work in particular (Beatson, 1995). Certainly many mothers do want part-time work, but for others it is a second-best choice dictated by lack of childcare. Reasons why anyone would positively prefer a temporary job are harder to find, although students planning to return to college may not mind either way. In the UK, students have grown in number during the 1980s and 1990s, and cuts in student grants have driven more of them to take part-time and temporary jobs. Around one in six British part-time workers are college or school students (*Labour Market Trends*, July 2000, p. S19). Across the EU only just over 65 per cent of part-time workers are part-time by choice,[9] ranging from over 85 per cent in the UK to less than 10 per cent in Spain and Belgium. Part-time work is often all unemployed jobseekers can get; in Belgium around one in six unemployed are 'chômeurs occupés' – people who claim benefits part-time while looking for a full-time job. In France, a recent government study found that job creation subsidies to promote part-time employment had increased 'involuntary' part-time work, fortunately reversed a little in 1998–2001.[10]

Throughout the EU, part-time workers more often receive low hourly pay than full-timers, and lack training or promotion prospects. Low pay for part-time workers goes together with inequality for women, and in most countries (the UK excepted) part-time jobs are often also temporary.[11] The ease with which employers can find cheap female and student labour often leads them to create part-time instead of full-time jobs, in particular jobs with very short hours. The Equal Opportunities Commission's 1998 report[12] on workers with very short part-time hours shows how employers cut costs by splitting full-time posts into 'mini-jobs' with hours too low to pay National Insurance contributions. This prejudices workers' future pension and other benefit rights – but some are so desperate that they ask for contribution-exempt jobs to have a higher net wage. Many short hours employees are students; others have two or more 'mini-jobs'. The EOC finds such jobs are particularly common in hotels and catering; other sources note them in retailing. For example at Asda, the supermarket chain since taken over by the American group Wal-Mart, 80 per cent of the workforce were part-time in 1997.[13] Many of these were earning less than the National Insurance threshold; when the company wanted to reduce excessive staff turnover, it offered these workers longer hours and found that more of them stayed. Employers use 'mini-jobs' to recruit students, who compete with mothers wanting longer part-time hours and with unemployed jobseekers wanting full-time work. Over half the new jobs created in the UK during the economic recovery of 1992–95 were part-time, compared to only 30 per cent of extra jobs created in the previous recovery of 1984–90. Given a limited number of mothers and students, there is a risk of under-employment of those seeking full-time work if this trend continues.

These problems illustrate how employers can take advantage of the huge increase in the number of mothers seeking employment in recent years. Mothers tend to be a captive labour supply with few job choices, particularly where there is poor provision of publicly funded childcare, as in the UK and in southern Europe. But at least there are enough part-time jobs in the UK for mothers who want them; part-time employment is 44 per cent of the female total in the UK compared to 33 per cent in the whole EU and only 17 per cent in Spain. Sweden in the 1980s provided ample good-quality jobs for women in the state sector – sometimes part-time but with good pay and conditions – including jobs in childcare services, which permitted other women to have more choices and work longer hours. This shows the value of a large public sector in sustaining the growth rate of quality employment opportunities. Unfortunately, Swedish state employment was forced to contract somewhat in the early 1990s, as described in Chapter 3. However, Sweden retains a very high female employment rate and – along with the UK and Ireland – a lower unemployment rate for women than for men, in contrast to other EU countries where the opposite is true. Sweden, Denmark and to a lesser extent the UK illustrate how, on a macro-economic level, high female employment rates have been associated with low unemployment, for men as well as women.

In much of Europe, especially in the UK, jobs in the state sector have been severely eroded both in number and quality by privatisation. Both public and private sector organisations have increasingly contracted out functions such as cleaning, catering, and security guards. In the UK this subcontracted work is often more insecure and lower paid than the permanent jobs it replaced (Allen and Henry, 1996). An ILO report on municipal services notes that subcontracting tends to have this effect in the UK, particularly for women, and may do so elsewhere (ILO, 2001). Half of UK temporary workers are in public administration, education and health where fixed-term contracts and agency temps have become much more common during the 1990s. The public sector has offered fixed-term contracts more frequently in the last few years, to avoid an obligation to make redundancy compensation as public sector organisations are restructured or contract (Conley, 1999). This again affects women more than men.

RISING INEQUALITY

Associated with the higher unemployment and other labour market trends of the last 20–25 years of the twentieth century has been a widespread increase in income inequality between households. Fifteen out of seventeen OECD countries for which data were available showed a rise in inequality of household incomes (before taxes and benefits) during 1979–95.[14] The UK showed a larger increase in inequality of disposable income than any other country of the 17. More surprisingly, Sweden and Denmark, having begun the period with very low inequality, also showed a relatively large increase, perhaps as a result of globalisation pressures on their economies and welfare systems. Moreover, in Sweden, the UK and the USA the redistributive effect of taxes and transfer payments was reduced in the 1990s (Caminada and Goudswaard, 2002, p. 170).

The rise in household income inequality was accompanied in the UK and USA by an overall rise in individual wage dispersion – the ratio of the highest hourly labour incomes to the lowest. This did not take place in most EU countries between the mid-1980s and the mid-1990s (OECD, 1996a, pp. 62–3). However, the OECD's latest data show some increase in wage dispersion in the Netherlands (for the whole period since 1979) and more recently in Germany and Italy (OECD, 2003a). Within the EU, the UK stands out as having the highest inequality of household income and the greatest wage dispersion. Inequality in the UK increased steadily through the Tory years (1979–97); in fact, the gap between the top 10 per cent of wage levels and the bottom 10 per cent increased faster during the period 1980–95 than in any other OECD country for which data are available apart from the USA.[15] Low-paid jobs (those paying less than two-thirds of the median wage) were 20 per cent of the total during the early 1990s in UK, but only 5–13 per cent in the continental countries of the EU 15 (OECD, 1996a). This can be attributed to the weakening of trade union power under the Tories, and to ineffective minimum wage regulation even before the 1993 abolition of Wages Councils.

The OECD comments that 'there is little solid evidence to suggest that countries where low-paid work is less prevalent have achieved this at the cost of higher unemployment rates and lower employment rates for the more vulnerable groups in the labour market, such as youth and women' (OECD, 1996a, p. 76). Certainly the effect of the UK's National Minimum Wage, introduced in 1999, has not been to choke off job creation in lower-paid sectors.[16] During the 1980s and 1990s, there was a reduction in the male/female pay gap in most countries, but this did not stop women from increasing their share of employment.

FLEXPLOITATION AND THE THREAT TO LABOUR STANDARDS

Temporary jobs rate badly in the quality stakes, with some exceptions. Firstly, in terms of pay: the European Commission's analysis shows in temporary jobs without training and promotion prospects 37.5 per cent earned less than 75 per cent of national median hourly earnings, compared to only 18 per cent in all other jobs. In Spain, temporary workers earn 10 per cent less than permanent employees (Polavieja and Richards, 2002). In the UK, however, an overall temporary/permanent pay gap of similar magnitude conceals higher pay for temporary workers in some skilled groups while clerical workers, plant and machine operators get less (Gray, 2002b). Secondly, in terms of health and safety: stress, unhealthy conditions and accidents are more common among temporary workers.[17] Thirdly, temporary workers are less likely to be offered training by their employers: across Europe less than a third of them get any, compared to over half of permanent workers.[18]

The Minima Sociaux research in the UK illustrated the career-wrecking reality of the trend towards temporary work. In food processing, transport and public utilities workers had seen secure jobs replaced by fixed-term contracts and agency arrangements, as shown by these comments from a former railway worker in Brighton:

> Fixed term contracts are the thing of the day now, you're on six months or a year; that happened to me the last two jobs. I was made redundant twice in the last nine years. Before the redundancies came along our conditions were changed; we were more or less coerced into it ... it seems that's the way things are going now .... I can only speak for what I do, which is British Telecom, around 50,000 of us were made redundant together, and we'd been there

several years. And then the last job, it was British Rail, I was made redundant by … [a train operating company], and the same thing applied. In both of those jobs, we were more or less forced to change our conditions and sign a new contract … I'd never been unemployed in my life. I know other people in my position who've lost their jobs … and the only way back into the work system is to go onto a fixed-term contract. Any employer does it in the buildings, or telecoms, for example, and you're asked to go in via an agency; at a moment's notice you can be dropped from the books, they won't have to explain to you.

Agency temps are the most 'commodified' form of labour, corresponding to Jeremy Rifkin's description of 'throw-away workers', sought by the globalised company to cope with frequent changes in demand (Rifkin, 1995). This form of work is growing very rapidly in most EU countries, as detailed in Chapter 7. In an account of some particularly bad agency conditions in Chicago (Peck and Theodore, 1998), unskilled manual workers, mainly recent immigrants, are treated by recruiters as 'warm bodies', hired by the day at the minimum wage and told not to return if they protest about anything. At its worst, the European casual labour market approaches this; the 'gangmasters' who recruit crop-picking workers for Norfolk and other market gardening areas, may not always pay the minimum agricultural wage and are notorious for their neglect of tax and social security payments. Many of these workers are migrants from Eastern Europe or even China, some even more vulnerable for being illegal.[19] Casual farm workers in Spain, often from North Africa, suffer similar problems.

In most EU countries, trade unions are concerned that agency work may undermine collective agreements. For example, a German trade union report found that in 1995 agency temps received only 63.4 per cent of average pay in the user companies[20] – a situation hopefully improved by recent legislation, described in the next chapter. Research done for the European Commission suggests agency pay far below that for permanent workers, ranging from 22 per cent to 40 per cent less in Germany and on average 32 per cent less in the UK.[21] However in some skilled occupations in the UK (such as nurses and construction tradesmen) agency temps earn more than permanent workers (Gray, 2002b). This occurs where employers are turning to agencies more to meet skills shortages than to cut costs. Agency workers in the UK, where their conditions are less regulated than in most EU countries, often lack sick pay, shiftwork bonuses or overtime premia, and do not get access to company pension schemes (TUC, 2001). When agencies were first permitted in Spain in 1994, this measure was greeted by a storm of protest from the trade union movement, fearing that agencies would undercut union labour and increase the already very high proportion of temporary work.

Agency temp labour is used not only to deal with fluctuations in staff requirements or to save costs. It may also be a strategy for increasing management power or replacing unionised workers (TUC, 2001; Gray, 2002b; Costello and Levidow, 2002). Anecdotal evidence from Spain suggests that agencies question job applicants carefully to exclude union members. Temporary, especially agency, workers can be pressurised to work harder because they are afraid of not being rehired (Dale and Bamford, 1988; Forde, 2001). They are afraid to complain or to use grievance procedures (Conley, 1999). These pressures, and their frequent changes of job, make them intrinsically very hard to unionise.

UNEMPLOYED PEOPLE IN A TWO-TIER LABOUR MARKET

As it becomes more difficult to find a full-time, permanent job the labour market tends to 'segment' – the unwaged compete for those jobs that are vacant, disproportionately part-time and temporary. Wages tend to grow most slowly in these jobs, both because of the competition and because these workers intrinsically lack bargaining power compared to secure full-time employees. Employers then see even more cost advantage in part-time and temporary hirings. Conley (1999) shows that in the UK's fast-casualising public sector of the late 1990s, many temporary jobs (often also part-time) fell to ethnic minority workers, especially women. All over Europe, migrants get some of the worst casual jobs, such as crop-picking or seasonal restaurant work.

Throughout Europe during the 1990s, jobseekers with previous work experience often found they could not get another job at anything like their old wage. The 'cost of losing a job', as Gregg, Knight and Wadsworth (1999) describe it, averages over 9 per cent of previous earnings for all UK unemployed. It rises to 30 per cent for those who lose a job they have been in for over five years, since they may have built up seniority pay with their previous employer. Downward wage mobility has also been revealed in a study of eleven EU countries (EC, 1998c, p. 100). Men re-entering work after unemployment of at least three months earn on average 25 per cent less than before they were unemployed; women 17 per cent less. The loss is particularly high in France (over 30 per cent for both genders) but relatively low in Denmark (10 per cent for men, 5 per cent for women) and, according to this study, very low for women in the UK (5 per cent , compared to a 30 per cent loss for men). The longer people are unemployed in between, the greater the gap between the former wage and the new wage. In earnings-related benefit systems, moving back into work on much lower pay means less benefits if you lose the new job, so taking a temporary job on lower pay than before is particularly unattractive.

As mentioned in Chapter 5, seven out of nine EU countries for which data are available show a rise in the ratio of vacancies to unemployment since the 1980s. More jobs are available that are not being taken up. The problem is often presented as one of a 'benefits trap' or lack of financial incentive; but it is more complex than that. It is also about job insecurity, too long or 'unsocial' hours, or long journeys to work. Or the 'incentive' problem may consist of being 'downgraded' in pay and status from a former skilled job but with no real prospect of retraining and a risk of long-term damage to the CV. Obviously, the rise in unfilled vacancies must to some extent be due to 'mismatch' of skills. However, given the growth in unskilled service jobs as well as in those requiring new 'knowledge economy' skills, it is hard to see how the skills mismatch could have got so much worse. The 'hard to fill' vacancies are not just for computer technicians or teachers; they are often for security guards or waitresses. What Michie and Wilkinson (1994) said a decade ago may still, sadly, be true: 'low pay is the reason for lots of jobs advertised in job centres (which over-represent the lowest paid sectors) going unfilled .... Some employers ... take advantage of the large surplus of cheap labour to reduce wage rates and casualise their workforce.' Job centres pick up employers who like free advertising and do not mind hiring unemployed people, hence the pay in these vacancies is demonstrably less than average for most specific occupations (Gray, 2002b; GMB, 1994). Comments of unemployed people interviewed in the Minima Sociaux project (see Box 6.1; names are fictitious) illustrate how jobseekers define the kinds of work they would rather avoid.

Of all the EU unemployed who got a job in 1997–98, over half (56 per cent) went into temporary jobs. These include temporary jobs promoted or specially set up for them through job-creation schemes in the public and non-profit sectors, and jobs with wage subsidies in the private sector. Temporary jobs were a majority of those obtained

Box 6.1 The jobs nobody wants[22]

'Robots' and 'slave labour': young people on the New Deal in Bradford:

Mary: *They'd look on t'computer and it were all factory jobs, and I told them I'd been in factories and I didn't like it ... I'll try to get a job, but I won't take no factory work.*
Jamie: *I hate factory work.*
Alan: *It turns you into a robot*
Mary: *I personally won't work for less than £200 a week.*
Tim: *They send you for factory work, working for peanuts.*

New Deal Participants in Chesterfield:

Simon: *There are hardly any good jobs in Chesterfield – just ones that are slave labour.*
AG: *What sort?*
Mike: *Labouring jobs, agency temporary work, jobs everyone else rejects, jobs for robots.*
Simon: *With agencies you can be one week working, next week not. People want full-time jobs.*
Kevin: *With decent wages.*
Simon: *And satisfying work, work you can get interested in.*
AG: *What counts as decent wages for you?*
Mike: *£4.50.*
AG: *That's good round here?*
Mike: *Yes.*

Norwich and Lowestoft: not the chicken factory!

AG: *Are there any sorts of jobs you would not take?*
Jim: *Anything to do with food.*
Sarah: *A and Z [name of a local chicken factory].*
Helen: *Standing up to my ankles in cooked carrots – they stink; they're disgusting; the factory is dirty.*
Nick: *I wouldn't want to have to work with meat.*
Anthea *(formerly self-employed office worker): I'm way over-qualified, but if they [Job Centre staff] could stick me into the chicken factory to fill a quota they would.*

France:

A group of seven French women, redundant from a textile factory near Lille, were agreed on their criteria for an acceptable job: it had to be full-time, paying at least the monthly minimum wage, and not more than 20 km from home.
Some comments from other areas expressed the impossibility of surviving on the wages offered, or on casual work:
In the building industry, for example, people have more interest in underground work from time to time than in getting properly hired, because when you're properly hired, it's so badly paid.
Sometimes it's four days, you have to start at 10 at night, and there are no more buses; then I took an assignment for one day, you can't refuse it or they won't have you back.

by the unemployed in Spain, Belgium, France, Italy, Germany and Portugal, according to European Commission research.[23] The labour pool for temporary jobs consists disproportionately of unemployed people re-entering work, young people, migrants and ethnic minorities[24] (see Box 6.2). Although much less common in the UK than in most of Europe, temporary work is nonetheless very important for the unemployed and disadvantaged groups. About one in five jobs taken by unemployed people in the UK are temporary, compared to 6.8 per cent of all jobs.

Agency work is particularly important for unemployed people. Over half of the 435 British agency temps surveyed by Forde (2001)

Box 6.2 Who gets temporary jobs

Unemployed:

In the EU as a whole in 1997, over half of those who were unemployed a year before were in temporary jobs.[25]

Youth:

In 1996, around 16 per cent of EU workers aged under 25 were in temporary jobs with no training,[26] compared to only 8 per cent of all workers.

Women:

A disproportionate share of temporary jobs in the UK are taken by women, especially part-time women and particularly in teaching and other public services (TUC, 2001; Conley, 2001). In Spain also, women are more likely to be on temporary contracts, most of all in the public sector.[27]

Ethnic minorities and migrants:

- In the UK, 2.6 per cent of Black or Black British respondents in the Labour Force Survey have been sacked or made redundant in the last three months, double the proportion of whites.[28]
- UK fruit and vegetable growers depend on several thousand migrant casual workers, often recruited by 'gangmasters', informal employment agencies who are well known to government departments and trade unions for flouting minimum wage regulations and tax laws. Some of these workers are thought to be illegal immigrants, which makes them especially unlikely to resist or complain.[29]
- A quarter of refugees in the UK are in temporary jobs, compared to 11 per cent of ethnic minority workers and only 6.8 per cent of all workers.[30] Refugees earn only £7.29 per hour, compared to £9.26 per hour for all ethnic minority workers and over £10 per hour for the workforce in general.
- A Dutch temp agency brought several hundred young Spaniards to work in the Netherlands for one- to three-month contracts up to Christmas 1997. They were apparently willing to do jobs at the Dutch minimum wage, which few Dutch unemployed would accept for such short periods. But after finding their working day was extended from the agreed 9 hours to 11 or 12 hours, several gave up and went home.[31]

in Telford and Leeds said they could not get a permanent job, and agency work was their only alternative to unemployment. From the point of view of many agencies themselves, especially those supplying manual workers, unemployed people are an important labour supply. Although some agencies – especially those recruiting for better-paid office work – tend to reject unemployed candidates (Gray, 2002b), up to 10 per cent of the overall agency labour force in the UK, and rather more for unskilled work, probably consists of people leaving unemployment. The proportion is 61 per cent in Germany[32] and probably even more in the Netherlands and France, where agency work is particularly extensive.

Both in the UK and in France, most jobseekers saw temporary employment agencies as the worst employers. It was alleged in Norwich that 'agencies take a third of what you earn', although agencies themselves, when interviewed, said this was greatly exaggerated. Nonetheless agency workers in manual or unskilled service jobs often earn less even than directly hired temps in the same kind of work (Gray, 2002b). Not only this, but agency work is the most insecure, involves the most loss of autonomy over working time and a particular sense of isolation and powerlessness, as shown by the comments in Box 6.2. Conversely, agencies were a frequently used and well-regarded source of vacancies for women in London who were seeking office jobs. Statistical evidence on agency pay in clerical jobs supports their judgement; women agency workers in this sector are paid no less than other temps (Gray, 2002b). However, all pay comparisons between agency and other workers must take into account the agency employees' less favourable arrangements for holidays, sick pay and pensions, among other differences.

Isn't a temporary job better than no job? Our interviewees repeatedly pointed out several reasons why it may not be:

- the difficulty of renegotiating benefit entitlements when a job ends;
- in continental systems, the linking of the insurance benefit level to earnings in the last job;
- job centres expect that an unemployed person will accept work of the same kind as they did before, even if their last job was only a temporary, stop-gap solution at a lower level of skill or pay than their last long-term job;
- the fear that once temporary work is accepted, the job centre may pressurise someone into accepting a sequence of temporary jobs from which there is no escape;

- jobseekers' perception that temporary contracts are often associated with excessively long hours, lack of control over working hours and conditions, and even poor health and safety;
- temporary jobs often do not carry any entitlement to paid holidays[33] or sick pay.

Temporary contracts were seen as a strategy used by employers to enforce work discipline and make people work harder:

Everybody's so fearful when they've got a short-term contract; if you get the sack you haven't got a leg to stand on. It means people are less likely to challenge it; they know they're being ripped off, but they're powerless to do anything about it. [lone mother, Brighton]

Box 6.3 What's wrong with temporary work?

- It's got to be really secure, the job you're going in to, because if you haven't been to any work for some time, you appreciate that you've got to get into the job, and feel secure, and know that you're going to keep it. Because if you lose that job, you've got to sign back on, and they would give you loads of messing about in the process, your rent's all messed up and everything else too ... [Norwich]
- If people take short-term jobs, they have to cope with the whole rigmarole when they come off of that job to get all their benefits all over again ... it's not easy trying to get all these forms sorted out ... people may say, to hell with that; it took me long enough to get it in the first place .... With temporary contracts you don't get any sickness or holiday pay, so you can't make any plans at all ... [Lowestoft]
- I would prefer to work, but where can I get a job that won't dump me on the dole in a few months' time and cause me to lose my home? .... I said [to the job centre] somebody's offered me a job, it'll be about 18 weeks' work through the summer ... but they said, you do realise you'll probably lose your home if you do this? [lone father, Lowestoft, worried about not getting help with his mortgage reinstated fast enough at the end of a temporary job]

France (near Lille):[34]

- I've done short-term agency assignments, one month or two weeks, without getting the minimum time needed to build up any insurance rights.
- We were a lot of agency workers together, we didn't know each other and people kept changing. You had no connection with them and you could never discuss anything.
- I did locum care work. It's underpaid – you get 70 francs[35] for a 20-hour sleepover ending at 7 in the morning. It's a real form of exploitation which happens because of the competition between the poor.

There are employers who don't want to make the commitment of taking somebody on permanent straight away, so they offer three months' probation, then they'll give you another three months or six months. So at the back of your mind you're always trying ... your utmost to keep that job you want. [former office worker, Norwich]

In East Anglia, jobseekers had a keen sense of the divide in pay and conditions between 'temporary' and 'permanent' staff, a difference more of status than of actual contract duration. Local trade unionists confirmed that some food processing companies offered repeated three-month contracts, so that an employee might be there for several years without getting permanent status. Or, in one informant's experience, employees might be laid off after only six weeks if sales were bad. Temporary status excluded employees from the company pension scheme and certain shift allowances to which permanent workers were entitled. One factory, when replacing many directly hired temps by agency staff in 2000, promised there would be no loss of pay. Three years on there was a pay gap of over £1 per hour between 'non-perm' agency workers and 'flexi assignment staff', who were promised a mere 24 hours per week at the lower rate, with unpredictable hours. For years, formerly well-paid permanent jobs in vegetable processing had gradually been replaced in this and other food factories by temporary and agency hirings. One man in Lowestoft was painfully aware why: 'they can save pounds by taking on temporaries ... They know that when one leaves there's 200 down the road that can drop into their place.'

Health and safety, as well as union recognition, are also at stake in temporary and agency work. Box 6.4 illustrates the dilemmas – leading, in one extreme case, to sudden untimely death. Both in France and in the UK, the requirement for an agency to ensure appropriate safety training may be ignored, and jobseekers are powerless to take action against this. In Spain, however, regulations now debar agencies from supplying workers to certain jobs considered dangerous.

Time sovereignty was another issue for those clinging to the margins of the job market; employers' demands for long or unsocial hours seemed hard to resist, especially for those in temporary work. One Belgian woman had worked in a hotel, with hours up to the legal limit, but with 'unofficial' overtime on top:

Hotel jobs, it's exploitative. It's the extra hours they promise to let you take off later but you never can. Or you never get paid for them. It's a mad job, exhausting. You're standing up, standing, standing, never a minute to rest.

In the tourist industry in Brussels, 'you have a contract for eight hours a day, but in practice you do 10 or 12, and it's not paid'. Large international hotel chains were said to be worse for unpaid overtime than the small establishments (Lévy *et al.*, 2001a).

Agency work was particularly associated with losing control over one's own working hours:

Box 6.4 Agencies and safety

Construction worker, Brighton

Some agencies, where the health and safety checking is diabolical. I worked for Personnel Selection, which is the same agency that killed somebody I knew down Shoreham Docks [see story of Simon Jones, below], and that goes back to about ten years ago, on a building site, where there was no checking on health and safety ... and I organised a walkout, because health and safety was at risk ... obviously they weren't giving me work after that, but at least I made some sort of statement ... Another time, they sent me to the [bread] factory where you were picking hot tins really quickly off a conveyor belt, you got burnt on the arm easily like that, ... generally agencies don't do health and safety checking, especially for manual work, building site work ... the agencies get away with blue murder. A lot of them employ you on the basis that you're self-employed, and so they evade their responsibilities that way; B ... is one, they use that so as not to pay holiday pay, sick pay, because they say it's self-employed ... Another thing temp agencies have done is cut out trade unions, except for Manpower and Alfred Marks.

The tragedy of Simon Jones:

Simon Jones was killed in an accident at Shoreham docks in 1998.[36] Some people at the Brighton unemployed centre, where some of the Minima Sociaux research took place, knew him and had helped his family in campaigning for his employer to be prosecuted. Simon was claiming Jobseeker's Allowance, and according to his friends had been under some pressure from the Job Centre to take additional steps to look for work or his benefits would be stopped. He therefore went to a private employment agency, which in April 1998 sent him to a temporary job unloading cargo from a ship at Shoreham docks. He was killed on his first day at work when his head was crushed by a crane. Simon had received only a few minutes' 'training', and inadequate training and supervision of his two co-workers were said to have played a part in the accident.

Dominique, France:[37]

They pass over a rotten job without taking stock of the things you're not trained to do: I was driving a fork lift without any training, and I had an accident and they carpeted me. They said I was working badly.

You're working in horrible conditions, you're out there at their whim, day and night. You don't say the hours you're working, they say the hours you're working. [former railway maintenance worker, Brighton]

One time I did two months working as a locum [i.e. for absent permanent staff], and I was doing 200 km a day. They call you in the evening to go somewhere the next day and you don't even know the company. [French jobseeker near the Luxembourg border]

In East Anglian food processing, shifts of up to twelve hours sometimes had unpredictable finish times:

Paul (Norwich): These jobs involve very long shifts. You might have to work over 60 hours to make enough. They would probably want you to opt out of the 48-hour directive. Often the shift system is 'midday till finish' and they may not tell you that finish could be as late as 11.30 p.m., depending on the day.
AG: What happens if you refuse overtime and want to go early?
Paul: You couldn't anyway because you're dependent on workplace transport.

Not only food processing, but some other sectors in Norwich were reported to have especially unpleasant systems of working time. In a book distribution warehouse:

I was doing a 67-hour week ... they said, your contract is from 12 midday till finish, and sometimes that would be half past 11 at night, with two 15-minute breaks ... on a temporary contract you were paid not to have a dinner break ... you were paid for the two 15-minute breaks, that's all you had all day, and sometimes you were called in at half past 10 in the morning, and you wouldn't go home till quarter to 12.

A similar system of working was reported in the printing industry in Norwich, with shifts of twelve hours per day containing only two 15-minutes breaks. (Some of these experiences may have been before the implementation of the Working Time Directive in 1999.)

UK law now requires that where the working week will regularly be over 48 hours, the employer must invite workers to sign an 'opt out' agreement, to say that they agree voluntarily to work more than the limit. Many people felt that if they wanted a job at all in food processing or warehouse work, they would have to 'voluntarily' opt out of the rights given to them by the Working Time Directive. In the UK sample for the Minima Sociaux research 13 out of 89 people (14.6 per cent) had worked over 48 hours in their last job, and eleven (12.3 per cent) between 44 and 48 hours. Sometimes, however, this was a choice dictated by low hourly pay.

If employers took liberties in stretching contract hours, they could be breaking the minimum wage law, as recognised by two women in Brighton:

Teresa: I know in [two national retail chains], they'll get paid so much for the hour, and then told that they're employed for 35–40 hours a week or whatever, and they'll get that minimum wage, but they'll actually be expected to turn up earlier, stay behind later, and it doesn't get classed as overtime …

Jenny: They stay behind for hours to clean up … an hour and a half, two hours, sometimes.

AG: So you don't get paid for that time?

Teresa: I think that's happening in a lot of places.

TEMP WORK – STEPPING STONE OR DEAD END?

It is sometimes argued that the creation of low-quality jobs at the margin of the 'stock' of job opportunities is no bad thing if people soon progress to something better. But in fact a barrier often goes up between full-time permanent positions and 'precarious' work – insecure, low-paid, sometimes under-employment in very short hours. A 'segmented' or 'dual' labour market tends to occur. 'Disadvantaged' individuals – those with a broken work record, or caring obligations, and generally ethnic minorities – are more likely to stick in the precarious jobs.

Rather than becoming a ladder for advancement, temporary jobs are for many ex-unemployed people merely an interlude between one spell out of work and the next. Throughout the EU, of those in temporary jobs in 1997, only 35 per cent moved into permanent work during the following year, while 44 per cent moved into other temporary jobs and 13 per cent into unemployment.[38] By contrast only 2.3 per cent of those who had a permanent job became unemployed. Looking at the problem the other way round, losing a temporary job is a frequent cause of becoming unemployed. Even in the UK where temporary jobs are rather less common than in most other EU countries, probably at least a third of those who become unemployed, do so when a temporary contract ends.[39] No wonder, then, that the Euromarches took up the cause not only of unemployed people but also of 'precarious workers' (Mathers, 1999).

Once people are in temporary jobs, their chances of moving to permanent work are quite poor in most EU countries. Only in Austria was the proportion who did so more than half within a year (during 1997–98). In Denmark, the Netherlands, Italy, the UK and Germany, just under half moved from temporary to permanent jobs within twelve months, but in Spain it was only 27 per cent and in France a mere 21 per cent . Some informants for the Minima Sociaux research were well aware of their poor chances of getting secure contracts; employers had many motives for not giving them. Employers often use temporary contracts as a form of probation – but the insecurity may go on and on:

> Most of their staff, they have up to 600 at any one time, are on temporary contracts, for three months only. At the end of three months they get another three-month contract. I know some people who have been there two years, and they still haven't been given a full-time contract, and they're still on the minimum wage. [Former book warehouse worker, Norwich]

In the course of this research, the author came across food factory workers who had been over six years in the same position, on a sequence of temporary contracts – never acquiring rights to compensation for unfair dismissal or redundancy. Even those who apparently please their employer may still not get permanent work:

> I worked at [major food processing factory] last year, didn't have any problem with them. I was given a 13-week contract, completed that, and then I was given another 13-week contract in another department, and then they laid me off. This year they contacted me again, and said, would I like to do the same sort of procedures as I done last year, 13 weeks, and I was given a 13-week contract, but it's not worth the paper it was written on, they had to lay me off after six weeks, because the sales were down. They had to lay everybody off basically, 300 to 400 people they'd taken on for that particular contract. I've since contacted them, to see if they need support, because the vegetable season's started again, but they told

me that they can't employ people until 12 weeks after they last laid you off. [Young woman, Lowestoft]

Those who take temporary work tend to have lower earnings over several years, even if they later get a permanent job (Booth, Francesconi and Frank, 2000).

CONCLUSION

Recent changes in European labour markets have made it increasingly difficult for the unwaged to find secure work at a wage that lifts them off dependence on benefits or tax credits. A secular trend towards greater job insecurity is apparent, despite some cyclical fluctuations in the share of temporary jobs in the total. The problem is not merely that many of the extra jobs created are temporary and part-time. There is also substitution of existing jobs; many employers are replacing former permanent contracts with temporary or agency hirings, and full-time jobs by ones with very short part-time hours.

Especially in France and Spain, the large increase in temporary contracts has led to little extra employment; the shift to temporary contracts over the last decade seems to have been less a question of growth at the margins than a substitution of temporary for permanent work.[40] This is consistent with the view that flexibilisation is an employers' cost-cutting strategy, and evidence that it has been taking place in declining sectors like manufacturing as well as growing service sectors. It is also encouraged by the form of some wage subsidies introduced to encourage hiring of unemployed people. Sometimes subsidies encourage job splitting; sometimes employers create a job to run for as long as the subsidy – usually a year or less. During the 1990s, fixed-term contracts increased their share of all EU jobs by three percentage points, and part-time jobs by 4.2 percentage points. Perhaps not much, but large by comparison with the 7.4 per cent of EU workers who were unemployed in 2001. Since most unemployed need a full-time wage, and short-term jobs often return them to the 'dole' before long, how much better would their chances have been if these changes in the labour market had not taken place?

Flexibilisation has tended to create a divide between 'good jobs' and 'bad jobs'. Unemployed people move mainly into 'bad' jobs, with insufficient chances of progression from the bad to the good. Although temporary jobs are less than one in six of the European total – and a lot less in the UK – they are a much larger share of the jobs that go to unemployed people, and a much larger share still of the vacancies that jobseekers have to consider. When temporary jobs end, a majority of those who moved into them from unemployment go back to the 'dole'. The most short-term, and in unskilled occupations the most badly paid, of these temporary jobs are with employment agencies. Agency work, although still a fraction of temporary jobs and a mere 1.4–2 per cent of total European employment, is increasingly very rapidly and features prominently in the stock of jobs the unwaged can and do get. Altogether, the regulation of temporary work and the role permitted to temporary work agencies has a profound impact on the quality of opportunities accessible to unemployed people and the way in which the 'reserve army' affects wages and conditions in the labour market as a whole.

A growing role is also played by temporary work agencies in policy measures for the placement of the unemployed. In France, 215,000 unemployed, almost 10 per cent of the national total, are registered for erratic short assignments with non-profit temporary help agencies, a form of intermediate labour market or 'entreprise d'insertion' (Lévy *et al.*, 2000a), which enjoy tax concessions in recognition of their 'welfare to work' role. In the UK, several (though not all) Employment Zones have been run by employment agencies since 1999, often in partnership with the Employment Service and other organisations. The 'stock' of jobs they offer in Employment Zones contains many permanent positions and is quite separate from the agencies' normal business. Notwithstanding this, jobseekers are not always happy with the agencies' approach, which is very strongly oriented to the placement targets in their contracts with the government, rather than to the needs of individuals. Special temporary work agencies or 'job pools' were established in the Netherlands in the late 1980s, working on a non-profit basis in partnership with the public employment service, to hire out jobseekers until they could get long-term work (ERGO, 1992; Finn, 1998/99). Similar non-profit agencies have been set up in Germany in the 1990s, receiving state subsidies if they take at least one in four of their workforce from the long-term unemployed and other disadvantaged groups. Beyond these special arrangements, unemployed people form an important source of labour supply for commercial agency business in some countries; as stated earlier, they are over 60 per cent of agency recruits in the Netherlands and Germany.

In Germany, the Hartz Commission in 2002[41] made proposals for 'personnel service agencies' attached to local employment service offices, to hire out unemployed people for temporary work. Some of the contracts for this work will be going to non-profit agencies, but many are likely to be won by large commercial agencies. This policy is a major new development, which links agency work to workfare arrangements, and will substantially increase the power of agencies over unemployed people – an issue to which we return in Chapter 8. While it was being implemented in 2003, similar provisions were under consideration in Belgium. The rapid growth of agency jobs, the scale and power of multinational employment agencies, which include some of the largest employers in the world,[42] and their huge bargaining power over the unemployed labour pool, raise important issues about the regulation of temporary work, which will be addressed in the next chapter.

7

Labour Market Deregulation: Debates and Struggles

DEREGULATION TO MEET EMPLOYERS' DEMANDS

The quest for labour flexibility by European governments began after the oil price increases of 1973, as a response to economic crisis (Treu, 1992). Flexibilisation is upheld in OECD and EC documents as essential to the growth and survival of western economies (OECD, 1994; EC, 1993), and as a way to create jobs. Responding to employers' requirements, governments have sought to make it easier to hire temporary labour. Since the 1980s, restrictions on the use of temporary contracts and on temporary work agencies have been eased in several countries, and protection against dismissal also relaxed. Some countries also swept away social security or working time regulations that impeded part-time hirings or working at atypical hours. In contrast to the USA, individual dismissals in most European countries can be challenged in law unless the employer gives a justifiable reason. Since the mid-1980s, the UK, Germany, Portugal, Spain and Sweden increased the range of permissible reasons or exceptions to these rules (OECD, 1999b, p. 52). However, in Germany and the UK, some important changes were reversed in 1999.[1] Several European countries relaxed or simplified procedures for consultation or administrative authorisation prior to collective redundancies; for example, rules on redundancy notice and compensation were eased in Germany and Belgium in 1985, and in France in 1987.

As noted in Chapter 6, flexibilisation is generally employer-led – although there are some exceptions, such as job-sharing negotiations at employees' request. Hiring temporary workers means employers only pay for labour when it is needed – they can keep fixed labour costs low and hire extra people when demand is high. Part-time and temporary workers often earn less per hour, with fewer fringe benefits (Heery and Salmon, 2000). They can also work evenings and weekends without an unsocial hours premium – a point of increasing importance in service trades where the employer's competitive strategy often includes extending opening hours. Employers save money by taking advantage of exemptions from social security charges for workers with very short part-time hours. In the UK, around 40 per cent of part-time workers earn so little they are exempt from National Insurance contributions,[2] and much of the growth in part-time jobs has been in positions of this kind.

Flexibilisation also weakens workers' capacity to organise, which in turn facilitates a further erosion of pay and conditions. Part-time and temporary workers are less likely than permanent full-timers to join trade unions. Without job security, workers are more fearful of being sacked. This enables employers to enforce stricter labour discipline and deters workers from risking conflict – about their right to join a union, or to be active in one, or about asserting their contractual rights. Part-timers are often women with caring responsibilities, which means they have less choice of jobs and lower wage expectations. Thus the overall effect of flexibilisation is to create a more difficult environment for workers to improve or defend their conditions. Later in this chapter, we examine the evidence on how the shift to 'atypical' contracts affects workers' bargaining power.

Before the mid-1970s part-time contracts were little used in continental Europe. They usually carried disproportionately high social security costs, which have since been reduced. Employers in the 1970s often faced national restrictions on variable working hours, which impeded shift-working, extended customer service hours or seasonal variations in working time. This led to some modifications of labour law in France, Spain, Belgium and Italy during the late 1970s and 1980s. Variable working hours have often been traded for a shorter working week. For example, when the French working week was further reduced to 35 hours by the 'Loi Aubry' of 1999, company and sector-level agreements to implement the details often included further employee concessions about variable or annualised working hours.

In most EU countries, fixed term contracts have historically been limited to a range of special circumstances. Gradually these were broadened in the 1980s, making it easier for employers to hire on short-term contracts in Belgium, France, Germany, Spain, Italy and Sweden.[3] In all these countries, especially Sweden, the 1990s saw a substantial increase in the proportion of temporary workers. There has also been some increase in the UK, which had no restrictions on the use of temporary hiring until the EU Fixed Term Work Directive entered UK law in 2002. Until the 1990s Italy, Sweden and Spain prohibited temporary work agencies; Greece still did until 2001. Rules regarding temporary work agencies have been gradually relaxed in many countries, easing restrictions on the length of time or the purpose for which employers can use agency labour. However, regulations about agency workers' relative pay and contract arrangements have tightened, reflecting a need for greater state intervention in this very rapidly growing form of work.

International variations in the use of temporary contracts reflect differences in the regulatory environment. Employers weigh up the relative costs of permanent and temporary hirings in the light of requirements about redundancy pay, how easily they can dismiss permanent workers, restrictions on the use of fixed-term contracts or agency workers. The more difficult or expensive it is to terminate permanent contracts, the more employers tend to hire short-term. For example, temporary jobs are almost a third of the total in Spain, where redundancy attracts over five weeks' pay after two years in a 'permanent' job, but only 9.2 per cent of all jobs in Denmark where redundancy pay is confined to white collar workers with long service. Danish employers make little use of temporary contracts because 'the general flexibility in the standard employment relationship fulfils the employer's needs' (Madsen, 2003, p. 71). Danish manual workers can be dismissed without notice during their first nine months if they are no longer needed or lack competence (Madsen, 2003, p. 72), whereas in many European countries, employers can dismiss permanent workers only after meeting various procedural and notice requirements.[4] Danish employees consequently tend to change jobs rather frequently, but survey evidence suggests that they do not fear insecurity so much as in many other countries, partly because of relatively high unemployment benefits.

In the UK, where the right to redundancy compensation begins after two years in post, the public sector in the 1990s turned increasingly to temporary contacts as a way of minimising redundancy payments when organisations shrink or are contracted out. Otherwise, British employers perhaps see less need for making contracts explicitly temporary, since they face few restrictions on sacking anyone who has been in a job less than a year.[5] Thus temporary contracts are a relatively small share of all jobs in the UK (6.8 per cent in 2001 against an EU average of 13.4 per cent); the type of contract makes little difference to either side's rights in the first year. Because of this, the number of workers whose formal status is that of 'temporary' may underestimate the extent of job insecurity in the UK. Around one in five of all workers have been less than one year in their present job, compared to the EU average of 14.8 per cent.[6]

In the UK, France, Spain and the Netherlands, temporary work agencies have doubled or trebled their business in the 1990s as employers have turned to them to save recruitment costs and provide 'disposable' workers (Gray, 2002b; Forde, 2001). Agency temps were expected to grow from 1.4 per cent of the EU labour force to around 2 per cent in the five to seven years from 1999.[7] The EC has estimated their share of employment in 1999 at around 2.1 per cent in the UK, 2.7 per cent in France, 1.6 per cent in Belgium, less than 1 per cent in Spain, Sweden and Denmark but around 4 per cent in the Netherlands.[8] Agencies' own figures suggest between two and four times as many temps in the UK as the total shown in the Labour Force Survey (Walby, 2002) – possibly because some agency workers regard themselves as self-employed, or register with more than one agency. However, some agency claims about the large share of the workforce they control may relate to the volume of placements or vacancies handled rather than to the share of employment. Because of the high turnover of agency staff, agency work is a far higher share of vacancies than of jobs. For example, by 1994 all types of temporary work agency controlled over 10 per cent of recruitment in the Netherlands[9] and by 1998 about 5 per cent in Spain.

In the 1980s, most of agencies' UK business was to provide 'cover' for absent staff. However, now they often supply dozens, sometimes hundreds of workers at once to a call centre or a factory. Financial and business services have seen the most rapid growth of temporary work (Gray, 2002b); the huge expansion of call centres involves many fixed-term and agency workers. The pace of work is so intensive that in any case workers have high sickness rates and many do not stay long.[10] Privatisation of former municipal and government services has transferred many jobs to temporary work agencies (Allen and Henry, 1996), as has subcontracting or 'outsourcing' of catering, cleaning, security, etc., which is increasing in both public and private sectors, in France as well as in the UK (Galtier and Gautié, 2003). In France and Germany, the engineering industries, especially car plants, turned to agencies for a large share of their manual workforce in the 1990s. In Peugeot, 30 per cent of employees are agency temps; in Renault, 10 per cent.[11] Young agency workers in France alternate between temping on the assembly lines and unemployment, feeling that the agency takes an unfairly large share of the car firm's payment for their work (Beaud, 1999).

Temp agencies compete with others to sell labour; sometimes this leads them to drive wages down, but more often and especially where a few agencies dominate the market, they try to push the basic wage up (Gray, 2002b). This is in their interests since their profit comes from a percentage mark-up on the temp's pay. They often try to secure equal basic pay for their employees with those of the user company; thus agencies do not necessarily resent or challenge the introduction of regulations requiring equal pay with direct hires or with rates laid down in relevant collective agreements. Such regulations were introduced in Spain in 1999, Greece in 2001 and in Germany in 2002, having existed earlier in Belgium, France, and several other EU countries.[12] They will form part of the proposed EU Agency Work Directive, currently in draft in 2003, if and when it eventually goes ahead. But the principle of equal pay is open to interpretation. In the UK, temps often have less remuneration overall, even if they get the same basic hourly rate as directly hired workers, lacking shift payments, bonuses and some overtime premia (Gray, 2002b; TUC, 2001). This is illustrated by the case of the food industry workers mentioned in Chapter 6. Danish agency workers do not have the same rights to pensions, sick and maternity pay as workers in the user undertaking even though the main Danish employers' federation has agreed equal basic pay for agency workers.[13]

DOES FLEXIBILISATION CREATE JOBS?

Western Europe's tradition of relatively heavy labour market regulation has been lampooned as the disease of 'Eurosclerosis' by a number of economists.[14] 'Rigidity' has been alleged in regulations about unfair dismissal, redundancy compensation (severance pay) or consultation, the use of temporary contracts and minimum wage laws. Most forms of worker protection come under suspicion in the 'flexibilisation' debate. The accusation of excessive 'rigidity' in Europe's labour laws was readily taken up by employer lobbies (Treu, 1992) and is echoed in the OECD's highly influential Jobs Study of 1994. Comparisons are constantly made with the USA, which has very few restrictions on employers' power to hire and fire. It also has a very low federal minimum wage – just 38 per cent of median earnings,[15] compared to minimum wages of 50–60 per cent of the median in most of the EU. These policies are often credited with the success of the American economy in creating a large number of new jobs over the last 20 years, albeit low-paid and insecure.

The USA has thus come to be held up as a model of successful labour market performance through labour 'flexibility'. The message is clear: deregulation of labour contracts, minimal trade union rights and low minimum wage levels are supposed to create more jobs. But the apparent success of the US economy comes at a high social cost. Real wage levels for the American poor actually fell during the 1980s and early 1990s.[16] The rising employment rate was achieved by drawing in women – reflecting the need for two incomes to keep many households going because of low wages.[17] There is also a high level of insecurity – in 1995, 15 per cent of male American workers had lost their job in the previous three years.

The US unemployment rate has been lower than the EU average since 1983 (Lazar and Stoyko, 1998, p. 11). This is partly because more Americans are in prison or employed in running prisons (Wilkinson, 2000, p. 66). Some European economies have been more successful at creating jobs than the USA, although the EU as a whole has not. However, the legacy of a crude comparison with the EU as a whole has been widespread admiration for the American 'model', tempered by disquiet at the growing inequality it entails. While the American employment rate (for men plus women) has exceeded the EU's since the mid-1970s, Denmark and Sweden have shown higher employment rates than the USA over most of that period. Mostly the EU has a lower employment rate for older workers, who are increasingly taking early retirement. In the EU's southern states, women's labour force participation has been low for historic and cultural reasons rather than labour regulations. However, a large though declining number of women, youth and older people there are unpaid workers in small farms and other family businesses, so that statistics on paid employment may be artificially low.

Among EU countries, the UK comes closest to the US model of labour regulation, and has reduced unemployment much more rapidly than the EU average in recent years. Australia and New Zealand have also shown rapid job growth and declining unemployment, following new policies to permit widespread casualisation of labour in the 1990s (Nickell, 1997). It has been argued that the British flexibilisation measures of the Tory years – such as the reduction of unfair dismissal protection, restriction of trade union rights, abolition of Wages Councils and deregulation of temporary work agencies – led to some job creation. As in the deregulated labour market of the USA, this was growth in low-quality jobs, mainly in low-paid service sectors like retailing and hospitality.

Workers who are hard to get rid of mean unwanted costs for a firm that is contracting, so there is an argument that employers will more readily take the risk of creating jobs in countries where 'sackability' is high. Conversely, the harder it is to sack people who have a secure job, the more likely they are to keep their jobs through a recession, with companies often reducing hours rather than payroll numbers as a way of keeping costs down. Making long-term jobs very secure will divert employers into using fixed term contracts or agency workers, or if that is not legally possible, into informal hirings with no contract at all or into using 'self-employed' labour. Conversely, making long-term contracts less secure may actually increase employers' use of them, relative to temporary contracts; Spain reduced redundancy compensation in 1994 and introduced a new, less protected form of permanent contract in 1997 (Perez-Diaz, 1998) to address the excessive use of temporary contracts, which has led to a huge divide in pay, prospects and experience of unemployment between those with secure jobs and those without (Polavieja and Richards, 2002). However, measures to improve conditions and security in fixed-term contracts – the objective of the EU's Fixed Term Work Directive of 2001 – may make employers use agency temps instead.[18]

Strict job security laws mean fewer terminations but also fewer vacancies; fewer people enter unemployment but those who do, stay unemployed for longer. They may end up with eroded and rusty skills, becoming gradually 'unemployable'. It has often been argued that 'too much' job security means youth and women returners become 'outsiders'; with no job they cannot benefit from job security laws like the 'insiders' and lose out from the infrequent filling of vacancies. Hence the OECD suggested in its Jobs Study of 1994 that relaxing employment protection legislation would reduce long-term unemployment and share job opportunities more equitably by age and gender. The Jobs Study has been a major influence on the 'flexibilising' labour market reforms in the EU during the 1990s, both through the EU Employment Guidelines and through OECD recommendations to individual governments in its regular 'country reports'.

In 1993 the OECD drew up an index of the strictness of employment protection legislation (EPL), scoring countries on various aspects of their regulations: redundancy pay; how long someone must be in a job before getting it or being protected against unfair dismissal; restrictions on fixed-term contracts and agency work, and so on (OECD, 1993). Countries were ranked in order of strictness of their rules. Although what to put into such an index and how to combine and weight its several elements must clearly be a matter of judgement, it gives a rough idea of the relative extent of 'commodification' of labour in different countries, or the 'sackability' of workers. In line with several previous studies both by the OECD and others, the OECD's 1993 research found that strict EPL, although it does not increase overall unemployment, is associated with a relatively high rate of *long-term* unemployment. This was confirmed by more recent OECD research, based on data from 1990–97.[19]

This recent OECD research showed that although strict EPL raises long-term unemployment, it has no influence on overall employment or unemployment rates, once a number of contextual variables are taken into account – such as wage bargaining systems,[20] the unemployed benefits system, tax rates on labour, and the stage of the economic cycle.[21]

However, on the 'insider/outsider' effect the OECD's 1999 work questioned some of the 1993 analysis. It found no significant association between EPL and lower employment rates of women and youth although the 1993 work had found one. Whereas earlier studies, including those by the OECD itself in 1993–94, had suggested that strict EPL is associated with a growth of temporary contracts (because employers move towards the type of hirings that are least regulated), the OECD's 1999 research finds no evidence for this. Nor do strict controls on the use and nature of temporary contracts tend to raise long-term unemployment.

The OECD's overall index is rather 'broad brush'; the authors of its more recent (1999b) research recognise this and examine the different kinds of regulation separately. They also widened the concept of EPL to include provisions relating to collective dismissal – such as consultation, and the 1989 'social plans' requirement in France.[22] This refinement of the data, as well as time passing, may underlie the slightly changed conclusion. Its overall message seems to reduce the justification for 'flexibilising' labour markets, paring away workers' rights to create more jobs. If the problem is merely the *distribution* of jobs between different kinds of jobseekers, other measures can address that – such as training, childcare provision and anti-discrimination measures.

Another important aspect of labour market regulation is minimum wage laws. Whether low minimum wage levels permit more low-skilled people to get jobs has been a live issue in both France and the UK in recent years. In 1995, the French government sought to ease the minimum wage requirement for young people, in the hope that fewer of them would be out of work if they were cheaper to hire. After massive protests, the government desisted, and the minimum wage, about 60 per cent of median earnings, remained the same for all age groups. It is sometimes said that high minimum wages mean no jobs for low-productivity workers, and that this at least partly explains the higher unemployment in the EU compared to the USA (Begg and Berghman, 2002, p. 183). Such arguments were used to defend the abolition of Wages Councils in the UK in 1993, and are still being used to permit extra-low starting pay for ex-unemployed people in Germany. Any argument that competitiveness requires low wages must also confront the already low wage costs in some EU countries as well as the rather weak relationship between wages and labour costs per unit of output. The UK, Ireland, Spain, Greece and Portugal all had lower hourly labour costs than the USA in 1996 (Abraham, 1999). How much lower would they have to fall to maintain manufacturing jobs, and with what consequences? In defence of the majority West European 'model', European Commission researchers (EC, 1998a, p. 73) have argued that while low wage rates may facilitate hiring of unskilled workers, they do reduce workers' motivation and probably productivity, as well as 'promoting popular unrest about the size of wage differentials'.

As mentioned in Chapter 6, the OECD's investigation based on a set of 19 countries through the 1980s and early 1990s found little evidence of a positive link between low pay and employment rates.[23] This work casts doubt on the argument that letting wage rates fall at the lower end of the scale helps to create more jobs. Esping-Andersen (2002), in an informative assessment of the effects of minimum wages and EPL, finds that high minimum wages do not affect the overall unemployment rate, although they may redistribute jobs away from the groups employers might have thought 'deserved' a lower wage, namely youth and the unskilled. Moreover, if the minimum wage level is high, the *outflow* from unemployment is also high – suggesting that a reasonable wage is needed to enable jobseekers to come off benefits. According to Michie and Wilkinson (1994), low pay is not the answer to unemployment; rather, unemployed people accept low-paid jobs out of desperation, but leave them if and when job prospects improve. Thus employers have little incentive to train. Low pay then leads to low skills; and may be the cause of lower productivity, rather than vice versa (Heery and Salmon, 2000, p. 6).

Recent research by the EC[24] shows that those EU countries with a higher share of good-quality jobs (that is, where secure work paying at least 75 per cent of median earnings is over 25 per cent of all employment) have higher employment rates than the ones with a lower share of good-quality jobs. However, it does find some support for a trade-off between job quality and employment quantity; looking at men alone, countries having a low share of high-quality jobs for men have higher male employment rates. Moreover, a high employment rate of people aged 55–64 goes with low job quality for this age group. But that might be a question of who, and how many, can afford to retire. One might argue that that low job quality goes with poor pension rights and inability to retire before 65; such a relationship for older men might influence the statistical relationship between job quality and employment rate for all men.

In Nickell's work (1997), certain other worker-friendly features of the labour market scene appeared to be associated with higher unemployment: the 'density' of union membership and the proportion of workers covered by trade union agreements, as well as the ratio of unemployment benefits to average wages and the duration of benefit entitlements. However, when the degree of coordination or centralisation of trade union bargaining is ranked on a scale of high/medium/low, high coordination seems to be associated with lower unemployment. This is thought to be because coordinated bargaining prevents 'leapfrogging' wage claims, thus reducing inflation. Against Nickell's verdict on the effect of trade unions, Nolan (1994) argues that in the USA, individual states with high union density have at least as much employment growth as those with less union members. Moreover, Nolan points out that in contrast to the legal shackles on trade unions enacted in the UK in the mid-1980s, Germany at the same period pursued a policy of high wages based on high productivity growth, without restricting union rights..

In short, there seems little evidence that either EPL or minimum wage levels affect unemployment, and the 'Eurosclerosis' hypothesis falls. Rather, Esping-Andersen (2000b, p. 105) has argued that the main cause of the relatively high unemployment in Europe compared to the USA since the early 1980s has been the combination of 'deruralisation' of the population – especially in France, Spain and Italy – with the rise in demand for paid employment for women.

THE EFFECTS OF FLEXIBILISATION ON WORKERS' STRUGGLES

Insecurity at work is a weapon in the class struggle; it affects the prospects for effective workers' organisation, not only in the workplace but through the interface between work and unemployment. Insecure work is creating a group of intermittently unemployed people on the margin of the labour force, unlikely to become unionised because of short job durations and fear of victimisation, and under pressure from the job centre system to accept a succession of insecure and low-paid jobs. The fear of job loss plays an increasing role in the bargaining environment. The use of temporary agency workers can be a way of undermining trade union organisation, as shown in some important UK labour disputes in the 1990s (see Box 7.1).

Box 7.1 Some key UK disputes about casualisation

The Liverpool dockers' dispute, which began in September 1995, attracted solidarity action by dockers/longshoremen all over the world. Eighty men working for Torside, a private subcontractor of the harbour company, were sacked for refusing to work overtime at a rate of pay they rejected. A further 329 employees of the Mersey Docks and Harbour Company itself (still partly state-owned) were sacked ostensibly for engaging in 'illegal secondary action', that is, refusing to cross the picket line of the sacked 80. When the harbour company's men sought to return to work, they found their jobs had been taken by temp agency casual workers at much lower wages. Later, some of the sacked men were offered, but refused, new individual contracts on worse conditions than before.

Source: John Pilger, *Guardian*, 23.11.96

Hillingdon Hospital

A second example of long-established unionised workers being replaced by cheaper, non-union staff on short-term contract comes from the West London suburbs, where a strike picket has continued since October 1995. The Hillingdon Hospital cleaners and catering workers were sacked after refusing to sign a new employment contract with an agency to whom the hospital had just contracted out certain services. The new contract envisaged a pay cut of more than 25 per cent, with abolition of pension rights, unsocial hours allowances and employer sick pay. Their places were taken by agency workers, few of whom were apparently interested in joining the union.

Source: UNISON leaflets of the period, and Costello and Levidow (2002)

Turning lecturers into self-employed subcontractors

In spring 1997, several further education colleges around London developed plans to terminate contracts for part-time staff and replace some posts through an employment agency, Educational Lecturing Services. Under the ELS regime, part-time staff would become officially 'self-employed', suffer a pay cut and lose their rights under employment protection laws as well as to parity of conditions with full-timers on issues like holiday pay. Kingsway College and others had strikes about these plans.

Source: NATFHE Kingsway College leaflet 1997

There is no legal bar to replacement of directly hired workers by agency ones while the direct hires are still in post (see the example in Box 7.2). Where this happens, agency workers have a different employer from the one running the host workplace, so under UK law they cannot strike against the host employer, only against their own. So even if agency workers have their own union and the agency recognises it (as was the case in this example) its bargaining power is automatically limited and the agency workers cannot easily join forces with direct hires.

Since the mid-1970s trade union membership and union density have declined rapidly, both in the UK and in most other European countries (Visser, 2002). Falling union strength following the recession of the 1980s extended to Australasia, the USA and Canada (OECD, 1991). In Sweden, Finland and Belgium the decline did not begin till the early 1990s. In Denmark, density began to fall only in 2001, and may fall further as the government introduces a ban on closed shop agreements.[25] Trade union membership in the UK revived slightly after Labour's election in 1997 but then fell again after 2000 (Brook, 2002). Despite the Employment Relations Act 1999, which introduced a legal right to trade union recognition,[26] union density, and the proportion of workplaces with union recognition, have fallen considerably since the 1980s (Bryson and Gomay, 2002). The 1999 Act may have encouraged avoidance strategies by employers, such as outsourcing.

Although the proportion of workers covered by collective agreements fell only in the USA and the UK (Esping-Andersen, 1996b),

---

Box 7.2 The employer's right to switch to agency hiring

In 2000, a food processing company in East Anglia decided to hire all its temporary workers in future through an employment agency. A number of directly hired temps were told they could no longer be on the company's own payroll, and to keep their jobs they would have to reapply through the agency. Some of them had been in continuous service for over two years. Although the agency paid the same basic hourly rate, the temps would lose shiftwork bonuses and other extras, in some cases amounting to up to £3,000 per year. An industrial tribunal ruled that they had no case against the employer for unfair dismissal; in other words, it was perfectly legal for the employer to replace direct hiring with agency arrangements, even if in practice this meant having some of the same people back with worse conditions. What had happened was deemed to be redundancy, rather than unfair dismissal. Because not all the agreed redundancy procedures had been followed, the former employees obtained an offer of some compensation.

the question remains how far agreements can be effectively enforced in the absence of former membership numbers. Trade unions have historically been stronger in manufacturing and in the public sector than in private service industries and in large workplaces than in small ones (OECD, 1991, pp. 117–18; *Labour Research*, May 1995, p. 16). Thus, sector shift in employment, including the declining size of the public sector and the replacement of manufacturing industry by service sector jobs, with the associated shift to smaller workplaces, accounts for part of the change in union density (OECD, 1991; Mason and Bain, 1993; Visser, 2002; Brook, 2002). The experience of low-skilled youth, characterised by frequent job changes punctuated by spells of unemployment, working often in small service sector establishments, impedes the transmission of the knowledge and practice of trade unionism to a 'new' generation of workers. New establishments are less likely to recognise unions than older ones; although one factor is that they are more likely to be in the service sector, another is a higher proportion of part-time employees.

Independently of the sector shift and establishment size factors, several writers have suggested that the increase in part-time work can help explain the decline in trade union density (Beaumont and Harris, 1995; Brook, 2002). Sinclair (1995) found that only 58 per cent of part-time women workers in a UK survey were union members, compared to 77 per cent of female full-timers and 85 per cent of male full-timers. For several reasons part-time workers are more difficult to unionise: caring commitments at home are a constraint on attending meetings, they are more likely to work unsocial hours, they have less meal-break periods than full-timers to talk to colleagues. Disney, Gosling and Machin (1995) found that the percentage of part-time workers was also one of the main factors explaining de-recognitions of trade unions by UK employers in the period 1984–90.

Temporary workers are less likely to join unions than those who have job security. Beaumont and Harris (1992) showed that union density is inversely related to the growth of temporary jobs within a workplace. In the UK Sinclair (1995) found that perceived permanence of job was one of the four main attitudinal factors determining the 'propensity' to join a union. Polavieja and Richards (2002) encountered a similar disaffection from trade unions among young temporary workers in Spain. In French car plants, young agency temps felt the unions have nothing to offer them (Beaud, 1999). Where the presence of a large proportion of insecure employees in a workplace impedes trade union organisation, this in turn may enable the employer to move further in the direction of casualisation without meeting employee resistance, gradually weakening union organisation still further.

Those in non-union workplaces suffer a higher incidence of low pay (Stewart, 1999) and some proportion of the rise in inequality in the UK during the period since 1970 can be attributed to the declining power of trade unions (Machin, 1999). Trade union bargaining power was adversely affected by legal restrictions placed on the unions during the period of the Conservative government, including in particular the prohibition of 'solidarity' actions in which workers strike against their employers to support other workers who have a different employer. The fragmentation of the labour force through extensive outsourcing and subcontracting of various functions of both public and private sector organisations has made this prohibition of particular relevance. Outsourcing of various municipal and other public services to private subcontractors has already been referred to in Chapter 6 as a cause of decline in wages and conditions. Workers' capacity to resist is hampered by the associated loss of job security, but also by the increase in the use of agency temps, whose unionisation rate is very low (Allen and Henry, 1996).

The shake-out of manufacturing employment in the 1980s set off a sequence of adverse effects on wages and conditions, especially of the lower-skilled. It led to a rise in the share of temporary and part-time jobs, both because of changed hiring practices in manufacturing and the increased share of employment in service sectors, which have always tended to use more contingent labour. It led to a buyers' market for employers in the face of high unemployment. Privatisation and shrinkage of the public sector labour force also helped to break up centres of trade union strength (Visser, 2002). All these factors led to a falling-off of unionisation and bargaining power, making it more difficult to preserve relative wage levels and job security. Flexibilisation – the rise in temporary and part-time work – was an employer's strategy to cut costs, and was helped along by changes in labour law. These were justified by arguments – not entirely founded on good evidence, as we have seen – that it would preserve jobs in the face of adverse market pressures and would help unemployed people, mothers and young people to get work. All too frequently, flexibilisation became flexploitation. It threatens to set up a vicious circle of eroding labour standards, as shown in Figure 7.1.

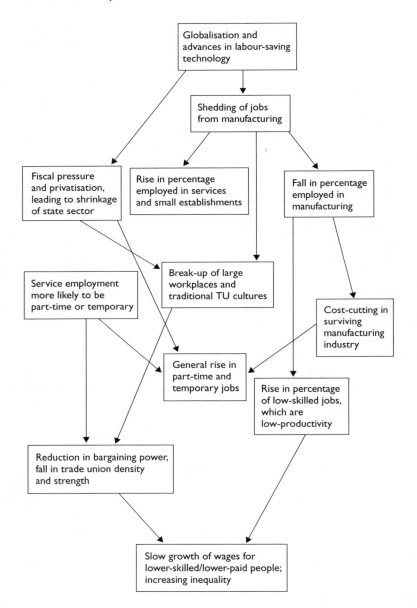

Figure 7.1   Flexibilisation and the degradation of labour standards

REGULATION AND ITS SHORTCOMINGS

Flexibilisation is a market-generated process, and changes in labour law at national level have tended to follow employers' quest for cheaper forms of labour supply. EU governments during the post-Maastricht period have tried to facilitate the development of flexible labour resources while regulating atypical work to make it acceptable. At national level, restrictions on fixed-term contracts and on temporary agency work have been eased, and in some cases also the rules about redundancy or individual dismissal. However, new EU directives have sought to secure equality of conditions for part-timers with full-timers, for fixed-term contract employees with permanent employees, and of agency workers with comparable direct employees, the last being still in draft in 2003.[27] These directives seek to prevent competition between countries and national economies through worsening labour standards. This objective can only work if they are effectively implemented, which depends not only on national states but on trade unions. But one should not, of course, assume that state and union objectives are always the same. The state seeks at best class compromise, at worst (as under Thatcher) a frontal attack on the unions' role. Danish trade unions have recently objected to regulatory proposals by the Liberal-Conservative government on part-time work, as interfering with collective bargaining.[28]

The EU's agenda, which might be described as 'acceptable flexibilisation', requires a change in the role of trade unions. It requires that they should not stand in the way of flexibilisation, but must be partners in the design and implementation of measures to legitimate flexibility. At national level, trade union strength and practices affect both employers' capacity to flexibilise labour and the force of legislation to secure rights at work; this can and does often bring them into acute conflict, as recent struggles over labour law in Spain and France have shown. At EU level, the ETUC participates in the 'social dialogue' where the draft directives emerge – possibly with some loss of independence from the employer side, although unusually, the social partners failed to agree on a text for the proposed directive on agency work, and the Commission had to write its own draft. There is a view among the trade union left[29] that social dialogue at EU level compromises the ETUC and brings it into a consensus relationship with capital and with globalisation.

In prescribing equality of conditions between workers with different kinds of employment contract, the EU directives invoke the notion of a 'comparable worker'. How this is defined depends to some extent on national situations. The first way is to refer to union agreements: a comparable worker may be one whose job would be covered by exactly the same collective agreement were it not for the difference in hours or employment contract status. France, Belgium and Germany, 'corporatist' countries where collective agreements play a large role in labour market regulation, have generally transposed EU equal conditions directives into national law in a way that makes use of this principle. Where sector-wide or company-level collective agreements exist, therefore, the directives in effect extend their coverage to those who were not previously covered just because of being part-time or temporary. This form of comparability is essentially union-driven; it is up to the trade unions to negotiate the scope of collective agreements and the job descriptions to which particular pay and conditions requirements shall apply. If a trade union agrees that certain temporary workers are on pay grade B rather than grade A, then they are different from grade A permanent workers – perhaps because they do different things, or because they are recently hired, or because a concession is being made to the employer to encourage hiring of unemployed people.

A second form of comparability is that used in the implementation of the part-time and fixed-term work directives in the UK. This relies on the notion of an individual 'comparable worker' who works for the same employer and does the same or an effectively equivalent job description. The individual comparability principle is vulnerable to small differences in job descriptions between part-time and full-time, or temporary and permanent workers. It is also vulnerable to employers deliberately making all workers on a certain grade or job description 'part-time' in name, even if they frequently do overtime amounting to a full week.

Whichever definition of comparability is used, the employer can often avoid the force of the directives by using self-employed labour-only subcontractors. They do not work for the same employer – they work for themselves – and they are rarely covered by collective agreements. Agency workers also have a different employer, and in the UK cannot claim comparability with user company employees in relation to the Part Time Work Directive until and unless the Temporary Agency Work Directive is enacted and effectively transposed into national law. Until then, agency work constitutes a loophole in the other directives in all countries except those where national law already provides, for example, for equal pay between agency workers and user company employees, or where (unusually) collective agreements concerning the user undertaking effectively cover agency workers too. Even if the same union agreement could be negotiated to cover both the user undertaking and the agency, it may be difficult to enforce equal conditions across the two employers. The greater the extent of casualisation, the higher the risk that there will be no comparable worker; all the employees doing a particular job description may be fixed-term or agency workers rather than permanents.

Both ways of defining a 'comparable worker' imply certain weaknesses and loopholes in the EU directives. The first definition, referring to collective agreements, depends on effective trade union organisation. Where there is no relevant agreement, equality may be unenforceable. But where there is, equality can be claimed with employees of other companies covered by the same agreement. By contrast, the second notion, the individual comparable worker, permits equality only with other employees of the same undertaking. On the other hand, the principle of individual comparability does enable individuals to bring action against an employer to secure their rights, even where no collective agreement is in force. This might be useful where coverage of collective bargaining is low, or where collective agreements are with individual firms rather than whole sectors. In practice, however, few underprivileged workers are likely to have the financial resources and know-how to bring such actions unless they work in a unionised workplace.

There are thus two styles of implementation of EU labour law: one 'strong', union-driven and union-dependent; the other 'weak', and framed in terms of individual rights. It is easy to see how employers will favour the second. Even the 'strong' elements of EU labour law depend heavily on the effectiveness of collective bargaining (Supiot, 2003), so that the gradual weakening of trade unions both through flexibilisation of labour and through globalisation of economies threatens to undermine the regulatory process. Supiot argues that new pressures may be needed, from social movements, from the 'ethical investment' movement and from consumer boycotts where necessary, to bring to bear enough pressure to enforce labour standards.

Despite the Stockholm Council's concern with job quality, and despite an apparent commitment to regulating for equality for 'flexible' workers, a distinct anti-union project is developing within some EU countries. For years this has been an important aspect of the UK deregulationist thrust in the EU; the Tories not only rejected the Maastricht social protocol but tried to 'weaken the power of the trade unions, deregulate the labour market and dismantle many of the tripartite institutions of corporatism in which trade unions played a major part' (Millward *et al.*, 2000, p. 224). New Labour has continued to be the spearhead of this project, and Blair is on record for his pride in the UK's continued very tough laws to contain trade union action;[30] the key laws on secondary action and on pre-strike ballots remain, despite the introduction of a muted right to trade union recognition in 1999.[31]

As Loic Wacquant (2001) has argued, Blairism represents a 'Trojan horse of Americanisation' and thus a danger for Europe in so far as it seeks to generalise the extreme inequality and insecurity shared by UK and American workers and seeks 'the imposition of desocialised labour as the new norm of employment and as a requirement of full citizenship'. A degree of corporatism is still a key feature of most EU states, and there is a clear assumption that the method of implementing labour policy directives will reflect the institution of 'social dialogue' at the level of the European Union itself. That is, the policy process in most member states and at the EU level is one that brings trade unions and employers' organisations together in a process of consultation, argument and compromise. Such is not the situation in the USA. If the USA represents the 'pure' neo-liberal model, that is one way in which it differs from the mainstream European model: the absence of trade unions from the political process of formation of labour market policy, and the absence of a notion of social 'partnership' enshrined in or brokered by state practice. What is different about Blairism is that it is much closer to this model than to the mainstream European model of labour market governance. There are now indications that this model is spreading to other governments towards the right of the EU spectrum, under Blair's influence. In France, changes to the law on collective bargaining are being proposed by the Chirac government that bring the right to trade union recognition closer to the UK and American models.[32] Spanish workers brought half a million people on to the streets in October 2002 protesting changes in the law on unfair dismissal and cuts in some forms of unemployment benefits.[33] In Italy, protection against unfair dismissal has historically depended on the right to trade union recognition. That right is being taken away by abolition of a key part of labour law.[34]

Blair's growing emphasis on the need for a 'flexible' labour force, even before his election in 1997, revealed a fundamental commitment to neo-liberalism that placed him closer to the former Tory government than to social democratic tradition. Several of the main concerns of the European centre-left parties – and of the trade unions – for job quality and for working time reductions are absent from New Labour thinking on labour markets. New requirements for employment agencies fall well short of those that are common in other EU countries; for example, there is no requirement for equal pay between temps and direct hires nor for the user undertaking to demonstrate the need for agency labour rather than direct recruitment. The Scandinavian and French concern with job quality, highlighted in the discussions of the Stockholm European Council in March 2001 (*European Industrial Relations Review*, May 2001, p. 16) has found little expression in New Labour's approach to the labour market, which has accepted EU directives in principle but watered them down severely in implementation. The British example shows how vulnerable are the concepts of EU-level labour regulation to the emasculation of trade union power and to weak transposition of EU directives into national law.

Although the UK's adoption of the Fixed Term Work Directive means significant gains for employees, it has been introduced in a weak form. There is entitlement to transfer to an open-ended contract only after four years, longer than in most other EU states. The definition of a 'comparable worker' for determining equality of pay and conditions is limited to workers for the same employer. The sudden postponement of the date on which this directive came into force, from July 2002 to October 2002, gave employers a (deliberate?) window of opportunity to arrange new temporary contracts for those who might otherwise have benefited from the right to transfer to a permanent contract because their first four years were almost up. Since the regulations were not retrospective, new contracts made just before the operative date escape the new provisions.

The Working Time Directive, like the Fixed Term Work Directive, has been introduced in a form very undemanding of employers. From January 1999, employees have been allowed to limit their working hours to 48 per week, but there has been extensive use of the provision permitted in the early years of implementation of the directive for voluntary 'opting out' by individual workers. A report for the Department of Trade and Industry (Neathy and Arrowsmith, 2001) found that in one company, out of 20 case studies, employees felt pressurised to sign the 'opt out' from the 48-hour limit; and that workers who later wanted to work less than 48 hours were more likely to be asked to leave. This is echoed in the interviews with unemployed people in Norwich, reported in the last chapter; they felt that many jobs were only available to them if they agreed to work more than 48 hours. Around 4 million UK workers worked over 48 hours per week in 1998, according to the TUC.[35] Thus even three years after the implementation of the Working Time directive, the Directive had had apparently little impact.

The Part Time Work Directive was implemented in the UK with what Stephen Byers, the minister responsible, described as a 'light touch',[36] attracting criticism from the TUC. Regulations permit comparison to be made only with another employee of the same organisation, who must also be of the same contractual status. That is, part-time temporary workers cannot demand equal treatment with full-time permanent workers. Again the 'representational deficit' in UK industrial relations is felt; whereas the EU directive permits reference to collective agreements covering several companies to enable part-time workers to find full-timers' conditions with which they can demand equality, such agreements cover a smaller proportion of the workforce in the UK than in most other EU states. The UK's narrow definition of 'full-time comparator' means that only one part-time worker in six may be able to find a 'full-time comparator', according to government estimates. A further shortcoming is that the UK regulations give workers no right to refuse to change their hours.

The EU Directive on Parental Leave was introduced in the UK in a weak form through the Employment Relations Act 1999, giving parental leave rights for employees with at least one year's service. Initially, the right was restricted to parents of children born after the new legislation came into force, and the rules provided no pay for fathers' leave. After pressure from the TUC and the Maternity Alliance, whose approaches to the European Commission led to an opinion expressed from the Commission to the UK government that the directive was being incorrectly transposed into UK law,[37] the right to parental leave was extended to all parents who already had a child under 5 in December 1999. From April 2003, employers also have to pay fathers of newborn children £100 per week for two weeks' paternity leave.

Both EU directives and national legislation about equality between workers on different kinds of contracts are vulnerable to a number of loopholes. For example, in the French car industry, employers find ways of evading the national 18-month limit on fixed-term contracts and temporary agency assignments,[38] which MEDEF, the French employers' organisation, has been trying to change.[39] Employers alternate 18-month direct hire contracts with agency assignments for the same individual, or alter job descriptions so that temporary workers can remain on a slightly different one after 18 months is up. Any new regulation risks pre-emptive action by employers to avoid its full effects. For example, the Flexibility and Security Act, introduced in the Netherlands in January 1999, gave new rights to agency workers depending on their seniority, including permanent contracts for some long-standing employees. Trade unions alleged that large-scale dismissals of temps took place just before its implementation, an apparently deliberate move by employers so that fewer temps would qualify. Moreover, employers are likely to make fullest possible use of any exemptions in equal rights requirements, in some cases leading to worse conditions for some groups of workers. The imminence of the Fixed Term Work Directive in the UK is said to have led to increased use of agency workers; since they do not have the same employer as the user undertaking's permanent workers, the directive cannot apply to them (Gray, 2002b). New German legislation to secure agency temps a rate of pay equal to that of direct hires from 2004 will not apply to temps in post less than six weeks – an exemption also inserted into the draft EU directive on agency workers. This might lead to typical assignments being shortened to take advantage of the exemption. Since the German legislation also permits a temp to be hired out several times to the same employer, in principle, a sequence of five-week assignments could be used to avoid the equal pay provisions for a year or two. The draft EU Directive on Agency Workers put forward by the Commission in March 2002 contains another most important loophole. Agency workers who have open-ended contracts with the agency and are paid between assignments, will *not* be able to claim equal pay with user company employees. If and when ministers reach political agreement to implement the directive, job security may thus be offered as an alternative to pay parity with comparable non-agency workers.

CONCLUSION

By whatever means, most of the EU appears as an island in which relative social justice has been, at least to some extent, preserved in the face of global trends. The traditions of relatively high unionisation, a strong economic and political role for trade unions, and a considerable degree of labour market regulation, appear to be vindicated – for all the questioning of the 'European model' by neo-liberal theorists.

Thirty years after the oil price shock of the 1970s, which marked the beginning of the troubled era for 'welfare' capitalism, inequality has grown dramatically in the USA and the UK, and also in Eastern Europe. But differentials between highest and lowest labour incomes remain much less in continental Western Europe, where trade unions have retained a significant role in governance and a strong tradition of labour regulation has been preserved. Job security has on the whole been better preserved in the EU than in the USA, and a host of rights to paid leave, limits on working time and gender equality have improved. However, these rights are under threat from trends in employers' practices, from deregulation and from the use of workfarist benefit systems to drive a wedge between secure, unionised workers and unemployed people, turning them into a lever to facilitate casualisation and 'flexploitation'.

There is no very strong evidence that strong labour regulation has damaged employment growth, although it has influenced the form of that growth. Employers naturally seek loopholes and gaps in labour law to minimise their costs. From the spread of temporary contracts in Spain to the proliferation in the UK of short-hours jobs which deprive women of pension rights, there are numerous examples of this. Regulation, to be effective, must avoid exemptions unless there is a clear case that employees or the unwaged will benefit.

Temporary and part-time work, once established, contribute to a decline in union strength and thus to further erosion of labour standards. Agency work poses an especially acute threat both to unions and to the gains they have achieved. Thus a potential vicious circle emerges of casualisation, declining union power, and more casualisation. State intervention is clearly needed to avoid this downward spiral, both to protect contractual rights and to uphold rights to trade union activity and recognition; but regulation also depends on unions to be effective. A coalition of the right is emerging among the leaders of EU member states, led by New Labour and backed by employer lobbies, to weaken the previous force of the EU 'social dialogue' and press for more deregulation of labour markets. To oppose this, and to press for effective implementation of EU labour directives at national and international level, is a challenge for trade unions across Europe for which they may call upon social movements and consumers to support their demands.

The future of labour market regulation in Europe, and its effective implementation, depends crucially on trade union bargaining power, especially on the extent of agreements covering more than one employer. Thus a major issue in the regulatory set-up will be the future interpretation of the right of collective bargaining and action under Article 28 of the Charter of Fundamental Rights of the European Union, which will be incorporated into the EU Constitution. An important qualification to this right in the charter is that collective action, including strike action, is to be defined and regulated by national laws and practices. This will become an even more acute issue as the EU enlarges to the east, taking in several countries where free collective bargaining has been slow to develop after the end of the 'socialist' era.

8
The Drift Towards Workfare in Europe

ACTIVATION: RE-COMMODIFICATION OR SOLIDARITY?

Alongside the greater conditionality of benefits that has swept Europe in recent years has been an increase in 'active labour market programmes' (ALMPs). These are intended to accelerate re-entry into jobs through training, or experience in 'work of community benefit', or intensified job search under close supervision (as in the New Deal Gateway). Such schemes are presented as an 'opportunity' by their architects and defenders, but some are regarded as a threat or a time-waster by many claimants. Critics such as Peck and Jones (2001), Jones (1996) and Peck and Theodore (2000b) regard Anglo-American ALMPs largely as a device for keeping wages low, whilst recognising that something more than just benefits and good macro-economic management are needed to help the unemployed. President Clinton described the expansion of American workfare measures in 1996 as 'tough love' – a rhetoric shown to be hollow by many accounts of harsh and punitive treatment on US workfare schemes.

In 1998 the European Employment Guidelines set a target that 20 per cent of the unemployed should participate in ALMPs. Member states are asked to provide some kind of action plan or other intervention for every young person who remains unemployed longer than six months, and every jobseeker over 25 after twelve months. The guidelines say nothing, however, about whether participation in such measures should or should not be compulsory, nor about the issue of fair remuneration. The Euromarch movement immediately became suspicious of the ALMP target; the possibility that it heralded a move towards workfare was much discussed at the 'counter-summit' meetings of unemployed people's movements in Cologne in May 1999.

WORKFARE AND THE RE-COMMODIFICATION OF LABOUR

Reflecting the historic concern of the unemployed about compulsion, and of trade unions about the unemployed being used as 'cheap labour', Costello (1993, p. 2) defined workfare as compulsory work or training on the job for less than the market wage. This is the definition we shall adopt here. But workfare is an ambiguous and much contested term. American terminology uses 'workfare' to describe not just mandatory work for benefit but a wide range of counselling, supervised job search, and training, and even subsidised jobs at full wages (Burghes, 1987; Mead, 1997). Lødemel and Trickey (2001) define workfare as 'compulsory ... and primarily about work' (p. xiv) but include as workfare some programmes that offer normal wages – such as the 'employer option' of the UK's New Deal and parts of the German HZA programme. Without ignoring the criticisms made of the 'work for benefit' principle, they adopt this wider definition to explore the objectives and outcomes of different kinds of mandatory work programmes.

However, theories of the workfare state as well as unemployed people's movements in Europe, associate workfare with the neo-liberal agenda of making labour cheaper (Peck and Jones, 2001; Jones and Peck, 1995). Programmes intended to reduce wage pressure can be distinguished from job creation schemes that maintain the demand for labour and prevent high unemployment from dragging wages down. The difference is between 'supply side' programmes concerned with work discipline and employability, and those that are broadly Keynesian or 'demand side'. ALMPs can be analysed within the same perspective as benefits systems, along the spectrum of de-commodification/re-commodification. Table 8.1 sets out a rough classification of the poles of this spectrum as 'ideal types'. Many actual ALMPs are not 'pure'; they have some elements in both columns. As we shall see later, the UK's New Deal is a hybrid package, with some Keynesian sub-programmes alongside some workfare ones. The key effect of reducing wage pressure is achieved by increasing the supply of labour for low-paid and temporary work, making it easier for employers to recruit. Some workfare programmes in the USA and Germany recruit directly for private employers; others drive people towards unattractive jobs by making compulsory work on 'schemes' even less attractive – in other words, using workfare as a deterrent. By contrast programmes that directly increase the demand for labour, for example by employing people at normal wages in community work, take jobseekers out of the labour reserve and reduce competition for other vacancies among those who are left. This holds up wage levels rather than depressing them.

American experience shows that mixed programmes that include training and job search can have a wage-reducing intention and

Table 8.1   Some key distinctions among active labour market programmes

	Re-commodifying; workfarist	De-commodifying; Keynesian
Effect on wage levels in the wider economy	Keeps wages low or reduces them	None or helps to raise wages
Effect on overall balance of supply and demand in the labour market	Redistributes existing jobs; 'created' posts replace others or would have been created anyway. Private employers hire more labour only if and when the wage-reducing effect makes it profitable for them to do so	Increases overall labour demand; net creation of new jobs
Wages in programme itself	Lower hourly rate than in comparable 'normal' jobs; often a benefit-based allowance rather than a wage	Normal pay for the job
Treatment of participants	Punitive, humiliating or stigmatising	More like a normal job
Voluntary participation?	No – compulsory, on pain of reduced/withdrawn benefits	Yes – can refuse without benefit penalty
Type of training	Deliberate limitation of training opportunities to a very basic level; severe restrictions on spending time in study rather than job search. 'Training' on how to search for jobs often applied to discipline people, keep them 'busy' and reduce their wage expectations	Longer, more advanced courses offered; less restrictions on courses claimants find for themselves
Effect on participants' skill level and future prospects	Minimal improvement in skill level	Participant improves skills and long-term choices
Examples (see text for details)	American 'work for benefit' programmes; New Deal 'ETF' option; parts of German 'HZA'; work for benefit within Danish and Swedish ' activation' systems for social assistance claimants	Most French job-creation programmes, e.g. CES, CRE, TRACE; the former Community Programme in the UK; Danish and Swedish 'job offer' schemes

effect through the 'deterrent' effect. The Euromarches' argument that European 'active labour market programmes' were workfare in disguise had some justification, particularly in view of the growing workfare elements in Scandinavian and German packages, as discussed later. But workfare requirements are not the only way of driving people towards low-paid jobs. Benefit sanctions for refusing to accept or apply for certain jobs in the 'open' market can be as effective. Peck and Theodore (2000b) see workfare itself as just the ultimate 'stick' in the workfarist approach to the unemployed. Their notion of 'workfarist' benefit systems is perhaps more central to any analysis of how benefits and ALMPs affect the low-paid labour supply than the precise definition of workfare itself.

The notion of 're-commodification' invites the question; relative to what? Workfare 're-commodifies' the jobseeker relative to cash benefits. But the offer even of workfare may improve income and choices for people who previously had no benefit rights, while arguably inferior to cash benefit while seeking a 'real' job. While French and Spanish employment and training programmes are generally voluntary, both countries have created schemes for people with no income maintenance rights, which must be considered as 'opportunities' for some although under 'take it or leave it' conditions. The TRACE programme, introduced in 1998, provides jobs with training for those youth who have no right to the RMI (that is, childless under-25s). In effect it extended existing employment programmes to people previously without benefits, training or jobs (Enjolras *et al.*, 2001). This is of some value, although TRACE has been criticised by French unemployed groups for offering too few places and inadequate wages. In Spain, regional minimum income schemes that have been developing in the 1990s are more strongly conditioned on work or work-like activity than the RMI. Access is at the discretion of a social worker who may impose an obligation to seek work, attend training or in some cases (especially in Andalucia) arrange employment for the participant in municipal road repairs or similar tasks – heavy and unpleasant work at the minimum wage.[1] Unemployed and without income maintenance, many French and Spanish youth turn to the lowest tiers of the casual labour market, often working in the 'informal economy' without social insurance or contracts. The TRACE programme, offering formal jobs with training to some of them, clearly has some de-commodification effect. The effect of the Spanish 'renda minima de insercion', available generally only to the over-25s, is however more ambiguous. In Catalunya, it has been said that the minimum income is insufficient, but that the course attendance conditions for receiving it may prevent the recipient from taking work in the informal economy (Ronneling and Gabás i Gasa, 2003, p. 120).

THE AMERICAN MODEL

Workfare is generally regarded as an American invention, although it has independent roots in Europe and Australia, as discussed later. It was promoted by President Nixon from 1969 (Peck and Jones, 2001, p. 90) and after small-scale experiments in the 1970s workfare increasingly took the place of cash social assistance through successive milestones of American legislation,[2] culminating in Clinton's Personal Responsibility and Work Opportunities Reconciliation Act of 1996. This took the drastic step of limiting welfare payments to two years at a time or five years in a lifetime, and gave state authorities targets for getting recipients into work or work-like activities. Failure to meet them means loss of federal funds. States have cut back on training, since the federal targets are defined largely in terms of work. Many states now use a 'work first' approach; training is offered only as a last resort to those who fail to get hired after a period of intensive job search, and then usually under various restrictions about the amount of training time relative to work time. Without training, workfare participants have no option but the worst jobs in the 'formal' sector.

A critique of the American programmes began to develop in the USA and in the UK in the 1980s. Louise Burghes (1987) pointed to American claimants 'working off' their grants at the inadequate federal minimum wage, raising the spectre of workfare being used to undermine established wages and displace normal jobs. As American workfare programmes expanded, so did the evidence of these effects, well documented by Piven and Cloward (2002):

- acute poverty often occurs in workfare jobs, even when working full-time;
- large-scale substitution of workfare labour for other workers has taken place; for example, in municipal street cleaning and parks jobs in New York, most of the labour force has been replaced by workfare participants paid far below the regular wage. Some large food processing companies have found workfare programmes an ideal source for recruiting very cheap

casual workers. This creates a particularly slave-like form of the benefits trap: they dare not leave or risk sacking, because they would lose Medicaid health insurance;

- workfare arrangements speed entry or re-entry into 'dead-end' jobs, often temporary, with poor wages and little prospect of advancement;
- the cheapest programmes, becoming more widespread, are based on the 'work first' principle. This means that workfare fails to give people the skills they need to hold a steady and reasonably paid job with any chance of upward mobility. They may get a job quickly, but they often remain partly dependent on welfare payments or food stamps. Throughout the USA, many participants return to the welfare rolls several times, perhaps not surprisingly in view of the extreme casualisation of low-skilled American jobs (Handler, 2003);
- job search sessions become workhouse-like, with discipline the main rationale for strict attendance rules, rigorous dress codes and unreasonably high targets for the number of employer contacts;
- compulsion has negative effects on personal and family life: women claimants are required to prioritise paid work over their responsibilities as mothers, spending too little time with their children. They are given no time off to care for children who are sick, and insufficient childcare funding to arrange quality care (White, 1999; Wittman, 1998). Some child injuries and even deaths have occurred in Wisconsin because mothers cannot afford adequate childcare, or are afraid to stay away from their workfare placements when childcare arrangements break down;[3]
- compulsory work is especially harsh for those with health problems. For example, in 1997 a 50-year-old New York woman with a history of heart disease died during a workfare assignment at the Coney Island Parks Department. She had been reassessed as 'fit' for work after three years on disability benefits, and given manual work as a condition of receiving welfare.[4]

The American experience shows how workfare serves capital by making it easier to recruit contingent labour, both directly and by inducing even non-participants to settle for lower wages as they seek to avoid workfare (Peck and Theodore, 2000a). One American study predicted that the 1996 programmes would generate a dramatic drop of 11.9 per cent in the wages of the unskilled.[5] In practice, their wages began to rise again in the late 1990s for the first time in many years – but this was probably due to boom conditions and despite workfare programmes. Even if wages do drop, will this reduce unemployment? Solow (1998) argues that workfare can only raise employment by causing a substantial drop in wages, enough to make it profitable for employers to expand their payrolls; otherwise it must cause displacement of existing workers into unemployment. In practice, given constant budget pressures, extra hiring within the public sector seems less likely than displacement; for example, the New York Parks Department is said to have replaced most regular staff with workfare participants. Within the private sector, even if wages fall it may still be cheaper to outsource to China or India. Moreover, creating additional jobs by reducing wages does not address the poverty trap problem, allegedly the reason why some remain unemployed in the first place. These additional jobs will probably be taken by students or second earners in the family; but parents and others on benefits may not be able to survive unassisted on wages that are lower than ever. Lastly, there are many people who are manifestly not being hired in the open market at any wage, because employers reject them, or they lack transport or childcare.

Early results from the 1980s workfare programmes, especially GAIN in California, produced a flurry of reports arguing that workfare was effective in redistributing jobs to the most disadvantaged.[6] However, other commentaries highlight the more negative points from the well-known evaluations of GAIN by the Manpower Demonstration Research Corporation (MDRC).[7] Tracked over three years, programme participants did earn a little more on average than 'controls' who did not go on workfare. But they also got less welfare money, so many were actually worse off in terms of their total income. Since the 1996 reforms California (and other states) have cut back on the training element of the GAIN package, reducing any value it had for helping people into long-term self-reliance in better-paid jobs. Overall, the 'successes' of workfare in the USA have been over-written; falling benefit dependency during the late 1990s is thought to have occurred as much because of economic revival and the introduction of tax credits as because of workfare programmes (Handler, 2003).

As workfare has expanded so has the use of sanctions, attaining a scale in the USA unheard of in Europe. In seven states over 20 per cent of welfare claimants are denied benefit for breaches of the rules (Handler, 2003). In New York in 1999, more people were being considered for sanctions than were actually engaged in workfare work (Wiseman, 2001). If fewer people claim assistance, the state's budget keeps any saving provided Federal workfare enrolment targets are met. So there is a double incentive to cut off aid from refuseniks and non-attenders – to save money and to meet enrolment targets more easily. Handler (2003) has questioned the effectiveness of sanctions in relation to the most disadvantaged groups in the US population, who often face racial discrimination, or have criminal records or drug addiction problems. The use of sanctions makes the questionable assumption that jobseekers would get a job if they tried harder. If their difficulty lies with employers or intractable personal problems, sanctions may simply push them from jobseeking into vagrancy or crime.

TOWARDS WORKFARE IN THE UK?

Before the New Deal, Tory 'work for benefit' schemes drew sharp opposition from some quarters. The 'Charter Against Workfare', promoted during 1987 by unions and Labour-controlled London boroughs, attacked government plans to introduce on-the-job training for benefit.[8] The New Job Training Scheme (NJTS), introduced in 1987–88, placed unemployed trainees in work experience for benefit plus a small allowance, often with private employers. While not compulsory, it was introduced in the context of a benefit regime that emphasised strict 'availability for work' requirements, so that officials could challenge someone to accept a training place on penalty of benefit sanctions. The 'charter' set out four criteria for an employment scheme to be acceptable: any future UK scheme should pay 'the rate for the job', be voluntary, offer participants full employment rights (to holiday and sick pay, against discrimination, etc.) and should be subject to trade union approval. NJTS was rapidly replaced by 'Employment Training', the design of which paid lip service to trade union demands and finally gained the TUC's acceptance. But several major unions continued their opposition, so that some companies and local authorities refused to provide places.

'Employment Training' stood in contrast to the Keynesian approach of the Community Programme in the 1980s. Employing at its height over 250,000 people, the Community Programme was voluntary and provided usually three days' work per week, which participants could supplement with other part-time work if they wished. Although there were some criticisms of the programme's organisation and quality, in many areas it provided work of real social value, in particular supporting the growth of 'community businesses', mostly in Scotland, and providing much-needed labour and funding for many community organisations, including unemployed workers' centres. Its rules were designed to these minimise displacement of existing jobs; the programme should involve 'work which would not otherwise have been done' and pay the rate for the job (Gray, 1999b). Sometimes these rules were broken, and in London the 'rate for the job' arrangements were less credible, given that funding limits meant only the lowest local wage rates could be supported. This led to criticism that it was used as 'cheap labour' to displace normal local authority workers. In response, left-wing authorities such as Hackney and Waltham Forest boycotted the programme. However, econometric evidence of displacement was small, and some critics accused the programme of actually increasing wage pressure by removing a share of the 'reserve army' into community sector jobs.[9] In some areas many participants were unionised and were able to organise for better conditions. Whatever the intentions of its Tory founders, the Community Programme in effect created a refuge from market pressures, offering an alternative to the worst private sector jobs.

Notwithstanding unions' aversion to the American model, its British advocates such as MPs Sir Ralph Howell and Frank Field captured the ears of the Commons Select Committee on Employment, and by 1997 there was an all-party consensus that something like workfare was needed in the UK. This led towards the introduction of the New Deal by the New Labour government in 1998. Its immediate predecessor was Project Work, piloted in certain areas by the Tory government in 1996, with a period of counselling and placement followed by work for benefit for those who had not found a job after 13 weeks.[10] In Brighton, unemployed people mobilised demonstrations against organisations using the labour of workfare participants. Project Work was resented by unemployed people interviewed by Finn and Blackmore (1998, pp. 107–8) because the work was paid on a 'benefit-plus' basis rather than a wage, and particularly in those cases where participants were offered no choice of placements. Although a 'Workstart' hiring subsidy – very similar to the hiring subsidy later offered under the New Deal's 'Employer Option' – was available to employers in some Project Work areas, few participants benefited and those who did mainly displaced other workers (Fletcher, 1997).

The New Deal family of programmes involve mandatory participation for the long-term unemployed (under-25s after six months, older JSA claimants after 18 months) as well as voluntary training for lone parents, disabled people and the over-50s. For JSA claimants, the New Deals are hybrids of Keynesian and supply side elements. On the one hand, they are the UK's version of 'work first', a forced intensification of job search to induce people into open-market vacancies, with workfare to follow for some of those who do not succeed. On the other hand, unlike Project Work they remove a number of people from the labour force for off-the-job training. The Employer Option – offering employers a hiring subsidy – has the capacity to create new vacancies in the non-profit sector, and does achieve this in a small way. However, most employers involved merely take advantage of the New Deal's 'captive' labour supply to recruit for vacancies they already had, probably at lower wages than would have been paid to other candidates (Hales *et al.*, 2000). The New Deal is credited with having raised employment and GDP largely because it helped to reduce wage pressure, rather than because the wage subsidy created jobs (Riley and Young, 2001). New Labour's programme has not attracted much opposition from the trade union movement, although the TUC has criticised the principle of compulsion and the heavy sanctions regime.[11]

The New Deal is designed to move as many people as possible into regular jobs before they get as far as an expensive programme. The initial counselling phase (the 'Gateway') involves an intensification of the normal job search process required of JSA claimants (Hales and Collins, 1999). The 'Gateway' is a period of particularly strict application of the normal JSA sanctions regime, with around 9 per cent of participants having benefits suspended for not seeking or accepting work. Surveys show that participants often experience the Gateway as a period of pressure to reduce their reservation wages.[12] For the majority of New Deal participants, the Gateway is their whole experience of the programme, since up to two-thirds leave from the youth programme and 85 per cent from the over-25s programme before the end of the counselling stage. Only 15 per cent of young people on the New Deal, and rather less of the over-25s, actually work for a 'benefit-plus' allowance.[13] More common is skills training, mainly off the job (around 17 per cent of youth and 13 per cent of over-25s). A few enter subsidised jobs at normal wages (around 6 per cent of both age groups). These jobs are usually popular, albeit often at the national minimum wage level or not much more,[14] but they are scarce. Young people at a training centre in Bradford, in the course of the Minima Sociaux research, complained they had not even been offered an interview for a subsidised job. During the Gateway they had been told that if they found no job by its end, they would be sent to the centre in preparation for a 'benefit-plus' placement.

Even though the number of workfare places in the UK is very small,[15] the risk of being sent to work for 'benefit-plus' adds to the overall pressure to accept a low-paid job. 'Benefit-plus' placements are generally unpopular, according to a national survey of New Deal participants (Bryson *et al.*, 2000). Many participants are sanctioned for refusing a place, for non-attendance or misconduct.[16] More than five days' unjustified absence, or ten days' sick can result in being 'sacked' from an option, and suspension of benefits. A young man in Chesterfield, set to rebuilding stone walls on hill farms, showed how people fear sanctions if they complain or insist on their rights:

> We were supposed to get a 15-minute break morning and afternoon, with one hour for dinner, but no break was given apart from 20 minutes for dinner. One day I wasn't well, I wanted to stop for five minutes, eat a sandwich, have a fag, and the supervisor threatened that he'd go to my New Deal adviser and get me sanctioned.

According to the National Participant Survey, 'those who subsequently suffered hardship (i.e., after sanctions) were least likely to be in jobs by the time of the survey interview' (Bryson *et al.*, 2000). While not all 'benefit-plus' experiences are negative, some participants find them meaningless in terms of work experience (see Box 8.1). The Environmental Task Force, predominantly involving outdoor manual labour, is the least popular of the four 'options' on the New Deal for Young People (Hasluck, 2000a). People with a criminal record are often directed to this 'option' after other providers reject them, adding a cruel turn of the screw to the discrimination already faced by ex-offenders in the labour market.[17]

WORKFARE: THE EUROPEAN AND AUSTRALIAN TRADITIONS

The inspiration for the New Deal came not only from the USA. Both Tory and New Labour politicians made some study of Australian measures (Finn, 1997). From Australia came the term 'Jobseekers' Allowance', adopted there during the early 1990s for a highly conditional benefits system backed by a tough sanctions regime. The

---

Box 8.1 Workfare placements on the New Deal in Chesterfield

- I was told to identify trees by bark, berry and leaf – it was rubbish – I can't find words to describe my feelings. The supervisor was patronising and I disliked this immensely. No, it was not useful work experience. I spoke to my New Deal Adviser, who told me to stick it out. [a man who eventually walked out and had his benefit stopped]

- It was a laugh because some of the work was interesting – but I don't like digging trenches. It was not as useful as proper work experience. There was not enough equipment so you had to take turns.

- I was doing clerical work. Yes, it was useful experience. But it was a s*** deal, cheap workforce. We were treated like naughty children. The quality of training was poor, there were double standards in the work practice. There was little or no help with job search.

- First I was sent to a charity shop at ... I learnt how to work the till, it was useful to be dealing with cash. She was quite good at training me for the tasks in the shop. Then I was ill, I had time off. The shop ... said they wanted someone more reliable (which I thought was fair enough because I had had a lot of time off). Then I was placed with another charity shop in ... I walked out after three days – I wasn't allowed to do anything other than hang clothes. I couldn't stick it. Then ... I was sent on the ETF. Some of the time we did some work but the placement officer didn't want to be there either. So you had barbecues and slept in the minibus half the time. We knew when we were going to be spot-checked so we knew when to work. I walked out with seven weeks left after an argument with the manager. I went on the sick and was treated for depression.

Job Compact of 1994–95 coupled this with a 'job guarantee' for the long-term unemployed (Burgess *et al.*, 1998). Refusal meant loss of benefit, for which the overt rationale was the 'reciprocal obligation' of state and jobseeker. Like the Swedish job guarantee, the Job Compact involved work at trade union rates; but employers failed to come forward with sufficient subsidised jobs. Difficulty in fulfilling the guarantee led to charges of programme failure and paved the way for a later right-wing government to replace the job guarantee by workfare obligations (Finn, 1997). The Australian experience shows that once a strong sanctions regime is in place, a job guarantee can easily be replaced by workfare given adverse macro-economic conditions or budgetary pressures. Thus one must ask, could the training and employer options of the New Deal wither away in recession, leaving only 'work first' and benefit-plus schemes?

A third influence on the development of UK labour market programmes from the early 1990s onwards came from Sweden. The 1980s Swedish system guaranteed job offers to those unemployed over six months; but during that six months they had to accept intensive help with finding work, and to be willing to retrain or move house. Layard and Philpott's (1991) interpretation of the Swedish 'job guarantee' was used to argue the case for more intensive job search discipline in the UK and for a definable exchange of obligations against rights, which has become the hallmark of New Labour's welfare to work policies. Layard, later a New Labour economic adviser, perhaps neglected the strong trade union orientation of the Swedish system of social protection. Unemployment insurance in Sweden is voluntary, and is trade union-run. The sanctions powers that exist in theory are rarely used in practice, as mentioned in Chapter 5.

Workfare in continental Europe is rooted in the traditions of poor relief, from which have developed social assistance benefits for the uninsured – mainly youth, long-term unemployed, lone parents, migrants and refugees. Outside the realm of social rights negotiated as part of the wage, social assistance follows a logic both of deterrence and control of idleness, of which workfare is a historic element. The Weimar Republic provided for a workfare obligation in the 1924 law concerning social assistance given by local authorities. Under this law was developed the Nazi practice of forced labour, described by Sergio Bologna (1994) – an unfortunate precedent, which has not been forgotten by today's unemployed when they criticise the harsh social assistance rule of 'take any job or no benefits'.[18] The Federal Social Assistance Act of 1961, introducing national rates and conditions for benefits for the uninsured, again empowered German municipalities to require claimants to work in exchange for social assistance (Voges *et al.*, 2001). For many years this power was hardly used, since most claimants were not in a position to work. But as unemployment rose in the 1980s, some local authorities were attracted to the apparent cost saving if social assistance claimants did municipal service tasks. This work also helped them re-enter the unemployment insurance system, when they were no longer the municipality's financial responsibility.

In Scandinavia, social assistance for the uninsured unemployed contrasts with the strongly de-commodifying approach of the insurance schemes and is associated with 'extensive social control' (Kildal, 2000). These municipally-run residual benefit schemes have provided a vehicle for the development of workfare in the 1990s, away from the sphere of influence of trade union-managed social insurance. Sweden still had workhouses until the 1930s, but unemployed people were excluded from them in case they might escape low-paid jobs (Lindqvist and Marklund, 1995); work was provided, rather than cash assistance. During the post-war period of full employment, the form of social assistance for the unemployed was barely an issue. But in the high unemployment of the early 1990s, many needed to claim assistance from municipalities, and poor law traditions were revived in the form of local workfare schemes (Cousins and Michel, 2000).

Danish local authorities were empowered to provide subsidised work or training for social assistance claimants in 1978, although some did so earlier. The notion of 'activation' of unemployed people and reduced duration of 'passive' insurance rights was taken up by Danish authorities under the influence of OECD recommendations in the late 1980s. Social assistance claims rose as an increasing share of unemployed in the 1990s were uninsured. Municipalities were then given wider powers to impose compulsory 'activation', providing work and/or training with a variety of different organisations, some private, some non-profit, to lead people towards regular jobs. After the Danish labour market reforms of 1994, this became a model also for Sweden. The Scandinavian programmes emphasise skills development more than elsewhere, and there is some debate about whether they constitute workfare in the same sense as American work-for-benefit programmes.

FROM JOB GUARANTEE TO WORKFARE:
THE DECLINE OF SCANDINAVIAN SOCIAL RIGHTS

Kildal (2000) argues that both Swedish and Danish systems have undergone degradation towards workfare in the 1990s. In both countries, the high benefits regimes of the 1980s and earlier provided a right for insured unemployed to receive a guaranteed job offer at normal wage rates when they reached the end of their insurance entitlement. This helped people to remain within the unemployment insurance system for life, alternating if necessary between benefits and labour market programmes, because 'programme' jobs or courses requalified them for insurance benefits. The right to 'requalification' was ended in Denmark in 1994, and in Sweden in 2001. Together with Lofhager (1998) and Goul-Andersen (2000), Kildal identifies the 1980s regimes with the notion of 'citizen's income' and the later 'activation' regimes with an obligation to work for sub-normal remuneration to obtain social assistance.

Prior to the crisis of the early 1990s, the Swedish state had a historic commitment to maintaining both high wages *and* full employment, which were presented as compatible rather than conflicting objectives. These were the twin pillars of the Rehn-Meidner model of macroeconomic management, which was the cornerstone of Swedish labour market policy from the 1940s to the late 1980s (Swedish Ministry of Labour, 1988). They implied a range of services to support the right to work, of which the 'job guarantee' for people at the end of their unemployment insurance rights was only one part. Another was and remains skills retraining, not just to maintain or establish basic employability, but to enable the worker to maintain his or her former occupational status when new skills are required to do so. In the 1980s, Sweden retrained redundant workers on a large scale, and participants in government retraining programmes were usually paid at their previous wage; but as unemployment rose in the early 1990s, this became unsustainable and benefit-based allowances were paid.

Both job guarantee and the commitment to full employment fell away as Swedish unemployment soared in the early 1990s. The authorities just could not provide enough placements to meet the job guarantee, and offered training instead. As more jobseekers exhausted their insurance rights and turned to local authorities for social assistance, the financial burden led some municipalities to impose work requirements (Kildal, 2000; Cousins and Michel, 1995). In some cases these were designed to have a deterrent effect, while in others the objective was skills development. In 1998 municipalities were given new, wider powers to impose both training and work on social assistance claimants, and to reduce or stop the benefits of any who refused. This policy was modelled on Danish legislation of 1993–94, which made similar provisions in order to deter a dependency culture. For youths aged 20–24, Swedish municipalities were given a responsibility to provide work or training for benefits after 90 days of unemployment, under contracts with central government; however, about one-fifth of local authorities declined to enter into contracts. Work of this kind, usually in local work experience projects, is outside normal labour contract arrangements and does not build the individual's rights to social insurance, including childcare services, parental leave and pension rights. Exit is often into temporary jobs, which are growing rapidly in Sweden (Cousins and Michel, 1995). Trade unions have been critical of the harsher approaches to unemployed people involved in recent policy developments.

The 'activity guarantee' introduced in 2000 requires all persons who have been unemployed or on labour market programmes for over two years to take part in 'competence development and training'.[19] They must take part in training for at least six months; further six-month periods can be imposed if they still do not find a job outside a programme. A deterrent effect seems to be intended; the OECD (2001a) regards this measure as 'a shift of emphasis in ALMPs, giving more weight to stronger incentives to search for unsubsidised jobs'. While the bulk of Swedish ALMPs for insured unemployed are still concerned with skills training rather than work, there has been a degradation of the Swedish model from the essentially Keynesian 'job guarantee' at normal wages to 'activation' on benefits. 'Workfare', as used by some right-wing British writers in the 1980s (e.g. Burton, 1987), was an inaccurate description of the earlier job guarantee system, but fits what was happening to some Swedish youth by the end of the century. However, the maximum value of social assistance benefits for adults remains high – although means-tested, it is at least as much as unemployment benefit for many families with children.[20] This makes work for benefit in Sweden more palatable than in Denmark, where social assistance rates are now considerably less than unemployment benefit rates.

The Danish 'job offer' scheme in the 1970s and 1980s was similar to the Swedish job guarantee; its aim was to help those reaching the end of their insurance rights to start afresh and obtain a new entitlement. Lasting seven to nine months, these jobs were provided in either public or private sector through wage subsidy arrangements (Jensen, 1999) and were paid at trade union rates. Although anyone refusing one would have been denied even social assistance, the job offers were a right, rather than an obligation, valued partly for the fact that (until 1994) they provided a re-entry route to very high unemployment insurance benefits.[21] In 1990, things began to change. Workfare, entitled 'activation', was introduced for all Danish social assistance claimants aged under 20, requiring them to take part in work or training for a wage deliberately set below normal collectively agreed rates. This requirement was extended to all under-25s in 1992 (Rosdahl and Weise, 2001). For older social assistance claimants, 'activation' was not widespread until after the labour market reforms of 1994, which extended 'activation' requirements to all those over 25 who had been at least a year on social assistance. The reforms also required activation of insurance claimants after four years (Madsen, 2003). From 1998 young people under 30 had to be 'activated' after only three months. Although some 'activation' places are trainee posts paid at normal wages, around two-thirds of those in 'activation' are engaged in 'individual job training', receiving a 'benefit-plus' allowance. This is usually on-the-job training in municipal employment projects. Some local authorities make use of the 'deterrent' effect of unattractive job training projects to persuade people to leave social assistance quickly (Rosdahl and Weise, 2001, p. 176), although other projects may provide more interesting and satisfying work than routine jobs in the open labour market (p. 174). Both Torfing (1999) and Madsen (2003) argue that the 'activation' strategy has played a major role in reducing Danish unemployment during the 1990s, especially youth unemployment; and in doing so without raising inflation significantly. Torfing is agnostic about the source of this achievement: the value of skills development, or the 'deterrent' effect of unattractive projects and lower benefits during activation or just economic growth. Madsen, however, attributes some importance to the 'deterrent' or 'motivation' effect. However, he points out an unpleasant paradox for policy-makers: to increase the deterrent effect by making activation less attractive would be to reduce its skills development value.

In some interpretations, even if Danish labour market policies are moving towards workfare, it is distinctively different from American workfare. Thus Torfing (1999) argues that Danish workfare 'is disarticulated from the neo-liberal context within which it is located in the UK and the US and re-articulated with the social-democratic and universalistic welfare model'. The difference, he argues, lies partly in the attempts to 'empower' the claimant rather than to control or punish, and in the emphasis on reskilling through training and education within Danish programmes, which differentiate them from 'work first' welfare to work systems. In support of the first point, Jensen (1999) points out that claimants tend to regard the activation plan positively and that it is drawn up by consensus between claimant and adviser. There is also a legal requirement for choice of 'activation' offers (Torfing, 1999, p. 18). However, Christensen (2000) agrees with Kildal (2000) that the changes of the 1990s reduce the 'decommodification' capacity of Danish support systems for unemployed people. For Christensen, the most distinctive feature of the change is the replacement of a citizen's right to income maintenance by a contractual discourse of benefits in exchange for activity. Against Torfing, he argues that 'Danish workfare ... builds on ... control and punishment'; since it is *compulsory* work in return for benefits, it can hardly 'empower'.

One can agree with Kildal about the degradation of both Swedish and Danish social rights of unemployed people, while recognising that this is a mild or 'soft' version of workfare compared to Germany, the UK or the USA. This degradation can be traced to the increased role of local authority social assistance administrations in income maintenance, so that their logic gained ground over that of the trade union-run insurance funds. In Sweden, this began with the economic crisis of the early 1990s and the sudden rise in the numbers of unemployed beyond the capacity of the 'job offer' scheme. However, in Denmark, it was more owing to deliberate reduction of unemployment insurance rights, casting more people into the social assistance net; and to the extension of 'activation' requirements to long-term insurance claimants. The 1994 reforms did this without the former guarantee that any last-resort job offer would be at normal wages. A further issue in Denmark was the composition of unemployment. Inexperienced youth and recent migrants were a high share of the total in the early 1990s, falling inevitably on to social assistance because they lacked an insurance record, and also hard to place. As the Danish unemployment rate fell to one of the lowest in the EU by the century's end, caseloads were dominated by the hardest to help, difficult to place in normal jobs even with hiring subsidies (Torfing, 1999, p. 21; Rosedahl and Weise, 2001, p. 174). Often they needed the sheltered work experience opportunities, which are offered by some of the 'individual job training' projects. But while this may explain the apparent need for special placements, it hardly explains or justifies a 'benefit-plus' arrangement – recalling Handler's argument that the 'deterrent' effect does not work for those who are constantly rejected by employers.

'CUMUL': THE TOLERABLE FACE OF WORKFARE?

Belgium is a curiosity in the spectrum of workfare policies. Claimants can escape the risk of benefit sanctions by signing up for casual work provided by the Agences Locales d'Emploi (ALEs). These are short-term assignments as domestic helps, childcare workers or gardeners in private households; or in some local authority or non-profit jobs. ALE work is regarded as an extreme form of 'cheap labour', especially since it is exempt from employers' social contributions, normally high in Belgium; the hourly wage is well below collectively agreed minimum rates. But a part-time ALE job avoids the possibility of having benefits terminated for being unemployed too long, and it also means the claimant need not be 'available' for other work, which they might be sent to apply for under a 'contrat d'insertion'. ALE workfare provides a paltry wage, which can be *added* to benefits, rather than being instead of benefits. Curiously, 'cumul' for social assistance claimants is permitted to a much greater extent if they take ALE jobs than if they take other jobs. Thus a combination of part-time work with the 'minimex' offered a higher income in the late 1990s than many full-time jobs accessible to 'minimex' claimants (Ballal and Bouquin, 2000). This trapped them into a severely underpaid form of work and created a captive labour supply for the local authorities, NGOs and households who use it. Far from shunning such work, many unemployed in 1999–2000 wanted it and, much as they complained about its low pay and bureaucratic pay claim systems, felt it was better than nothing. A Belgian government report in 1998[22] questioned the value of ALE work as a bridge to normal jobs, because people tended to stick in it for very long periods. But increased workfare requirements for social assistance claimants under 25, introduced in October 2002, may now be changing this situation (Nicaise and Groenez, 2003). Workfare placements may now become full-time, and possibly in the private sector, a prospect received with alarm by Belgian unemployed activists (Pozzo de Borgo, 2003). Social assistance offices in Belgium are increasingly turning to partnership arrangements with private employment agencies to find claimants temporary jobs (European Foundation, 2002).

GERMANY: THE USE OF WORKFARE TO PROMOTE A LOW-WAGE SECTOR

In the late 1990s, wage subsidies to private employers began to be used to create a specific 'low-wage sector' in Germany, into which unemployed people are increasingly required to move on pain of losing benefits. Of all the countries considered here, the German approach is most explicitly based on the rationale that only a fall in 'entry-level' wages can resolve the intractable unemployment crisis following reunification. Certain types of hiring subsidies are conditional on the wage being 20 per cent lower than normal in relevant collective agreements, a rule that outraged the German claimants interviewed for the Minima Sociaux project (Lévy et al., 2000b). The threat of sanctions is used to drive social assistance claimants into low-wage sector jobs, or into unpopular forms of casual work, or into jobs for which minimum wage controls – dependent in Germany on sector-level trade union agreements – have fallen away. Large-scale provision of workfare placements has become expensive, and policy developments associated with the Hartz Commission in 2002 have greatly increased the role of placement into private sector temporary jobs.

The German programme, Hilfe zur Arbeit (HZA), in which 3–5 per cent of unemployed participated in most regions at the end of the century (Voges *et al.*, 2001) includes work for benefits, or wages at not more than 80 per cent of normal rates. This may be in municipal services like refuse disposal or in non-profit organisations. It also includes 'normal' private sector jobs for which the employer receives a subsidy, often subject to the '80 per cent of normal wage' rule. In the late 1990s unemployed people could be required to participate in three-month subsidised work placements, including very low-paid work such as crop picking. They involved about one unemployed person in six at some time during their unemployment spell (Gueck, 2000). Temporary jobs of this kind may form an increasing share of placements under the Hartz Commission regime. All of these workfare variants were most unpopular with interviewees. German claimants felt humiliated by the menial nature of compulsory work placements. Imparting no useful skills, such assignments were seen both as a punishment for being unemployed and as a way of driving jobseekers into the worst jobs (see Box 8.2).

The Hartz Commission proposals, now being implemented under the Job-Aqtiv Act 2002, may be a very significant development for the future of workfare in Europe. The official employment service

---

Box 8.2 German unemployed people's comments on workfare assignment:

- I rather felt like an innocent victim of criminal justice. I was trained for office work, and now I find myself condemned to heavy labour. These measures undoubtedly are meant to crush our refusal of lousy job offers.
- They want to wear us down by these humiliating practices ... they are quite aware of the deterrent effect of their unreasonable demands ... I actually feel treated like an outlaw.
- They do not combat unemployment but the unemployed.
- I was detailed for a road-sweeper job – allegedly to show my willingness to work ... I am trying my best to find a decent job, but they load such a senseless test on me ... Just guess where I was supposed to sweep up ... in the midst of downtown, right in our pedestrian zone! This is a really humiliating punishment.
- ... the guy at the social assistance office wanted to find out whether I could get up early and show up at work on time. I was told to present myself at the municipal waste disposal site at a quarter to six in the morning for the next two weeks. Each morning I had to register at the time-clock and after that I had to supervise the mechanical cleaning of the dustbins for four hours a day, and that was it. I suppose that because I was always on time the social assistance office never picked this up again ...

Source: Interviews by Martin Gueck, presented in Lévy *et al.*, 2000b

will set up 'personnel service agencies' to place unemployed people as soon as possible into temporary jobs, and they must accept a lower wage than before or lose benefits.[23] Appointed by competitive tender, some of these agencies may be non-profit, but much of the work is expected to go to commercial temporary work agencies, alone or in partnership with the public sector. At the same time, steps are being taken to privatise parts of the employment service itself.[24]

The new laws of 2002 inspired by the Hartz Commission also involve a new regulatory regime for temporary work agencies. Agency temps are now entitled to the same wage rate as comparable employees in the host company.[25] They previously earned on average 30 per cent less than host company workers, so on the face of it this provision means a considerable improvement. However, there is an exception for agency workers who were formerly unemployed; during their first six weeks, their agency wage may be as low as their former unemployment benefit. Subtly, therefore, the new rules provide for agency-based workfare. At this stage the long-term effects of the policy cannot be known. But there is a risk that companies will come forward with a large number of six-week assignments, possibly expanding agency hiring of unemployed people where they might formerly have created longer-term and better paid jobs. At the same time, restrictions on the repeated use of agency temps in the same post, and on agency placements exceeding 24 months, have been lifted. Through the expansion of agency labour the German government hopes to create at least 50,000 jobs. If so, situations may become more common in which the collective agreements relevant to agency temps are those made with the temp agencies themselves rather than the host companies. Such agreements are unlikely to be influenced by groups of workers in any strong bargaining position. Moreover, as the use of agency labour increases, so also will the proportion of jobs for which there is no 'comparable permanent worker' with whom agency employees can have pay equality under the new regulations.

Workfare is dissolving into an extreme form of workfarist benefit system, with employment agencies as placement agents. The emerging German model of workfare is the European form that perhaps comes closest to the US model, with a significant volume of placements with private employers. The new German system, now also being considered in Belgium, performs exactly the role attributed to workfare by Peck and Theodore (2000b): that of making more labour available for agency and temporary jobs, thus facilitating their substitution for permanent jobs. Whereas more traditional forms of workfare increase the contingent labour supply through the 'deterrence' effect and through disciplining or controlling unemployed people in their job search process, the Job-Aqtiv Act does it much more directly. Agency-led workfare could become a major force for casualisation of the German labour market and for de-unionisation. Trade union opposition to the Hartz Commission proposals has on the whole been muted. But in some areas – such as IG Metall in Rhine-Westphalia – unions have joined with unemployed organisations in coalitions to fight the new policies.

Agency-led workfarism may be the ultimate in supply side policies – any residual Keynesianism in the creation of jobs, either as work experience schemes in the third sector, or through wage subsidies offered to the private sector, is likely to be stripped away. 'Make-work' schemes have a high cost, even where private employers or the voluntary sector contribute part of the wage required. Even provision of work for 'benefit-plus' has high administration and programme overhead expenses. Increasingly, therefore, workfarist benefit regimes are recognised as cheaper to run than workfare itself. The Hartz Commission proposals in Germany may become an inspiration for other governments to resolve the problem of workfare costs. What better than to place employment agencies, with a constant supply of new assignments, at the heart of the system of 'availability for work' testing – and to induce flexibilisation of the labour market at the same time?

Would agency-led workfarism be acceptable if conditions of agency workers were sufficiently regulated? There must be some doubt about whether this can be sustained in the face of difficulties of union organisation among agency workers, and inherent weaknesses in 'comparable worker' regulation. Moreover unemployed people need secure jobs. As in the USA, the experience of the Working Nation policy in Australia, where a stricter benefit regime was imposed on an already rapidly casualising labour market, was that although people found jobs, a considerable proportion returned quickly to unemployment (Finn, 1997).

WORKFARE, ACTIVATION AND SKILLS DEVELOPMENT

As the American experience shows, training is crucial to 'de-commodification'; many unemployed people need additional qualifications to access a wider range of jobs. Training reduces competition at the bottom of the jobs ladder and consequently reduces the pressure of the labour reserve on wages in the least skilled jobs. In both the UK and Germany, claimants thirst for good-quality learning opportunities but are often disappointed in the range, quality and level of programmes available to them. Sweden and Denmark, on the other hand, have retained longer courses, with an emphasis on empowering jobseekers to progress to different sectors or to a high level of the occupational ladder.

Neither workfare nor tight benefit conditions provide a helpful environment for improving jobseekers' skills. Where training is used as an activation device, it is often too basic or poorly chosen. Moreover, training that is compulsory leaves the trainee powerless to complain about quality. At the same time, training that jobseekers choose for themselves is often restricted by availability for work conditions. Complaints about the quality and choice of courses were widespread in all four of the countries studied by the Minima Sociaux research. But if claimants choose their own courses, they are often accused of not being 'available for work'. In the UK this is a long-standing issue, with the JSA rule that study must usually be limited to 16 hours per week[26] and must not interfere with job search or availability to take a job. The weekly limit on study time hinders jobseekers' own efforts to improve their employability. Claimants may give up training in order to take short-term or low-skilled jobs, because they have to be continuously available for work at short notice. Stricter benefit conditions have now made this an issue in France and Belgium also. The French PARE programme, rather like the UK's JSA, and the 'contrat d'insertion' for Belgian youth make it more difficult to study on benefits without offending the new rules. In Belgium, referral to compulsory basic training sometimes forms part of the 'contrat d'insertion'. Yet some claimants who have chosen their own course of study are told that they must desist or their availability for work will be challenged.

In Germany's two-tier welfare system, many training schemes are reserved for the insured unemployed. In the late 1990s many local workfare schemes (HZA) offered a training element or phase, but not to have access to the national schemes is, in claimants' eyes, to be a 'second-class unemployed' with fewer choices. Even those who were claiming insurance benefit complained that 'assignment to the [training] measures can be arbitrary and random and thus often does not correspond to the stated interests and preferences of the claimants' (Gueck, 2000). Training was often used as an 'activation' device, which individuals could not refuse, and which did not take them forward much in terms of skills or work experience. Those who already had high skills seemed to be offered most choice to obtain more. But older or lower-skilled jobseekers felt that officials limited their access to training, just as employers discriminated against them in the job market itself. The new policy of placing claimants in temporary work appears to prioritise mobilisation of unemployed people for temporary work over reskilling.

The vast majority of UK informants – over four out of five – thought that more training opportunities would help them. Most of these wanted to go on a more advanced or longer course than the ones offered to unemployed people. There was considerable frustration at the low level of qualifications offered in government training schemes they had experienced. 'Training for Work', the main programme of the late 1990s, was progressively cut back in length from six months to three or four, and oriented more and more to basic employability, to getting people into the lowest level of jobs. It rarely offered access to a qualification level above NVQ2. Initially, this was the intention on the New Deal, but in practice a considerable number of exceptions seem to be made; up to 20 per cent of participants on the Training Option are permitted to follow NVQ3 courses or vocational qualifications that fall outside the NVQ structure (Bryson et al., 2000). Training on the New Deal is longer than in any other programme seen since in the UK since the late 1980s, and represents a substantial increase in government training investment.

In the 'Minima Sociaux' research, informants who had attended labour market training programmes prior to the New Deal often found them of poor quality . There was a view that the private training companies who often run such programmes made a lot of money at public expense, being driven by targets rather than providing a service, and using poorly qualified instructors who taught them little. Claimants preferred to attend further education colleges, which offer a wider range of courses not limited to unemployed students. Sometimes, however, Job Centres said they should not attend these courses full time; they were often suspected of breaking the rule that they should not study at the expense of looking for work. The New Deal attracted less complaints about training quality than the older UK programmes, but did not necessarily secure continuity of previous training. On joining the New Deal, some people were required to give up courses they had found for themselves. Others had to take courses equivalent to ones they had done before, rather than progressing to a higher level. A compulsory programme clearly constrains trainees' capacity to complain about their advisers' choice of course or level, or about the quality of what is provided. The high drop-out rate from the New Deal Training Option may reflect these factors. But it is also an issue of inadequate financial support for the trainees themselves; a year is a long time to remain on benefits with no extra allowances to pay for bus fares and lunches. Whereas most full-time students do part-time jobs to make ends meet, New Deal trainees cannot do so without losing their benefits.

French and Belgian caseworkers often used an offer of on-the-job training places to test claimants' willingness to work. The various financial inducements to employers to hire unemployed people appear to have encouraged an excess supply of poorly paid on-the-job training offers, with a corresponding shortage of long-term vacancies. Unemployed people reported that often ANPE could only offer them a succession of 'stages', which they associated with inferior pay. Yet off-the-job training of the kinds they wanted was often too expensive, and they could not always obtain support from the employment service to fund it.

Scandinavian labour market programmes are often noted for their 'human capital' approach. Compulsory activation in Sweden emphasises skills improvement rather than work, with the bulk of programmes concerned with education and training; the main place of work experience is within the municipal programmes for youth. The OECD would prefer a shift towards 'work first' policies and complains that Swedish training programmes hold people off the labour market until they have finished their course, so that they increase wage pressure rather than reducing it. The Danish 'job offer' scheme, introduced in 1978, was augmented by an offer of two years' education in 1985 (Torfing, 1999). There was an increased emphasis on training from 1994; some subsidised apprenticeship places were provided for uninsured youth, and unemployed people could apply for educational 'leave' from jobseeking to undertake courses they themselves chose (Madsen, 2003). Until 1999, two years' educational leave was permitted for the insured unemployed (Etherington, 1998); but since then only one year. In 1999 13 per cent of 'activated' persons were on educational leave and a further 39 per cent on vocational training courses organised within ALMPs. From 1994 to 2001 educational leave was also permitted for up to a year to employed persons, who could claim 70 per cent of unemployment benefits while studying, and gave rise to valuable vacancies for training and experience on the job for unemployed persons. Sadly, this scheme was closed in 2001. If it were not for leave schemes and early retirement measures, Danish unemployment would have been around four times as large as it was by 1999 (Madsen, 2002).

The Danish system of 'job rotation' whereby an unemployed person stands in for a worker on educational or parental leave has been highly successful (Compston and Madsen, 2001; Etherington, 1998), and is regarded as a model for other parts of Europe. But under a new Liberal-Conservative government from 2001, it diminished in scale. Torfing (1999) noted that 'mobility-enhancing benefits and job-searching courses play a limited role in the Danish workfare strategy, as priority is given to education and high-quality private or public job training'. However, this priority may now be diminishing somewhat in favour of 'work first'.

Intermediate labour markets

Some people do not get hired by the capitalist sector at any reasonable wage. Falling unemployment generates a focus on the 'hard core' of very long-term unemployed, for whom workfare is regarded by its defenders as a solution to the 'culture of dependency' (Mead, 1997) and by its critics as a wholly inappropriate solution (Handler, 2003). Training is a way forward for some of these people, but not for all, especially for the over-50s who are a high share of the long-term unemployed in some areas. Nor can wage supplements or subsidies help the most disadvantaged; there are some people who are unlikely to be hired even if their services are very cheap. Some fraction of unemployed people will always need a considerable period of help to resolve social problems, including released prisoners, those with broken work records through mental illness or substance abuse, and the homeless; a few have more than one such problem.

To provide a path back to normal employment for the most disadvantaged, several 'intermediate labour markets' or ILMs have been set up in the UK Deal (Simmonds and Emmerich, 1996; McGregor, Ferguson *et al.*, 1997). These non-profit organisations offer a sequence of counselling, training and work experience on real wages (rather than 'benefit-plus'), all under one roof. The idea is to provide a bridge between unemployment and the open labour market in a holistic framework. Some similar ventures (empresas de insercion) are found in Spain (ERGO, 1992; Gray 1999b). What these enterprises share with ILMs in the UK is the concept of preparing people for the open labour market, but they often also offer a longer-term refuge for the most disadvantaged. For example, some Spanish cooperatives have been founded by ex-prisoners. The international Emmaus organisation has created several 'enterprises d'insertion' in France, which offer jobs to homeless people, often in recycling activities such as turning crates into furniture, or preparing donated sacks of old clothes for resale in second-hand shops. Employees can stay as long as they need to; in effect these organisations provide a form of sheltered employment. This type of reinsertion enterprise is preferable to subsidised temporary work, which risks undermining established labour standards in the normal labour market, as already discussed in Chapters 6 and 8.

Fighting discrimination

However, those with difficulty in gaining acceptance by private employers should not be ghettoised into special employment programmes. A significant share of unemployed people face discrimination by employers, on grounds of disability, age, race or language. Ex-offenders also suffer serious discrimination by employers. What employers are afraid of is in many cases a definable risk that if they hire an ex-offender, s/he will steal or become violent at work. These are insurable risks and it would, in principle, be possible for the public employment service to offer insurance against these risks.

Racial discrimination in the USA affects around one-third of welfare claimants who are black and another third who are Hispanic. It is a growing issue in Scandinavia, where migrants have swelled historically 'white' dole queues in recent years. As long as people of colour, or those who speak other languages, can only access the lowest layers of the job market they will be especially vulnerable to disincentives to work and to frequent redundancies. Discrimination – against minorities and against other vulnerable groups – is a broad cultural and legal issue, which cannot be left to individual projects and training providers. Sadly, the tendency for 'welfare to work' systems to reward service providers on their results may lead to 'creaming' by them rather than district-wide attempts to change employers' hiring practices, such as the equal opportunities campaigns run in the late 1990s by some Training and Enterprise Councils in London. It is important that such campaigns take an inclusive view of the many forms of disadvantage; focusing on one alone may simply shift the problem to another.

CONCLUSION

This chapter has challenged the notion of workfare as 'tough love' – and indeed its appropriateness for anything but reducing wage pressure and browbeating the jobless to accept flexploitation. There are three possible reasons why people don't get jobs: they won't, they can't, or there are none – at least at any wage that will keep the household afloat. Workfare deals with the first group, which is probably tiny – but only by punishing the innocent with the 'guilty'. Except perhaps in the Danish or Swedish versions, it does little to help the second group, who need training and measures to combat employer discrimination. A workfare framework in fact makes training measures less effective, in so far as instructors have to spend time dealing with the disruption and demoralisation caused by reluctant trainees. It also impedes jobseekers from finding their own appropriate training outside labour market programmes. As for the third problem, it may actually make things worse – any jobs created because labour becomes cheaper are likely to be worse paid than the ones that gave jobseekers a disincentive to work in the first place. Those unemployed people who take them still need public money to survive, through tax credits or in-work benefits of some kind.

The trajectory of degeneration of the Keynesian model intersects, in Scandinavia and Germany, with the growth of workfarist benefits. Indeed, the prior existence of the Keynesian job-creation model provides a reference point and a legitimation for the notion of 'creating work' for unemployed people. Had it not been for this history, workfarist benefits might have been used alone, moving people into low-grade private sector jobs rather than make-work schemes. A considerable Keynesian element, taking people out of jobseeking for a period of training, survives in the hybrid ALMP packages of the UK and Denmark, and is still the major programme component in Sweden. However, current labour market trends provide new opportunities for 'work first' policies that may undermine not only surviving programmes for subsidised quality jobs but also the Scandinavian skills development approach. The huge mushrooming of private employment agencies in the 1990s provides a new vehicle for placement of unemployed people at minimal cost; partnerships between these agencies and the public employment service are now being developed in Germany, used in a small way in Belgium and being considered in Denmark. There are huge potential implications for the deterioration of labour standards, despite the reregulation of the agency labour market through the new EU directive and German national law.

9

Conclusion: Alternatives to Workfare and Flexploitation

This book has highlighted the growing tendency in European benefit systems to adopt what Peck and Theodore (2000b) describe as a 'workfarist' approach, obliging people to take any job however low paid, and often using compulsory 'activation' measures to drive them to do so. This approach places the main burden of adjustment in the labour market on unemployed people themselves. Workfare and workfarist benefit systems serve to increase the supply of labour to low-paid jobs; at best they help to increase the number of jobs by making labour cheaper. At worst, they simply make it easier for employers to substitute bad jobs for good. Many would say that workfarist approaches attack labour standards and are essentially unfair; do they nonetheless 'work' in terms of reducing unemployment? Handler (2003) argues that for many participants it has not in fact achieved lasting employment or independence from benefits. Both he and Peck and Jones (2001) have pointed out that what success can be attributed to workfare in the USA was achieved during a period of economic upturn.

At the heart of the workfarist approach is a contradiction. On the one hand, neo-liberal orthodoxy holds that wage pressure must be reduced to create more jobs. Conversely, it is frequently said – by commentators ranging from the poverty lobby to the OECD – that some people remain unemployed because of a 'benefits trap' or inadequate incentives to work. As one jobseeker in Brighton put it, 'there are a lot of unemployed people because wages are so low'. The apparent solution of making pressure from the employment service to accept low wages more palatable through the offer of tax credits or other 'in-work benefits' is potentially very expensive. It runs the risk that employers – including highly profitable firms with no need for subsidy to sustain payroll numbers – will take advantage of state wage supplements to freeze or even reduce wages in the long run, throwing more of their labour costs on to the taxpayer. If the bill for in-work benefits becomes too great, the history of the nineteenth-century Speenhamland system might repeat itself.

When in-work benefits become too costly and the lowest wage rates have meanwhile fallen lower than ever, the state's response might be to curtail wage supplements and revert to even fiercer workfare pressures on unemployed people, perhaps cutting out-of-work benefits as well.

Essentially, the incentive problem suggests that there is an element of unemployment that is due to a lack of distributive justice – to the incompatible expectations of employers and jobseekers about what wages are reasonable. If employers' requirements are assumed to be unchangeable, then it is jobseekers' expectations that must change; then wages must fall to clear the labour market. Jobseekers' reservation wages are theorised by neo-liberalism as behaviours, as demands, rather than as needs. However, if the employers' expectations are treated as a behaviour, rather than an objective necessity, one could equally argue that profits must fall in order for higher wages to be 'affordable' at a level of output and labour demand that would provide jobs for all. While the workfarist solution involves bullying jobseekers to accept lower wages, a redistributive solution, on the other hand, would require a reduction in profit per worker to permit a higher labour share of national income. This can be used to reduce working hours and permit more people to have a wage at a given level of productivity, through work-sharing. Or it can be used to increase output of non-market services, creating both use-values and jobs.

Normally if individual companies expect a reduction in profit per worker, they will hire fewer people; but what is proposed here is that if the 'norm' of expected profit per worker could be reduced across the board, higher wages would be possible at a given level of output or higher output for a given level of wages. To suggest that this 'norm' is negotiable rather than 'given' is not such a heresy as might at first appear, for four reasons. Firstly, the distribution between profits and wages is constantly being renegotiated; that is what trade unionism is all about. Secondly, the capital market is not perfect; rates of return vary considerably with the scale and monopoly power of individual companies. Thirdly – as noted by Will Hutton (2002) – considerable variation exists in the time horizon for maximising shareholder value, and short-termism is a peculiarly Anglo-American phenomenon. Paring labour costs to the minimum, in terms of both number and quality of jobs, is associated as much with pursuit of short-term shareholder value as with response to competition in the product market. Fourthly, the redistributive solution, while it has never been realised in a complete or stable way, does have some precedents in recent European history. It has both a public service variant and a work-sharing variant – exemplified in Sweden and France respectively – to which we return later.

The problem in Europe today is essentially that employment growth with good wages and conditions depends on raising the labour share of national income. The context of this problematic is that globalisation reveals itself as a distinct phase of capitalism, much more antithetical to the labour movement and the welfare state than the capitalism of the 1970s and earlier. Flexploitation, exemplified by the sad experiences of precarious work which have been documented in Chapter 6, is an expanding lowest layer of labour conditions under globalisation, in which those with a broken work record risk consignment to a virtual workhouse of low pay, stress, fatigue and frequent sackings. Flexploitation is twinned with workfarism for unemployed people through a vicious circle: the worst jobs become less attractive, so unemployed people reject them unless bullied, and these jobs are intrinsically insecure, casting more people on to the dole queue more often. The solution to higher unemployment, in the canon of neo-liberal policy prescriptions, is then perceived to be a relaxation of labour standards (deregulation and flexibilisation of labour markets) and a fall in wage pressure, achieved by mobilising the unwaged labour reserve to accept low-paid jobs. If we ask: is it globalisation that leads to flexploitation or government policies, the answer is in one sense that they are complementary; increased corporate power, under more intense international competition, begins a vicious circle that is compounded by reduced labour market regulation and workfarist pressures on unemployed people to take unsatisfactory jobs. In another sense, the answer is neither globalisation nor government, but employers; the case for corporate 'social responsibility' asserts that they have a choice.

As discussed in Chapter 3, workfarism is associated with the decline of the Keynesian Welfare National State (KWNS). Old-fashioned Keynesianism assumed that wages were 'sticky' and would rarely fall, basically because of working-class power. It then fell to the state to induce an outward shift in the demand for labour at the 'given' wage rate – either by more public spending or by inducing a fall in the cost of borrowing. Expansionary state spending, even if tax-financed, has been impeded in the European Union for over a decade by the Maastricht straitjacket, as discussed in Chapter 4. Instead the new benefits policies and the drive for deregulation of labour markets try to induce adjustment of labour supply to employers' demand – they attempt to increase employment by facilitating flexploitation.

The KWNS, where it survives, must be defended as an alternative to neo-liberalism; any revival of the KWNS, where feasible, would be a welcome springboard to move beyond neo-liberalism and its dangers. But to regard such a revival as a necessary 'first stage' or as a project in itself risks becoming a diversion into a minefield of dilemmas and contradictions that that project confronted in the 1980s. These include the tendency of the welfare state to crisis, as described in Chapter 3, and the potential slide from welfare to workfare in recession, of which something has been seen in Sweden. Moreover, the KWNS is now inevitably tainted with an admixture of privatisation and subcontracting and an assumption that this cannot be questioned or reversed. This assumption is likely to be reinforced by the General Agreement on Trade in Services (GATS), now being negotiated through the WTO, which creates a presumption in favour of privatisation and impedes its reversal.

The average rate of profit per employee in the economy as a whole is clearly affected by the relative size of the private and non-profit sectors. Privatisation and subcontracting are enemies of quality job creation. They transfer public money to shareholders, who spend more than low-paid people on second-hand assets (real estate, antiques, more shares) – forms of spending that do not create many jobs. Then the privatised or outsourced 'public' sector becomes less effective at creating jobs than before, on the familiar Keynesian maxim that the savings ratio is higher for the rich. Even if privatised services produce the same service level for less taxes – and there is little evidence that they do – this may well be because of lower wage bills. So privatisation may be bad for employment volume as well as quality. The deterioration of wages and job security often associated with privatisation creates a 'drag' effect on wages and conditions in the rest of the economy. This may exacerbate the apparent 'need' for workfare pressures to fill the lower-paid jobs. Privatisation thus represents a threat to any project to revive the role of the public sector as an employer of last resort, or as an engine for employment growth along the lines of the Swedish experience of the 1980s.

Private capital increasingly looks to ex-public services as a profit centre or source of capital accumulation. Big construction companies and major employment agencies now see a large share of their business from the public sector. Subcontracting and privatised provision involves a new breed of multi-function companies like SERCO, whose activities range from security through private prisons to schools management, and Capita, known as educational consultants and administrators of housing benefit and criminal record checks. This new breed of large private providers, often multinationals, is consolidating its hold on the ex-public sector across Europe. Capital now sees incursions into the public sector as a major new source of investment opportunities. In this environment the role of the state as a Keynesian provider of jobs will be available, if at all, only on the private contractors' terms. Their business is making profits, not providing employment; and like any other private companies, they will be concerned to minimise labour costs. Privatisation also means public services can be 'globalised' – profits can be expatriated, elements of services subcontracted to providers in other countries. As with globalisation in other sectors, this means that capital no longer has such an incentive to look after, train and maintain the 'social reproduction' of a particular national workforce. Nor can we envisage that this process of social reproduction can simply be transferred to the European level, because globalisation reaches beyond Europe.

The Keynesian project, if revived, needs to focus on growth of collective services that will be truly collective and non-capitalist. GATS makes this difficult, because it outlaws any privileging of the non-profit sector over the private sector. Given the many obstacles to the resuscitation and democratisation of the KWNS – as noted in Chapter 3 – the way forward lies in creating forms of non-profit production outside the state sector, whilst taking advantage of channels of support from the state where these are available. Such channels might even include subsidies to hire unemployed people; the Community Programme of the 1980s supported many voluntary organisations and social enterprises, as noted in the last chapter. However, a radical attempt to grow a non-profit sector needs to mobilise resources from many channels, certainly not depending on state programmes or charity. There may be some scope for reviving the tradition of mutual aid as a source of finance for housing construction, eldercare or childcare programmes. Non-profit production need not be confined to services that are provided free, or with tax funding; one can envisage a non-profit sector producing food, electricity and public transport as well as childcare, health services or refuse collection.

However, the question must be posed, why create more *work*? As one lone mother in Brighton put it, 'is there any point in creating any more jobs, because there's enough work to be done already?'

Seen from the viewpoint of mobilising people to make profits, which shouts out from the EU's Employment Guidelines, her comment is heresy. Seen from the perspective of how to allocate and reward socially necessary work, making more of it indeed seems a strange goal. The problem is partly that some work is unpaid, because it takes place within the family and community; to spend enough time in parenting, eldercare and community organisation alongside full-time employment is a continual struggle for many people. The problem is partly the maldistribution of work, for example, between the four million Britons who work over 48 hours per week and the one and a half million who want a wage but have none. The problem is also one of private affluence and public squalor; the resistance of people with six- and seven-figure salaries to higher taxation, and increasingly the resistance of middle-income people too as they lose confidence in a bureaucratised and increasingly privatised system of collective services. Rather than job creation for work's sake, the point is to ensure that all socially important work in these collective services gets done. That requires a fresh approach to taxation and to distribution of income. If gross profit margins were lower, wage-earners could make a satisfactory income in fewer hours, and people would have more time for family and community.

If profits remained constant, but were taxed more heavily, more investment in non-market services could be funded alongside a given level of net wages and a given level of production for the market. Between 1991 and 2001, the net rate of return on capital in the EU rose by rather more than a quarter; already by 1991 it was over 14 per cent more than the average during the 1980s.[1] Despite the setbacks since '9/11', there is scope for skimming the cream here. New forms of tax on profits and assets are needed to secure collective services, and there is no reason why this could not be part of a project of harmonisation of fiscal policy at EU level. The Tobin tax is only one – possibly not the best – alternative that has been suggested.

THE LAYERS OF THE ONION

A growing array of social movements, left and green parties and radical trade union currents, showing their strength in the two European Social Forums in Florence and Paris, has gathered behind the declaration that 'another Europe is possible'. A Europe, that is, committed to workers' rights and to using its wealth for good collective services. What would need to be done to make that vision possible, and what are the constraints? What can be achieved within capitalism, and what depends on a root-and-branch change in that system? In order to avoid a crude dialogue of the deaf between 'reformist' and 'revolutionary' perspectives, it may be helpful to think of the constraints rather like the layers of an onion. Just as the new plant needs to break through several layers of the old onion bulb before the shoot can grow, a revitalised, solidaristic and collectivist welfare state is a project that can only be realised by breaking through several layers of constraints. Some of these stem from particular forms of capitalism and capitalist governance; other derive from capitalism of any form. But here the analogy with the vegetable world ceases. The layers of the old onion are essentially dead; but in the human world all the actors – including employers, governments and international institutions – are alive and fighting back against opposition to their plans. Constraints on the breakthrough of a new social project can be strengthened when under threat, broken and then reimposed, or can change their form. To inform political action, we must understand their dynamism as well as their 'layered-ness'.

The different visions of 'another Europe' are not necessarily contradictory. The Keynesian vision still has many advocates, and to pursue it does not necessarily impede more radical perspectives. The future cannot be constructed as a neat series of alternative policy options, nor as a discrete series of stages along a one-way street. Rather, the future emerges from struggles in which the battle lines move to and fro, and in which new political configurations are constantly emerging.

As a first step towards a redistributive solution, one could argue for changes that have some recent precedent and form part of mainstream policy discourse, changes on which a consensus between 'social partners' can probably be reached. A framework for 'welfare to work' programmes that provides some long-term 'sheltered' work for the most desperate, and good-quality skills training with real choices, would be a good beginning. Training should not be a mere parking device to occupy idle hands in the waiting room with humiliating tasks. Nor should it be 'customised' to particular employers to the point of becoming a conveyor belt to low pay at the cash desk or call centre; training needs to impart transferable skills that will give the trainee more choices. Training for unemployed people has become, like every area of the welfare state in its present phase of fragmentation and privatisation, a profit centre for private contractors. Better to reduce restrictions on benefit-supported study, allowing the unwaged to choose their own courses and mingle with employed and young students, which is a widely supported demand from benefit claimants themselves. Better still would be the large-scale development of Danish-style job rotation programmes, which facilitate practical work experience for unemployed people on real wages by allowing them to take the place for a few months of workers going on educational or parental leave. Educational leave permits existing workers to improve their skills and promotion prospects, creating the possibility that they can move into better jobs, leaving behind more spaces for the unwaged. This 'musical chairs' pattern of moving up through skills development reduces the overcrowding at the bottom of the pay ladder that contributes to the 'flexploitation' problem.

The message is at last being widely heard in government circles across the EU that childcare for employed mothers, and especially for lone parents, needs to improve. Less clear is how to make employment and childcare compatible in an era of 24/7 working hours. Many jobs – particularly those the unwaged tend to get, as shown in Chapter 6 – require unpredictable shifts, evening and weekend work. But those providing childcare services outside the extended family rarely want to work 'atypical' hours. Shorter working hours, and greater control over them by individual employees, would make it much easier for parents to obtain and hold jobs. This is especially true for lone parents, around 10 per cent of whom in the UK are actually lone fathers with particularly severe childcare problems.

Childcare, together with quality education and training for adults, are forms of 'social investment', expenditure which receives every endorsement from current EU policy goals, as set out at the Lisbon Economic Council and subsequent European summits. They form part of the 'baseline' of essential social expenditures, which capital, even globalised capital, may support as the female labour supply gains importance and constant reskilling is essential for competitiveness. However, there is still a battle to be won about who pays: the employer, the state or the individual. There is a tendency for the cost of 'lifelong learning' to be thrust on to individual workers, penalising those with low pay or long hours.

To go beyond the arena of mainstream policy debate requires a challenge to the prevailing neo-liberal consensus. It requires a greater scale and scope of state intervention in the economy, but no more than the KWNS commonly assumed. It requires a return to the traditions of social protection rights built up in northern Europe from the 1950s through the 1980s. In terms of EU-level social policy, this means revisiting the 1980s vision of 'Social Europe' and giving centre stage to 'social dialogue', but without the concessions to neo-liberalism that characterised the EU policy documents of that period. What unemployed people themselves want is above all for lack of employment to be seen as a problem of the economy, not as their own responsibility. Moreover, there is a sense of being cheated of insurance protection, which has diminished during the many years for which some older workers have been making social security contributions. In terms of the regulation of jobs, better control of conditions for agency and other temporary workers would be a priority for many unwaged people, who rank casual work in the chicken factory or the warehouse alongside workfare in street sweeping or farm labour in their chamber of horrors. Improving pay levels is not enough; job security and time sovereignty are also important. So is a sense of dignity, of having a chance to use acquired skills and experience and to be respected for them.

To break the vicious circle of casualisation and declining union strength is an urgent precondition of sustaining labour standards in the enlarged Europe, in which competition from the low-wage new member states will threaten established wages and conditions in the west. Trade union recognition rights need to be preserved and extended, and there is a need to reassert and extend the political role of unions in economic and social policy, in particular in the governance of social security and labour market programmes. As Supiot (2003) suggests, to redress the power deficit of trade unions under globalisation requires a solid alliance of social movements and consumer groups to support their struggle against corporate giants. But this is a slow and difficult task; where a power deficit already exists, as in the UK, regulation must begin with the state, and the numerous loopholes and exemptions in the EU labour directives need to be tightened. Strongly implemented, the directives resulting from the social dialogue process over the last 20 years can provide a springboard for further advance. However, the lack of effective EU-wide regulation of temporary work agencies, through delays in the adoption of the proposed directive on agency work, leaves a major gap in the legal framework, which employers seeking to evade the force of the other directives will be ready to exploit.

This second layer of change would also involve an extension or revival of historic practice in the most worker-friendly member states of the EU. The constraint here is the uneven incidence of neo-liberal values and of the countervailing power of trade unions and social movements. Various countries contribute to a list of desiderata. From Denmark we can take extensive job rotation linked to expansion of parental leave and study leave, as well as sabbatical leave, which was available in the early years of the job rotation scheme. From Denmark also the model of high minimum wage rates set through collective agreements, which where union strength is adequate are on the whole preferable to state minimum wage regulations, permitting negotiated flexibility around exceptions and working time aspects. From France and Belgium in the 1990s, we draw the right to extensive 'cumul' of benefits with occasional or part-time employment, which needs to be coordinated with regulation of casual work. From Spain, we can highlight an extensive cooperative sector and considerable encouragement of unemployed people to become self-employed.

Sweden exemplifies the public service variant of a redistributive solution, with social expenditure over one-third of GDP at its peak in the early 1990s, and still the highest in the OECD (Kuhnle, 2000). Swedish social democracy of the 1970s and 1980s achieved a high level of public services, alongside high wages and a high employment rate. A large state sector was crucial to this model; it supported female employment through childcare services and family-friendly jobs in government employment. However, the keystone of the Swedish model was not merely high social expenditure but the enormous influence of organised labour, which underlay those policies. Social insurance, as in Denmark, was and remains trade union-managed, defending generous benefits as well as extensive retraining of redundant workers. The Rehn-Meidner model of economic policy, which was the expression of trade union-oriented Keynesianism, maintained that full employment was compatible with high wages through a principle of equal pay for equal work.

The work-sharing variant of the 'redistributive solution' is of a different order to the left Keynesian model; it represents one aspect of pay bargaining or labour regulation, rather than a comprehensive approach to economic policy. It is exemplified in the French 'Loi Aubry' of 1999, and in work-sharing 'deals' achieved by national bargaining in Belgium in the 1980s, which achieved working time reductions through educational leave, career breaks and sabbaticals, and cuts in weekly hours. In periods of strength trade unions often negotiate a shorter working week without loss of pay, or indeed alongside increased pay. Such deals were widespread in Germany in the 1970s and 1980s, moving towards a 35-hour week by 1995. Later, working time reductions were negotiated defensively by German unions as a way of saving jobs, accepting a weekly pay cut on condition hours were cut by a larger proportion. In France the cut in the national standard week from 39 hours to 35, under the 'Loi Aubry' of 1999, was intended as a job-creation measure. It is credited with having generated between 200,000 and 400,000 new jobs.[2] However, it was less redistributive than appeared; employers received substantial state subsidies to compensate them for maintaining hourly wage rates, the cost of which was borne largely by the working class through extra taxes. Moreover many employers intensified workloads, or introduced new flexibilities of working hours often against workers' interests.[3] Many low-paid employees resented the loss of overtime and overtime pay. The Loi Aubry, although it exempted employers with fewer than 20 staff, is alleged to have driven some small firms into financial difficulties, because the cut-away four hours per week of each person did not add up to a viable extra job, leading to a shortage of labour input or to impractical amalgamations of job descriptions. Its critics blamed the shorter working week for the decline in French competitiveness and for the excessive budget deficit of 2002–03, claims that have some element of truth but are doubtless exaggerated in view of the very rapid growth of the French economy in 2000–01. The Loi Aubry seems to have failed on points of detail, from which future lessons can be learnt. Chirac's effective reversal of the cut in hours by extending permitted annual overtime closed an experiment that might have worked better if it had been based more on local negotiations about what workers wanted, and if subsidies had been concentrated on small firms.

In the third layer of change we can place demands that are not totally without precedent, but seriously challenge capitalist interests. These would include the reversal of privatisations, notwithstanding any international agreements that stand in the way. They would also include a guaranteed basic income; much higher taxation of executive-level incomes, distributed profits, and various forms of tax on wealth and assets would be required to fund it. The limit on working hours in the Working Time Directive could be progressively reduced, and leave rights increased.

The widespread demand for an unconditional basic income demand reflects an exasperation with the increasing obligations attached to benefit rights, and a recognition that these impositions serve employers' interests and encourage the spread of flexploitation. The overall message is not a refusal of work, but rather than a demand for what has been portrayed in Chapter 5 as the ideal of a de-commodifying benefit system, one which enables people to refuse bad jobs and retrain for good ones. Underpinning income guarantees could be a demand for a minimum wage level throughout the EU, set at a standard percentage of GDP per capita. Basic income for the unwaged could be fixed at a certain percentage of the average wage. With relatively unconditional benefits over say 65 per cent of the average, comparable with Danish and Swedish benefit levels, low-paid or otherwise unattractive jobs in the capitalist sector would find no takers. However, many forms of unpaid work and partly paid work in the non-profit sector would flourish, creating a political and economic space for that sector to grow and to move an increasing share of production beyond the realm of exploited labour.

These are not stages in some planned and plannable journey; social change does not come in neat and plannable stages, nor is it a continuous drive down a one-way street. One must expect that changes at the second and third layers would be strongly resisted by capital. Some parts of the EU will inevitably have social forces capable of pushing through more layers of the onion than others. What is important is to find ways, within the complex institutions of EU governance and social dialogue, to secure harmonisation upwards in workers' interest rather than allowing the neo-liberal project of big business to continue to call the tune. Nor is it agreed, among the many supporters of the notion that 'another Europe is possible', where that journey would end. If some would be content with a revival of the KWNS, others would welcome their efforts to achieve that as a chance to pursue other battles, to paraphrase Gramsci, on more friendly terrain.

Notes

CHAPTER 1

1. 'Minima Sociaux et Condition Salariale: "l'Europe vue d'en bas"'. TSER project CT98–3071, 30.11.1998 to 30.12.2001.
2. The full list of continental fieldwork areas was: Normandie, Marseilles, Lorraine, Ile de France and Poitou-Charentes in France; Brussels, Charleroi and Anvers in Belgium; Ludwigshafen, Dresden, Mannheim, Frankfurt, Reutlingen, Mainz, Erfurt, Berlin, Munich and Bad Hersfeld in Germany.

CHAPTER 2

1. Portugal introduced a minimum income scheme in 1997, of which the main adult beneficiaries are lone parents (see EC (2002c), p. 40). A pilot scheme was being tested in selected municipalities in Italy in 2001–02 (EC (2001b), p. 35).
2. These complex debates are summarised in Cousins (1998).
3. EC, *Employment in Europe, 2003*, p. 79.
4. EC (1995), *InforMISEP*, no. 58.

CHAPTER 3

1. According to the well-known international financier, George Soros, it was a mistake to give the European Central Bank a mandate to focus on price stability as its central policy goal: 'to bring about full employment, an economy needs government policies specifically designed for the purpose; the invisible hand will not get us to a happy equilibrium' (see John Gray, 1998, p. 90).
2. See OECD (2001b), pp. 151–8.
3. OECD (1998c), Table 7.7.
4. Belgium and Germany: OECD (1998c), Table 7.7; France: Lodovici (2000), p. 61.
5. OECD (1998c), Table 7.3.
6. Ibid., Table 7.2.
7. This term was first used within anthropology to describe theories of why certain societies did things in particular ways; functionalist explanations argue that several different societies show apparently similar responses to certain needs or problems. The question is; do the practices or policies really respond to the needs, or do they become widespread because of missionaries, fashions or some other reason?

CHAPTER 4

1. EC (1993) (the 'Delors' White Paper).

2. EC (1994).
3. Union of Industrial and Employers' Confederations of Europe.
4. Of the EU 15, only the UK and Sweden had not adopted the euro by December 2003.
5. The Working Time Directive is a health and safety rather than an employment creation measure; it merely limits working hours to 48 per week and entitles all workers to four weeks' paid holiday per year. Only a small minority of European employees would not have these conditions anyway – although, as shown in Chapter 4, UK workers have among the longest hours in Europe.
6. See EIRO online (European Industrial Relations Observatory), <www.eiro. eurofound.ie/1998/12/InBrief/EU9812129N.html>.
7. Commission Staff Working Paper, 'The Lisbon Strategy: Making Change Happen', 2002 (COM (2002) 14 final), p. 12.
8. Although 38 per cent of the unemployed population of the EU and 25 per cent of the inactive are found to be in poverty, 6 per cent of employed persons are too. The EU in its Joint Report on Social Inclusion (2002c, p. 24) uses the definition of less than 60 per cent of median income.
9. *European Anti-Poverty Network (EAPN) News*, no. 87, 2001, p. 2.
10. See EIRO, feature EU0004241F of 2000, on <www.eiro.eurofound. ie/2000/04/Features/EU0004241F.html>.
11. What has become known as the 'Washington Consensus' refers to policy guidelines developed by the G8 group of countries in 1990, including balanced budgets and low government spending, privatisation of state enterprise, market determination of interest rates, and deregulation of labour, financial and other markets.
12. The ILO definition, also adopted in EU statistics, is that someone is unemployed if she or he wants work, has looked for work in the last four weeks, and would be available to take a job if offered one – that is, would not be prevented by lack of childcare, by a need to care for an elderly or sick person, or lack of support for the jobseeker's own disability issues.
13. European Commission (2002): *Impact Evaluation of the European Employment Strategy*, para. 2.2.2.
14. The indicators adopted by the Laeken summit in December 2001 are detailed in the European Commission (DGV)'s annual, *Employment in Europe, 2002*, p. 80.
15. European Commission (2002): *Recommendations on the Broad Guidelines of the Economic Policies of the Member States and the Community (for the 2002–2005 period)*.
16. For the full range of grounds, and other major provisions of the charter, see <www.eiro.eurofound.ie>.
17. 'Perspectives', editorial prepared by Patrick Bollé, *International Labour Review* (1997), 136/4: 577.
18. See *Financial Times*, 29.8.03, p. 6: 'More states ready to challenge stability pact, says Schröder'.
19. See Charlotte Denny and Larry Elliott, 'IMF warns trade gap could bring down dollar', *Guardian*, 19.9.03.

20. Existing childcare provision varies widely in extent and cost between member states, but is generally in short supply except in Scandinavia (Rubery and Fagan, 1999).
21. See EC (1994), p. 32.

CHAPTER 5

1. EC (1998a), p. 80.
2. Such a shift occurred in seven out of nine countries for which the European Commission presents evidence (2002b), pp. 71–2.
3. The OECD's data in columns 3 and 4 do not include most social assistance schemes that are locally administered, but do include national ones like UK Income Support.
4. OECD (2003a).
5. EC (2001b), p. 25.
6. Ibid., p. 22.
7. OECD (2001), *Economic Survey of Belgium, 2001.*
8. EIRO, June 2002: see <www.eiro.eurfound.ie/2002/06/feature/ES0206210F. html>.
9. Three months is the usual length of the 'permitted period' allowed for jobseekers with prior experience to search for similar work at their usual wage. Some pay cut must be accepted after the end of the permitted period and any job after six months.
10. OECD, *Employment Outlook, 2000*, ch. 4, pp. 135–6.
11. See also EC (1998c), p. 107.
12. OECD (1995b), pp. 64–5.
13. Bertelsmann Foundation, *International Reform Monitor*, issue 3, October 2000, p. 36. The penalty introduced for refusing a job offer was a 25 per cent benefit cut for 40 days on the first refusal, 50 per cent cut on the second, and complete suspension of benefit on the third refusal (see also EIRO December 1999, on <eiro.eurofound.ie/1999/12/InBrief/ SE9912108N.html>.
14. OECD (2001a).
15. EC (1998a), p. 43; OECD (1997a), p. 23.
16. ERGO (1992), Annex 1, p. 68.
17. See EIRO feature DK0301106F of 2003, on <www.eiro.eurofound.ie>.
18. With a minor concession that claimants can reject jobs below a certain wage for up to six months, provided they can show this does not affect their chances of getting work; see Unemployment Unit, *Unemployment and Training Rights Handbook* (1997), p. 43.
19. Bertelsmann Foundation, *International Reform Monitor*, issue 5, October 2001, p. 43.
20. *Guardian*, 9.7.2003.
21. *Guardian*, 18.10.03, p. 18.
22. See <www.eiro.eurofound.ie/2002/09/Feature/DE209205F.html>.
23. See <www.eiro.eurofound.ie/2002/06/feature/ES0206210F.html>.
24. OECD (2001), *Economic Survey of Belgium, 2001.*
25. Lévy *et al.* (2000b).

26. EC (1998c), p. 109.

27. See Danish National Action Plan for Employment, 2003, on <www.bm.dk/english/publications/napuk2003/default.asp>.

28. Incapacity Benefit for those with an insurance entitlement; means-tested Income Support for others who are tested as unable to work. The latter are technically counted as 'Incapacity Benefit claimants' since they are credited with National Insurance contributions as persons unfit for work (see Alcock *et al.*, 2003, p. 113).

29. In a survey of 200 unwaged people at Staveley, in Derbyshire, 17.5 per cent had experienced discrimination from employers owing to a health problem or disability, compared to over one-third who were claiming incapacity benefit (Derbyshire Unemployed Workers' Centres, 2003, pp. 17, 25).

30. Ibid., p. 21.

31. At the time of these focus groups, the National Minimum Wage was £3.60 for those over 22, and £3.20 for 18–21-year-olds.

32. Agence Nationale pour le promotion de l'Emploi, the French job centre network.

33. The period in which a jobseeker is permitted to look for the kind of work and level of earnings that s/he had before.

34. Unless the person leaves between five and twelve weeks after starting the job.

35. See WFTC Summary Statistics for February 2003, on <www.inlandrevenue.gov.uk/wftctables>. This figure is derived by multiplying the average weekly award by the number of claimants, grossed up to 52 weeks.

36. See TUC evidence to the Low Pay Commission, October 2002, on <www.tuc.org.uk>.

37. Since the time of the fieldwork (summer 1999) Family Credit was replaced (in November 1999) by the more generous Working Families Tax Credit; but the mortgage 'trap' may still remain.

38. This is a long-standing problem in the UK, which does not occur in Sweden or Germany where more people rent their homes (see Clasen *et al.*, 1997, pp. 27–8).

39. See *European Industrial Relations Review*, March 2001.

40. OECD (2003b).

41. Walwei (1998), cited in Lévy *et al.* (2001b).

42. See Finn *et al.* (1998); Jordan *et al.* (1992).

CHAPTER 6

1. Statistics derived from the annex on 'Key Employment Indicators' in EC (1998a, 2002b).

2. See EC (2001a), ch. 4; and (2002b), ch. 3.

3. EC (2001a), p. 75.

4. There are no data for Sweden, and France divides jobs only into 'low pay' and 'reasonable'.

5. The Dutch 'Flexibility and Security Act' of 1999 gave long-standing agency workers the right to permanent contracts, and also to training,

in certain circumstances: see <http://eiro.eurofound.ie/1999/01/features/ nl9901117f.html>.

6. EC (2002b), p. 92. Data for this analysis do not include Sweden, Finland or Luxembourg.
7. Ibid., p. 102.
8. In Austria, Belgium, France, Germany and Spain, the bulk of temporary agency work is in manufacturing, whereas in the UK, the Netherlands and Scandinavia it is more focused on services (see EC (1998a)).
9. EC (2001a), p. 69.
10. See EIRO feature FR0111102N on <www.eiro.eurofound.ie/2001/11/ InBrief/ FR0111102N.html>.
11. It is often held that this is less so in the UK than elsewhere, but Hazel Conley's case studies of local authorities, among the biggest employers of part-time women, suggest otherwise (see Conley, 1999).
12. See Purcell *et al.* (1999).
13. Vanessa Houlder, *Financial Times*, 29.1.97.
14. Data assembled by Gottschalk and Smeeding in 1998 and presented in Sigg and Behrendt (2002), p. 168. The 15 countries include Sweden, UK, USA, Germany, Denmark and France, and the exceptions were Ireland and Italy.
15. OECD (1999b), p. 64.
16. See TUC evidence to the Low Pay Commission, October 2002.
17. See EC (2001a), p. 74; and the European Foundation for the Improvement of Living and Working Conditions, Third European Survey on Working Conditions, available on <www.eiro.eurofound.ie>.
18. EC (2001a), p. 73.
19. See *Guardian*, 24.7.03; 25.7.03.
20. See EIRO briefing note, DE9711138F on <www.eiro.eurofound.ie/1997/11/ feature/DE9711138F.html>.
21. Explanatory Memorandum to the Proposal for a Directive on Working Conditions for Temporary Workers, com/2002/0149 final, accessed on <http://europa.eu.int> on 2.12.03.
22. See Chapter 1 for notes on the sources of these quotes from the Minima Sociaux fieldwork. Names are fictitious.
23. See EC (2002b), p. 89.
24. Ibid., p. 25.
25. EC (1998a), pp. 45–6.
26. EC (2001a), p. 75.
27. EIRO (2002).
29. Source: *Labour Market Trends*, March 2003, p. 130.
29. *Guardian*, 24.7.03, p. 3; Gray (2002b).
30. *Labour Market Trends*, February 2003, p. 57.
31. See EIRO, feature ES9710227NES of 1997 on <www.eiro.eurofound.ie>.
32. See <http://www.eiro.eurofound.ie/1997/11/feature/DE9711138F. html>.
33. In the UK the Employment Relations Act 1999 provided for a right to holiday pay for agency temps, but in practice this may just be added to the hourly rate rather than being a more visible payment for weeks off.
34. From Lévy *et al.* (2000b).

35. Less than 11 euros.
36. See <www.simonjones.org.uk> and *Guardian*, 23.2.99, for further details of this case.
37. From Lévy *et al*. (2000b).
38. See EC (2001a), ch. 4; data are based on the European Community Household Panel Survey. The remaining 8 per cent left the active labour force.
39. In the author's research sample of 98 long-term unemployed people in 1999, 32 (38 per cent of those who explained why they had lost their last job) had 'signed on' when a temporary job ended. Daniel (1990) found that the proportion was just under 22 per cent.
40. EC (2002b), ch. 1; see also more detailed information in ch. 2, pp. 59–60.
41. See <http://eiro.eurofound.ie/2002/09/Feature/DE0209205F.html>.
42. For example, Manpower plc operates in 48 countries with a workforce of around two and a half million, according to its company secretary, Keith Faulkner, speaking to a conference in London in January 1999.

CHAPTER 7

1. Germany had removed protection against unfair dismissal from employees in firms with under ten employees in 1996; in 1999 the threshold was restored to its old level of five employees. In the UK, until 1985 protection against unfair dismissal was available after six months in a job; the Tories then changed the threshold to two years, and New Labour in 1999 restored unfair dismissal protection after one year.
2. Over three-quarters of these social security-exempt jobs are held by women. Particular attention has been drawn to the hotel and catering sector, where a report for the Equal Opportunities Commission (Purcell *et al*., 1999) found that in pubs, bars and clubs over half the employees in 1995–96 earned less than the lowest wage at which National Insurance contributions must be paid.
3. OECD (1999b), p. 53.
4. Ibid., ch. 2; 'Employment Protection and Labour Market Performance', pp. 42–132.
5. See note 1.
6. See EC (2001a), Fig. 24, p. 72, and Gregg *et al*., (1999).
7. Eric Zoetmunder, of Bakkenist Management Consultants in the Netherlands, speaking to a conference entitled 'The Temporary and Agency Worker – Their Role in Europe's Workforce', organised by Manpower and the T&G Union in London in January 1999.
8. Explanatory Memorandum to the Proposal for the Agency Work Directive, COM/2002/0149 final.
9. See <http://www.eiro.eurofound.ie/1999/01/feature/NL9901117F.html;> and <http://www.eiro.eurofound.ie/1997/11/features/NL9711144F.html>.
10. Industrial Relations Services (1998), section entitled 'Employee Health Bulletin', pp. 10–12.

11. See EIRO briefing note, 'Challenging the general: Commonplace use of agency work', feature FR0202104F on <www.eiro.eurofound.ie/2002/02/Feature/FR0202104F.html>.
12. EIRO briefing notes, GR0111101, ES9907140FES and DE9711138F, on <www.eiro.eurofound.ie>.
13. See <http://www.eiro.eurofound.ie/about/2002/12/feature/DK0212103F.html>.
14. This term seems to have first been used by H. Giersch in a paper written at Kiel University in 1985, and was taken up by (among others) Samuel Bentolila and Giuseppe Bertola ('Firing costs and labour demand: How bad is Eurosclerosis?'; *Journal of Economic Studies* 1990, 57: 381–402.
15. OECD (1996a), ch. 3, p. 76.
16. See ibid., p. 63 and Chart 3.3, p. 67; also Dresser and Rogers (2003).
17. Hutton (2002).
18. This was argued by a senior executive of a major international temp agency, whom the author interviewed shortly before the Fixed Term Work Directive was enacted.
19. See OECD (1999b), ch. 2.
20. The actual situation faced by employers wanting to downsize or casualise their workforce may be affected by trade union agreements as well as labour law. The OECD's analysis controls for trade union density and bargaining coverage, to take this into account.
21. This is contrary to previous work by Stephen Nickell (1997), who found that during 1983–94, EPL had a negative effect on the employment rate of the population as a whole. However, Nickell had pointed out that this negative effect could be spurious; it just so happens that south European countries, especially Spain, had rather strict EPL during the period being studied but – for unrelated reasons – a relatively low employment rate of women.
22. For firms that lay off a large number of workers to develop a plan to help them find other jobs.
23. The low pay variable was defined as the proportion of workers earning less than two-thirds of the weekly or hourly median wage.
24. EC (2002b), ch. 3.
25. See EIRO feature DK0112147F of 2001, on <www.eiro.eurofound.ie>.
26. An employer can now be obliged to recognise a trade union where at least 50 per cent of the workforce are members, or where a majority of employees voting in a secret ballot request union recognition.
27. The draft directive on agency workers has had the most difficult passage of all the EU labour directives to date. After the 'social dialogue' process failed to agree on a proposal, the Commission itself put one forward (see <www.eiro.eurofound.ie/2002/04/Feature/EU0204205F.html>). But in June 2003 the European Council in Luxembourg failed to reach political agreement for its acceptance and implementation.
28. See EIRO feature DK0304101N of March 2003, at <http://www.eiro.eurofound.ie/2003/04/inbrief/dk0304101n.html>.
29. Put forward, for example, by some trade union speakers at the European Social Forum in Florence in November 2002.

30. Blair in opposition reassured the employers that even the planned changes to trade union law, eventually embodied in the Employment Relations Act 1999, would still 'leave British law the most restrictive on trade unions in the Western world' (*The Times*, 31.3.97).

31. Interestingly enough, the new right to recognition is closely modelled on American legislation. In the American context, it has been found wanting because outsourcing, agency hiring and subcontracting can easily be used by employers to fragment their workforce and minimise the risk of the 50 per cent threshold being attained.

32. See EIRO feature FR0304103N of 2003, on <www.eiro.eurofound.ie>.

33. See EIRO features ES0206210F of 2002, and ES0205204N ES0207201N, on <www.eiro.eurofound.ie>.

34. EIRO, 2002: 'Comparative overview of industrial relations in Europe', on <http://www.eiro.eurofound.ie>.

35. 'Six days a week', August 1999; see <www.tuc.org.uk /work_life/tuc-465-f0.cfm#P101_1117>.

36. EIRO feature UK0005175F of May 2000, on <http://www.eiro.eurofound.ie/2000/05/feature/uk0005175f.html>.

37. *European Industrial Relations Review* (2001), p. 2.

38. EIRO feature FR0203107FFR of 2003.

39. EIRO feature FR0005162.NFR of 2000.

CHAPTER 8

1. This makes use of a scheme dating from 1984 for mandatory work at the national minimum wage rate, so low that it is rarely used in the 'formal' labour market (Costello, 1993, p. 6).

2. See Piven and Cloward (2002) and Handler and Hasenfeld (1997) for a detailed account of these developments.

3. Communication from Laura Wittman, University of Wisconsin, to the e-mail list workfare-discuss (see archives on <www-pluto.informatik.uni-oldenburg.de>).

4. See the case of Marsha Motipersad, press release by the Association of Community Organisations for Reform Now, 28 July 1997 and reported to the e-mail list workfare-discuss; see archives on <www-pluto.informatik.uni-oldenburg.de>).

5. See Peck and Jones (2001) p. 185.

6. See for example Mead (1997). There is a hint that the MDRC, as evaluator, acted as spin doctor to promote these programmes (Peck and Jones, 2001, p. 96).

7. Handler and Hasenfeld (1997); Burghes (1987).

8. See Unemployment Unit (1988); Gray (1996); Peck and Jones (2001), pp. 267–8.

9. This argument was made by Michael Beenstock and David Brown, 'Economic Agenda', *Guardian*, 7.1.87. See also Normington *et al.* (1986) for the official evaluation of the Community Programme's effects.

10. See *Working Brief*, November (1996), p. 4; December (1996), pp. 8–9; February (1997), p. 5.

11. See TUC (2002).

12. See Gray (2001), on the survey done for the Minima Sociaux project in Chesterfield; and Bryson *et al.* (2000).
13. Details of the numbers of New Deal participants in various parts of the programmes can be found on the web site of the Centre for Economic and Social Inclusion, <www.cesi.org.uk> which is frequently updated.
14. See Bryson *et al.* (2000) for data on wage rates; this and several other surveys attest the popularity of 'real jobs'.
15. There are under 16,000 people on 'benefit-plus' placements within the New Deal, plus 11,400 people in subsidised jobs where the wage is generally low, but subject to minimum wage regulation.
16. This proportion attains almost 40 per cent on the Environmental Task Force and 22.7 per cent in the Voluntary Sector placements (Employment Service statistics, cited in TUC (2002)). The proportion sanctioned has increased substantially over the history of the programme.
17. See Fletcher (1999) and Watkinson (1999). Almost half those who leave the New Deal for Young People without getting work are ex-offenders or had received a police warning at some time (Hales and Collins, 1999).
18. See Lévy *et al.* (2000b).
19. Swedish Labour Market Board press release, 20.9.2000, on <www.ams. se/pdf./syssel_en.pdf>. See also OECD (2001a).
20. OECD (1999c), p. 123.
21. This right was removed to prevent people going through several rounds of insurance rights followed by a job offer and a new insurance entitlement. The maximum number of job offers had already been restricted to two in 1990.
22. The Jadot report: see <http://www.eiro.eurofound.ie/1998/12/feature/BE9812254F.html>.
23. See <http://www.eiro.eurofound.ie/2002/09/Feature?DE0209205F. html>.
24. See <http://www.eiro. eurofound.ie2002/03/feature/DE203204F.html.
25. See feature of 22.7.03 on <www.eiro.eurofound.ie>.
26. For schemes supported by the European Social Fund, the limit is 21 hours.

CHAPTER 9

1. EC (2000) *European Community Economic Data Pocket Book*, p. 29.
2. The upper limit was claimed in a French report in spring 2002, mentioned by Jim Pollard in the *Observer*, 24.3.02, available on <www.guardian. co.uk>. A figure of merely 200,000 was estimated by Jean-Paul Fitoussi, interviewed by Judith Larner in the *Guardian*, 11.10.03.
3. See Gray (1999a); John Henley in the *Guardian*, 29.8.01 and 10.10.03; John Crace, *Guardian* 11.8.01.s

Bibliography

Aaronovitch, S. and Grahl, J. (1997) 'Building on Maastricht' in Gowan, P. and Anderson, P., eds, *The Question of Europe* (London: Verso)

Abraham, F. (1999) 'A policy perspective on European unemployment', *Scottish Journal of Political Economy* 46/4: 350–69

Abramsky, K., ed. (2001) *Restructuring and Resistance: Diverse voices of struggle in Western Europe* (London: K. Abramsky)

Adema, W., Gray, D. and Kahl, S. (2001) *Social Assistance in Germany*, Labour Market and Social Policy Occasional Paper no. 58 (Paris: OECD)

Alber, J. and Standing, G. (2000) 'Social dumping, catch-up or convergence. Europe in a comparative global context', *Journal of European Social Policy* 10(2): 99–119

Alcock, P., Beatty, C., Fothergill, S., Macmillan, R. and Yeandle, S. (2003) *Work to Welfare: How men become detached from the labour market* (Cambridge: Cambridge University Press)

Allen, J. and Henry, N. (1996) 'Fragments of industry and employment: Contract service work and the shift towards precarious employment' in Crompton, R., Gallie, D. and Purcell, K., eds (1996) *Changing Forms of Employment: Organisations, skills and gender* (London: Routledge)

Atkinson, A.B. (1983) *The Economics of Inequality* (Oxford: Oxford University Press)

—— (1995) *Incomes and the Welfare State: Essays on Britain and Europe* (Cambridge: Cambridge University Press)

Balanyá, B., Doherty, A., Hoedeman, O., Ma'anit, A. and Wesselius, E. (2000) *Europe, Inc: Regional and global restructuring and the rise of corporate power* (London: Pluto Press)

Ballal, S. and Bouquin, S. (2000) 'Vers une rédefinition des logiques de droits collectifs incarnées par le travail et son statut', *Année Sociale*: 264–84 (Brussels: Université Libre de Bruxelles)

Barnard, C. and Deakin, S. (1999) 'A year of living dangerously? EU social rights, employment policy and EMU', *Industrial Relations Journal* 30(4): 355–72

Bastian, J. (1994) *A Matter of Time* (Aldershot: Gower)

Beatson, M. (1995) *Labour Market Flexibility*, Employment Department Research Series no. 48, April (Sheffield: Employment Department)

Beaud, S. (1999) 'The Temp's Dream' in Bourdieu, P. ed., *The Weight of the World: Social suffering in contemporary society* (Stanford: Stanford University Press): 282–96

Beaumont, P. and Harris, R. (1995) 'Union de-recognition and declining union density in Britain', *Industrial and Labor Relations Review* 48/3

Beenstock, M. and Brown, D. (1987) 'Economic Agenda', *Guardian*, 7 January

Begg, I. and Berghman, J. (2002) 'EU social (exclusion) policy revisited?' *Journal of European Social Policy* 12/3: 179–94

Benner, M. and Bundgaard Vad, T. (2000) 'Sweden and Denmark: Defending the Welfare State' in Scharpf, F.W. and Schmidt, V.A., eds, *Welfare and Work in the Open Economy* (Oxford; Oxford University Press)

Bennett, F. and Hirsh, D., eds (2001) *The Employment Tax Credit and Issues for the Future of In-Work Support* (York: Joseph Rowntree Foundation)

Bennett, F. and Walker, R. (1998) *Working with Work: An initial assessment of Welfare to Work* (York: Joseph Rowntree Foundation)

Birks, C. (1987) 'Social welfare provision in France' in Ford, R. and Chakrabarti, M., eds, *Welfare Abroad: An Introduction to social welfare in seven countries* (Edinburgh: Scottish Academic Press)

Bologna, S. (1994) 'Nazism and the working class', *Common Sense* 16 (Edinburgh: Conference of Socialist Economists).

Bonefeld, W. (2002) 'European integration – the political, the market and class', *Capital and Class* 77 (Summer): 117–44

Bonoli, G., George, V. and Taylor-Gooby, P. (2000) *European Welfare Futures: Towards a theory of retrenchment* (Cambridge: Polity Press)

Booth, A., Francesconi, M. and Frank, J. (2000) *Temporary Jobs: Who gets them, what are they worth and do they lead anywhere?*, University of Essex Institute for Labour Research (Colchester: UEILR)

Brook, K. (2002) 'Trade union membership: An analysis of data from the autumn 2001 LFS', *Labour Market Trends* (July): 343–52

Bruce, M. (1961) *The Coming of the Welfare State* (London: Batsford)

Bryson, A. and Gomay, R. (2002) 'Recent trends in union membership' in National Centre for Social Research and Park, Alison, eds, *British Social Attitudes: The 19th report* (London: Sage)

Bryson, A., Knight, G. and White, M. (2000) *New Deal for Young People: National Survey of Participants, stage 1*, Policy Studies Institute/Employment Service Research Report 44 (Sheffield: Employment Service)

Burgess, J., Mitchell, W., O'Brien, D. and Watts, M. (1998) 'Workfare in Australia and New Zealand: A critical assessment', paper given to the 5th National Conference on Unemployment (Melbourne: University of Melbourne)

Burghes, L. (1987) *Made in the USA* (London: Unemployment Unit)

Burton, J. (1987) *Would Workfare Work?* (Buckingham: University of Buckingham)

Caminada, K. and Goudswaard, K. (2002) 'Income distribution and social security in an OECD perspective' in Sigg, R. and Behrendt, C., eds, *Social Security in the Global Village* (London and New Jersey: Transaction Publishers)

Castles, F. and Pierson, C. (1996) 'A new convergence: Recent policy developments in the UK, Australia and New Zealand', *Policy and Politics* 24/3: 233–45

Christensen, E. (2000) 'The Rhetoric of Rights and Obligations in Workfare and Citizens' Income Paradigms/Discourses in Denmark in a Labour History Perspective', paper given to the 8th Basic Income European Network Conference, Berlin, October

Clarke, J. (2001) 'Globalisation and Welfare States: Some unsettling thoughts' in Sykes, R., Palier, B. and Prior, P., eds, *Globalisation and European Welfare States: Challenges and change* (Basingstoke: Palgrave)

Clarke, L., de Gijsel, P. and Janssen, J. (2000) *The Dynamics of Wage Relations in the New Europe* (Dordrecht: Kluwer)

Clasen, J. (2000) 'Motives, means and opportunities: Reforming unemployment compensation in the 1990s' in Ferrera, R. and Rhodes, M., eds, *Recasting European Welfare States* (Portland, Oregon: Frank Cass)

Clasen, J. and Freeman, R., eds (1994) *Social Policy in Germany* (Hemel Hempstead: Harvester Wheatsheaf)

Clasen, J., Gould, A. and Vincent, J. (1997) *Long-term Unemployment and the Threat of Social Exclusion* (Bristol: Policy Press)

Clerc, D. (2001) 'Un chèque pour l'emploi', *Alternatives Économiques* 189 (Février): 20–3

Coates, K. (1998) 'Introduction: Full Employment, a European Appeal', *Spokesman*, no. 64: 1–4

Collinson, D. (1987) 'Picking women: The recruitment of temporary workers into the mail order industry', *Work, Employment and Society* 1: 371–87

Compston, H. and Madsen, P.K. (2001) 'Conceptual innovations and public policy: Unemployment and paid leave schemes in Denmark', *Journal of European Social Policy* 11/2: 117–32

Concialdi, P. (2001) 'Un coup fatal au statut salarial', *Alternatives Économiques* 189 (Fevrier): 23

Conley, H. (1999) *Temporary Work in the Public Services: Implications for equal opportunities* (Cardiff: Cardiff University, mimeo)

Costello, A. (1993) *Workfare in Britain* (London: Unemployment Unit)

Costello, A. and Levidow, L. (2001) 'Flexploitation Strategies; UK lessons for Europe', in Abramsky, K., ed., *Restructuring and Resistance: Diverse voices of struggle in Western Europe* (London: K. Abramsky)

—— (2002) 'Flexploitation struggles: UK lessons from and for Europe', *Soundings*, no. 19 (Winter 2001–2): 74–97

Cousins, C. (1998) 'Social Exclusion in Europe: Paradigms of social disadvantage in Germany, Spain, Sweden and the UK', *Policy and Politics* 26/2: 127–46

—— (1999) *Society, Work and Welfare in Europe* (Basingstoke: Macmillan)

Cousins, C. and Michel, A. (2000) 'Recent welfare to work policies in the UK and Sweden', paper given to the Social Policy Association Conference at the University of Surrey (Roehampton: University of Surrey).

Crompton, R., Gallie, D. and Purcell, K., eds (1996) *Changing Forms of Employment: Organisations, skills and gender* (London; Routledge)

Dale, A. and Bamford, C. (1988) 'Temporary work: Cause for concern or complacency?', *Work, Employment and Society* 2: 191–209

Daly, Mary (2001) 'Globalisation and the Bismarckian Welfare States' in Sykes, R., Palier, B. and Prior, P., eds, *Globalisation and European Welfare States: Challenges and change* (Basingstoke: Palgrave): 79–102

Daniel, W.W. (1990) *The Unemployed Flow* (London: Policy Studies Institute)

Deacon, A. and Field, F., eds (1997) *From Welfare to Work: Lessons from America* (London: Institute of Economic Affairs)

Deacon, B. (2001) 'International Organisations, the European Union and Global Society' in Sykes, R., Palier, B. and Prior, P., eds, *Globalisation and European Welfare States: Challenges and change* (Basingstoke: Palgrave): 59–75

Dean, H. and Melrose, M. (1999) *Poverty, Riches and Social Citizenship* (Basingstoke: Macmillan)

Derbyshire Unemployed Workers' Centres (2003) *Barriers to Employment in Staveley* (Chesterfield: DUWC)

Dhillon, B. (2000) 'Minimising sanctions on JSA', *Working Brief* (June): 11–12

Dickens, R. (1999) 'Wage mobility in Great Britain' in Gregg, P. and Wadsworth, J., eds, *The State of Working Britain* (Manchester: Manchester University Press)

Disney, R., Gosling, A. and Machin, S. (1995) 'British unions in decline: Determinants of the 1980s fall in union recognition', *Industrial and Labor Relations Review* 48/3

Dresser, L. and Rogers, J. (2003) 'Part of the Solution: Emerging workforce intermediaries in the United States' in Zeitlin, J. and Trubeck, D., eds, *Governing Work and Welfare in a New Economy* (Oxford: Oxford University Press)

Duran, R.F. (1997) *Contra la Europa del Capital y la Globalizacion Economica* (Madrid: Talasa); extracts translated into English in Abramsky, K., ed. (2001) *Restructuring and Resistance: Diverse voices of struggle in Western Europe* (London: K. Abramsky)

Eardley, T., Bradshaw, J., Ditch, J., Gough, I. and Whiteford, P. (1996) *Social Assistance in OECD Countries*, Department of Social Security Research Report no. 46 (London: Department of Social Security)

Enjolras, B., Laville, J.L., Fraisse, L. and Trickey, H. (2001) 'Between Subsidiarity and social assistance – the French republican route to activation' in Lødemel, I. and Trickey, H., eds, *An Offer You Can't Refuse: Workfare in international perspective* (Bristol: Policy Press)

ERGO (1992), *ERGO Programme Report, Phase 1*, PA Cambridge Economic Consultants Report for European Commission, DG V

—— (1996) *ERGO Programme Report, Phase 2*, PA Cambridge Economic Consultants Report for European Commission, DG V

Esping-Andersen, G. (1990) *The Three Worlds of Welfare Capitalism* (Cambridge: Polity Press)

—— (1996a) 'After the Golden Age: Welfare State dilemmas in a global economy' in Esping-Andersen, G., ed., *Welfare States in Transition: National adaptations in global economies* (London/Thousand Oaks: Sage)

—— (1996b) 'Welfare states without work: The impasse of labour shedding and familialism in continental European social policy' in Esping-Andersen, G., ed., *Welfare States in Transition: National adaptations in global economies* (London/Thousand Oaks: Sage)

—— (1999) *Social Foundations of Post-industrial Economies* (Oxford: Oxford University Press)

—— (2000a) 'Regulation and context: Reconsidering the correlates of unemployment' in Esping-Andersen, G. and Regini, M., eds, *Why Deregulate Labour Markets?* (Oxford: Oxford University Press)

—— (2000b) 'Who is harmed by labour market regulation? Quantitative evidence' in Esping-Andersen, G. and Regini, M., eds, *Why Deregulate Labour Markets?* (Oxford: Oxford University Press)

Esping-Andersen, G., with Gallie, D., Hemerijck, A. and Myles, J. (2002) *Why We Need a New Welfare State* (Oxford: Oxford University Press)

Etherington, D. (1998) 'From Welfare to Work in Denmark', *Policy and Politics* 262: 147–61

European Commission (1993) *Growth, Competitiveness and Employment: The Challenges and Ways Forward into the 21st Century* [the 'Delors' White Paper] (Luxembourg: EU)

—— (1994) *European Social Policy: A Way Forward for the Union*, COM [94] 333 [White Paper] (Luxembourg: EU)

European Commission, DG V (1998a) *Employment in Europe, 1998* (Luxembourg: EU)

—— (1998b) *Proposal for Guidelines for Member States Employment Policies 1999*, Com 1998 574 Final (Luxembourg: EU)

—— (1998c) *Social Protection in Europe 1997*, Com 1998 243 (Luxembourg: EU)

—— (1999) *The 1999 Employment Guidelines* (Luxembourg: EU)

—— (2000) *The Social Situation in the European Union, 2000* (Luxembourg: Eurostat)

—— (2001a) *Employment in Europe, 2001* (Luxembourg: EU)

—— (2001b) *Social Protection in Europe, 2001* (Luxembourg: EU)

—— (2002a) *Communication on Building an Inclusive Europe* (Luxembourg: EU)

—— (2002b) *Employment in Europe, 2002* (Luxembourg: EU)

—— (2002c) *Joint Report on Social Inclusion* (Luxembourg: EU)

—— (2003) *Employment in Europe, 2002* (Luxembourg: EU)

European Foundation for the Improvement of Living and Working Conditions (2000) *Third Survey of Working Conditions in the EU 9* (Dublin: EFILWC)

—— (2002) *Integrated Approaches to Active Welfare and Employment Policies: Belgium* (published on the internet at <www.eurofound.eu.int/publications/files/EF0251EN.pdf>)

European Industrial Relations Review (2001) *New Employment Bonus Scheme to Benefit 8 million*

Euzéby, S. and Chapon, C. (2002) 'Towards a convergence of European social models', *International Social Security Review* 55/2: 37–55

Felstead, A. and Jewson, N., eds (1999) *Global Trends in Flexible Labour* (Basingstoke: Macmillan)

Fernie, S. and Metcalfe, D. (1996) *Low Pay and Minimum Wages: The British evidence* (London: London School of Economics, Centre for Economic Performance)

Ferrera, R. and Rhodes, M. (2000) 'Introduction' in Ferrera, R. and Rhodes, M., eds, *Recasting European Welfare States* (Portland, Oregon: Frank Cass)

Finn, D. (1995) 'The Job Seeker's Allowance: Workfare and the stricter benefit regime', *Capital and Class* 57: 7–12

—— (1997) *Working Nation: Welfare reform and the Australian Job Compact for the long-term unemployed* (London: Unemployment Unit)

—— (1998) 'Labour's New Deal for the unemployed and the stricter benefit regime', *Social Policy Review* 10: 105–22

—— (1998/99) 'Welfare Reform in the Netherlands', *Working Brief*, December/January: 17–20

—— (1999) 'Job Guarantees for the Unemployed; Lessons from Australian welfare reform', *Journal of Social Policy* 28/1: 53–71

Finn, D., Blackmore, M. and Nimmo, M. (1998) *Welfare to Work and the Long-Term Unemployed* (London: Unemployment Unit)

Fletcher, D. (1997) 'Evaluating special measures for the unemployed: Some reflections on recent UK experience', *Policy and Politics* 25/2: 173–84

—— (1999) 'Ex-offenders and the labour market: A review of the discourse of social exclusion and the consequences for crime and the New Deal', *Environment and Planning* C: *Government and Policy* 17: 431–44

Ford, R. and Millar, J., eds (1998) *Private Lives and Public Responses: Lone parenthood and future policy in the UK* (London: Policy Studies Institute)

Forde, Chris (2001) 'Temporary Arrangements: The activities of employment agencies in the UK', *Work, Employment & Society* 15/3: 631–44

Fraser, D. (1973) *The Evolution of the British Welfare State* (Basingstoke: Macmillan)

Galtier, B. and Gautié, J. (2003) 'Flexibility, stability and the interaction between employment protection and labour market policies in France' in Auer, P. and Cazes, S., eds, *Employment Stability in an Age of Flexibility* (Geneva: ILO): 59–107

Garrett, G. (2000) 'Shrinking States: Globalisation and national autonomy', in Woods, N., ed. *The Political Economy of Globalisation* (Basingstoke: Macmillan)

George, V. and Taylor-Gooby, P. (1996) *European Welfare Policy: Squaring the welfare circle* (Basingstoke: Macmillan)

Geyer, R.R. (2000) *Exploring European Social Policy* (Cambridge: Polity Press)

Gill, C., Gold, M. and Cressey, P.P., (1999) 'Social Europe: National initiatives and responses', *Industrial Relations Journal* 30/4: 313–29

Ginsberg, N. (1978) *Class, Capital and Social Policy* (London: Macmillan)

GMB Union (1994) *The Pay Rates of Young Workers* (London: GMB/Labour Research Department)

Godley, W. (1997) 'The hole in the treaty' in Gowan, P. and Anderson, P. eds, *The Question of Europe* (London: Verso)

Gold, M., Cressey, P. and Gill, C. (2000) 'Employment, employment, employment: Is Europe working?' *Industrial Relations Journal* 31/4: 275–90

Gorz, A. (1985) *Paths to Paradise: On the liberation from work* (London: Pluto)

Gottfried, H. (1992) 'In the margins: Flexibility as a mode of regulation in the temporary help service industry', *Work, Employment and Society* 6: 443–60

Gough, I. (1979) *The Political Economy of the Welfare State* (London: Macmillan)

Goul-Andersen, P. (2000) 'Welfare Crisis and beyond: Danish welfare policies in the 1980s and 1990s' in Kuhnle, S., ed., *Survival of the European Welfare State* (London/New York: Routledge)

Gould, A. (1999) 'The erosion of the welfare state: Swedish social policy and the EU', *Journal of European Social Policy* 9/2: 163–74

Gray, A. (1988) 'Resisting economic conscription', *Capital and Class* 34: 119–46

—— (1993) 'Integrating Citizens' Income with Social Insurance', *International Social Security Review* 46/2: 43–66

—— (1995) 'The flexibilisation of labour and the attack on living standards', *Common Sense* 18 (December)

—— (1996) *The Rights of the Unemployed: A Socialist Approach* (Nottingham: The Spokesman/European Labour Forum)

—— (1998) 'Missing rungs in the ladder', *'t'-mag* (November): 15–17 (Redruth, Cornwall: 't'-Magazine)

—— (1999a) *Time Off Pays Off: Shared opportunities for learning and earning* (London: Fabian Society)

—— (1999b) 'The Community Programme re-visited: Lessons for the New Deal era', *Local Economy* 14/1: 96–109

—— (2000) *The New Deal in Derbyshire* (London: Local Economy Policy Unit, South Bank University; published jointly with Derbyshire Unemployed Workers' Centres, Chesterfield)

—— (2001) 'The New Dealers who still have no jobs', *Competition and Change* 5: 375–393

—— (2002a) 'European perspectives on welfare reform – a tale of two vicious circles?' *European Societies* 4/4: 359–80

—— (2002b) 'Jobseekers and gatekeepers: The role of private employment agencies in the placement of the unemployed', *Work, Employment and Society* 16/4: 655–74

Gray, John (1998) *False Dawn: The delusions of global capitalism* (London: Granta)

Gregg, P., Knight, G. and Wadsworth, J. (1999) 'The cost of job loss' in Gregg, P. and Wadsworth, J., eds, *The State of Working Britain* (Manchester: Manchester University Press)

Gueck, M. (2000) 'Minima Sociaux et Conditions de Travail: German Report', unpublished working paper for Minima Sociaux project, University of Heidelberg, Germany

Guillén, A.M. and Alvarez, S. (2002) 'Southern European Welfare States Facing Globalisation, is there Social Dumping?' in Sigg, R. and Behrendt, C., eds, *Social Security in the Global Village* (London and New Jersey: Transaction Publishers): 67–84

Hales, J. and Collins, D. (1999) *New Deal for Young People: Leavers with unknown destinations* National Centre for Social Research, Employment Service Research Report 21 (Sheffield: Employment Service)

Hales, J., Collins, D., Hasluck, C. and Woodland, S. (2000) *New Deals for Young People and for Long-Term Unemployed People: Survey of Employers*, National Centre for Social Research/Employment Service, Employment Service Research Report 58 (Sheffield: Employment Service)

Handler, J. (2003) 'Social citizenship and workfare in the US and Western Europe: From status to contract', *Journal of European Social Policy* 13/3: 229–43

Handler, J. and Hasenfeld, Y. (1997) *We the Poor People: Work, poverty and welfare* (New Haven: Yale University Press)

Handler, J. and White, L., eds (1999) *Hard Labor: Women and work in the post-welfare era* (New York: M.E. Sharpe)

Hantrais, L. (1995) *Social Policy in the European Union* (London: Macmillan)

Hasluck, C. (1999) *Employers and the Employment Option of the NDYP: Employment additionality and its measurement*, Employment Service Report, ESR 14 (Sheffield: Employment Service)

—— (2000a) *The New Deal for Young People: Two years on*, Employment Service Research Report, ESR 41 (Sheffield: Employment Service)

—— (2000b) *The New Deal for the Long Term Unemployed: A survey of progress*, Employment Service Research Report, ESR 46 (Sheffield: Employment Service)

Heery, E. and Salmon, J., eds (1998) *The Insecure Workforce* (Parrington: Barmarick Publications)

Heery, E. and Salmon, J. (2000) *The Insecure Workforce* (London: Routledge)

Hoggett, P. (1994) 'The Politics of the Modernisation of the UK Welfare State' in Burrows, R. and Loader, B., eds, *Towards a Post-Fordist Welfare State?* (London: Routledge)

Holland, S. (1998) 'The feasibility of full employment', *Spokesman* 64: 12–37 (Nottingham: Spokesman Books)

Holmwood, J. (1998) *Europe and the 'Americanisation' of British Social Policy* (mimeo.) (Edinburgh: Department of Sociology, University of Edinburgh)

Hunter, L.C. and Robertson, D.J. (1969) *Economics of Wages and Labour* (London: Macmillan)

Hutton, W. (2002) *The World We're In* (London: LittleBrown/Time Warner Books)

ILO (2001) *The Impact of Decentralisation and Privatisation on Municipal Services* (Geneva: ILO)

Industrial Relations Services Employment Review (1998) 'Employee Health Bulletin' 653 (April) 10–12 (London: Industrial Relations Services [IRS] Ltd)

Jensen, P.H. (1999) 'Activation of the unemployed in Denmark since the early 1990s: Welfare or workfare?' at <www.socsci.auc.dk/ccws/workingpapers> (accessed on 20.8.2003)

Jessop, B. (1993) 'Towards a Schumpeterian Workfare State?', *Studies in Political Economy* 40: 7–39

—— (1994) 'The Transition to Post-Fordism and the Schumpeterian Workfare State' in Burrows, R. and Loader, B. eds, *Towards a Post-Fordist Welfare State?* (London: Routledge)

Jones, M. (1996) 'Full steam ahead to a workfare state?', *Policy and Politics* 24/2: 137–157

Jones, M. and Peck, J. (1995) 'Training and Enterprise Councils: Schumpeterian workfare state or what?', *Environment and Planning* A, 27: 1361–96

Jordan, B., James, S., Kay, H. and Redley, P. (1992) *Trapped in Poverty? Labour market decisions in low income households* (London: Routledge)

Kildal, N. (2000) 'Workfare tendencies in Scandinavian welfare policies', paper presented at 8th Basic Income European Network, Berlin, October, BIENOnline: <http://www.basicincome.org>

Kitson, M., Martin, R. and Wilkinson, F. (2000) 'Labour markets, social justice and economic efficiency', *Cambridge Journal of Economics* 24 (special issue published jointly with the Institute of Employment Rights): 631–41

Krzeslo, E. (2000) 'Danielle; se battre, c'est travailler', *Politique* 1 (October): 23–49 (Brussels: Fondation Jacques Gueux)

Kuhnle, S. (2000) 'The Scandinavian welfare state in the 1990s: Challenged but viable' in Ferrera, R. and Rhodes, M., eds, *Recasting European Welfare States* (Portland, Oregon: Frank Cass)

Kvist, Jon (1998) 'Complexities in assessing unemployment benefits and policies', *International Social Security Review* 51/4: 33–55

Labour Research Department (1987) *Temporary Workers: A negotiators' guide* (London: LRD)

Layard, R. (1998) 'Getting people back to work', *Centre Piece*, Autumn: 24–27 (London: London School of Economics)

Layard, R. and Philpott, J. (1991) *Stopping Unemployment* (London: Employment Institute [later renamed Employment Policy Institute])

Layard, R., Nickell, S. and Jackman, R. (1991) *Unemployment* (Oxford: Oxford University Press)

Lazar, H. and Stoyko, P. (1998) 'The future of the welfare state', *International Social Security Review* 51/3: 3–36

Legard, R. and Ritchie, J. (1999) *New Deal for Young Unemployed People. The Gateway*, Employment Service Research Report, ESR 16 (Sheffield: Employment Service).

Legard, R., Ritchie, J., Keegan, J. and Turner, R. (1998) *New Deal for Young Unemployed People*, Sheffield CPR/Employment Service Research Report, ESR 8 (Sheffield: Employment Service)

Lévy, C. (2000) 'Un plein emploi précaire', *Politique* 1 (October): 22–37 (Brussels: Fondation Jacques Gueux)

Lévy, C., Bouquin, S., Gray, A., Gueck, M. and Krzeslo, E. (2000a) 'Minima Sociaux et Condition Salariale, rapport de juin 2000', unpublished working paper for 'Minima Sociaux' project (Paris: CNRS).

—— (2000b) 'Minima Sociaux et Condition Salariale, rapport de décembre 2000', unpublished working paper for 'Minima Sociaux' project (Paris: CNRS)

—— (2001) 'Minima Sociaux et Condition Salariale: "l'Europe vue d'en bas", rapport final' (Paris: CNRS)

Lindqvist, R. and Marklund, S. (1995) 'Forced to work and liberated from work: A historical perspective on work and welfare in Sweden', *Scandinavian Journal of Social Welfare* 4: 224–37

Linebaugh, P. (1991) *The London Hanged: Crime and civil society in the eighteenth century* (London: Verso)

Lødemel, I. and Trickey, H., eds (2001) *An Offer You Can't Refuse: Workfare in international perspective* (Bristol: Policy Press)

Lodovici, M.S. (2000) 'The dynamics of labour market reform in European countries' in Esping-Andersen, G. and Regini, M., eds, *Why Deregulate Labour Markets?* (Oxford: Oxford University Press)

Lofhager, J. (1998) 'Solidarity and universality in the Danish welfare state – empirical remarks and theoretical interpretations', paper given to the 7th International Congress of the Basic Income European Network (Amsterdam, September); BIENOnline: <http://www.basicincome.org>

Machin, S. (1999) 'Wage inequality in the 1970s, 1980s and 1990s' in Gregg, P. and Wadsworth, J., eds, *The State of Working Britain* (Manchester: Manchester University Press)

Madsen, P. (2002) 'The Danish model of flexicurity: A paradise with some snakes' in Sarfati, H. and Bonoli, G., eds, *Labour Market and Social Protection Perspectives in International Perspective* (Aldershot: Ashgate)

—— (2003) '"Flexicurity" through labour market policies and institutions in Denmark' in Auer, P. and Cazes, S., eds, *Employment Stability in an Age of Flexibility* (Geneva: ILO): 59–107

Manow, P. and Siels, E. (2001) 'The employment crisis of the German welfare state' in Ferrera, R. and Rhodes, M., eds (2000) *Recasting European Welfare States* (Portland, Oregon: Frank Cass)

Marsh, A., Callender, C., Finlayson, L., Ford, R. and White, M. (1999) *Low Paid Work in Britain: Baseline surveys from the earnings top-up evaluation*, Department of Social Security Research Report, no. 95 (London: DSS)

Mason, B. and Bain, P. (1993) 'The determinants of trade union membership in Britain: A survey of the literature', *Industrial and Labor Relations Review* 46/2 (January): 332–50

Mathers, A. (1999) 'Euromarch – the struggle for a social Europe', *Capital and Class* 68 (Summer): 15–20

Mathers, A. and Taylor, G. (1999) 'Between Global Capital and the Nation State: Social movement politics and the struggle for "Social Europe"' paper given at 'Will Europe Work?', European Sociological Association, 4th annual conference, Amsterdam

McGregor, A., Ferguson, Z., *et al.* (1997) *Bridging the Jobs Gap: An Evaluation of the Wise Group and the intermediate labour market* (York: Joseph Rowntree Foundation)

Mead, L. (1997) 'From Welfare to Work: Lessons from America' in Deacon, A. and Field, F., eds, *From Welfare to Work: Lessons from America* (London: Institute of Economic Affairs)

Merseyside Port Shop Stewards (1998) *Dockers Charter*, monthly magazine of the Liverpool dockers' disputes (Liverpool: Merseyside Port Shop Stewards, c/o TGWU)

Metcalfe, D. (1987) *Cutting Work Time as a Cure for Unemployment*, Occasional Paper in Employment Studies, no. 6 (Buckingham: University of Buckingham)

Michie, J. (1994) 'The growth of unemployment in the 1980s' in Grieve-Smith, J. and Michie, J., eds, *Unemployment in Europe* (London and San Diego: Academic Press)

Michie, J. and Wilkinson, F. (1994) 'The growth of unemployment in the 1980s' in Grieve-Smith, J. and Michie, J., eds, *Unemployment in Europe* (San Diego: Academic Press)

Millar, J., Cooke, K. and McLaughlin, E. (1989) 'The employment lottery: Risk and social security benefits', *Policy and Politics* 17/1: 75–82

Milward, A. (1997) 'The social bases of Monetary Union' in Gowan, P. and Anderson, P., eds, *The Question of Europe* (London: Verso)

Millward, N., Bryson, A. and Forth, J. (2000) *All Change at Work? British employment relations 1980–98*, Workplace Industrial Relations Survey series (London: Routledge)

Mishra, R. (1977) *Society and Social Welfare: Theoretical Perspectives on Welfare* (London: Macmillan)

—— (1984) *The Welfare State in Crisis: Social thought and social change* (Hemel Hempstead: Harvester Wheatsheaf)

MISSOC (1999) *Social protection in the member states of the European Union* (Luxembourg: EU)

Murray, I. (1996) 'Stricter benefit regimes scales new heights', *Working Brief* 77 (September)

Neathy, F. and Arrowsmith, J. (2001) 'Implementation of the Working Time Regulations', *Employment Relations Research Series* no. 11 (April) (London: Department of Trade and Industry [for summary, see <www.eiro.eurofound. ie/2001/05/features/UK0105133F.html>])

Nicaise, I. and Groenez, S. (2003) *The Belgian National Action Plan for Social Inclusion 2001–2003: A preliminary evaluation* (Louvain: HIVA, Catholic University of Louvain)

Nickell, Stephen (1997) 'Unemployment and labour market rigidities: Europe versus North America', *Journal of Economic Perspectives* 11/3: 55–74

Nimmo, M. (1997) 'Benefit traps and the potential for intermediate labour markets', *Working Brief* 89 (November): 17–19 (London: Centre for Social Inclusion [formerly the Unemployment Unit])

Nolan, P. (1994) 'Labour market institutions, industrial restructuring and unemployment in Europe' in Grieve-Smith, J. and Michie, J., eds, *Unemployment in Europe* (London and San Diego: Academic Press)

Normington, D., Brodie, H. and Munro, J. (1986) *Value for Money in the Community Programme* (Sheffield: Manpower Services Commission)

Novak, T. (1997) 'Hounding Delinquents', *Critical Social Policy*, 17/1: 99–109

O'Connor, J. (1973) *The Fiscal Crisis of the State* (New York: St Martin's Press)

OECD (Organisation for Economic Cooperation and Development) (1988) *Measures to assist the long-term unemployed* (Paris: OECD)

—— (1990a) *Measures to assist the long-term unemployed: Recent experience in some OECD countries* (Paris: OECD)

—— (1990b) *Labour market policies for the 1990s* (Paris: OECD)

—— (1991) *Employment Outlook* (Paris: OECD)

—— (1993) 'Atypical work', *Employment Outlook*, July: 13–30 (Paris: OECD)

—— (1994) *The OECD Jobs Study: Evidence and Explanations, Part II: The adjustment potential of the labour market* (Paris: OECD)

—— (1995a) *Labour Market Policies and the Public Employment Service: The Prague Conference* (Paris; OECD)

—— (1995b) *Economic Survey of Sweden, 1995* (Paris: OECD)

—— (1996a) *Employment Outlook, 1996* (Paris: OECD)

—— (1996b) *Benefits and Wages in OECD Countries* (Paris: OECD)

—— (1997a) *Labour market policies: New challenges: Policies for low paid workers and unskilled jobseekers* (Paris: OECD)

—— (1997b) *Making work pay: Taxation, benefits, employment and unemployment* (Paris: OECD)

—— (1997c) *Economic Survey: France* (Paris: OECD)

—— (1998a) *Occasional Paper 33: Social and health policies in OECD countries* (Paris: OECD)

—— (1998b) *Occasional Paper 35: What works among active labour market policies* (Paris: OECD)

—— (1998c) *Statistics at a Glance* (Paris: OECD)

—— (1999a) *Economic Survey: Belgium and Luxembourg* (Paris: OECD)

—— (1999b) 'Employment Protection and Labour Market Performance', *Employment Outlook*: 47–129

—— (1999c) *Economic Survey of Sweden, 1999* (Paris: OECD)

—— (2000) 'Eligibility criteria for unemployment benefits', *Employment Outlook*: 129–152

—— (2001a) *Economic Survey of Sweden, 2001* (Paris: OECD)

—— (2001b) *Retrospective Economic Indicators* (Paris: OECD)

—— (2003a) *Employment Outlook, 2003* (Paris: OECD)

—— (2003b) *Economic Survey of Germany, 2003* (Paris: OECD)

Ormerod, P. (1994) 'On inflation and unemployment' in Grieve-Smith, J. and Michie, J., eds, *Unemployment in Europe* (London and San Diego: Academic Press)

Palier, B. (2001) 'Defrosting the French welfare state' in Ferrera, R. and Rhodes, M. eds, *Recasting European Welfare States* (Portland, Oregon: Frank Cass)

Parker, H. (1993) *Citizens' Income and Women* (London: Citizen's Income Research Group)

Peck, J. and Jones, M. (2001) *Workfare States* (London: Guildford Press)

Peck, J. and Theodore, N. (1998) 'Trading warm bodies: Processing contingent labour in Chicago's temp industry', *Work, Employment and Society* 12/4: 655–674

—— (2000a) 'Beyond "employability"', *Cambridge Journal of Economics* 24/6: 729–740

—— (2000b) 'Work first: Workfare and the regulation of contingent labour markets', *Cambridge Journal of Economics* 24/1: 119–38

Perez-Diaz, V. (1998) 'The "soft side" of employment policy: The Spanish experience', *West European Politics* 21/4: 200–30

Pierson, Christopher (1991) *Beyond the Welfare State?* (Cambridge: Polity Press)

Pierson, C., Forster, A. and Jones, E. (1999) 'Politics of Europe 99: Changing the guard in the European Union. In with the new, out with the old?', *Industrial Relations Journal* 30/4: 277–90

Pierson, Paul (2001) 'Post-industrial Pressures on the Mature Welfare States' in Pierson, P., ed., *The New Politics of the Welfare State* (Oxford: Oxford University Press)

Pilger, J. (1996) 'They never walk alone', *Guardian Weekend*, 23 Nov.: 14–23

Piven, F.F. and Cloward, R. (2002) *Regulating the Poor* (London: Tavistock Publications)

—— eds (2002) *Work, Welfare and Politics: Confronting Poverty in the Wake of Welfare Reform* (Eugene: Oregon University Press)

Polanyi, K. (1957) *The Great Transformation* (Boston: Beacon Press)

Polavieja, J. and Richards, A. (2002) 'Unions and working-class fragmentation in Spain', in Bermeo, N., ed., *Unemployment in the New Europe*: 203–44 (Cambridge: Cambridge University Press)

Pozzo de Borgo, C. (2003) *Chomage et précarité* (film produced for CNRS and the Institut National de l'Audio-visuel, Paris)

Prideaux, S. (2001) 'New Labour, Old functionalism: The underlying contradictions of welfare reform in the US and the UK', *Social Policy and Administration* 35/1: 85–115

Purcell, K., McKnight, A. and Simm, C. (1999) *The lower earnings limit in practice: Part-time employment in hotels and catering* (Manchester: Equal Opportunities Commission)

Regini, M. (2000) 'The dilemmas of labour market regulation' in Esping-Andersen, G. and Regini, M., eds, *Why Deregulate Labour Markets?* (Oxford: Oxford University Press)

Rhodes, M. (2000) 'Globalisation, welfare states and employment: Is there a European "Third Way"?' in Bermeo, N., ed., *Unemployment in the New Europe*: 87–120 (Cambridge: Cambridge University Press)

Rifkin, J. (1995) *The End of Work* (New York: Tarcher/Putnam)

Riley, R. and Young, G. (2001) *The Macroeconomic Impact of the New Deal for Young People*, National Institute for Economic and Social Research, Discussion Paper no. 184 (London: NIESR)

Ronneling, A. and Gabàs i Gasa, A. (2003) 'Welfare or what?' in Steinert, H. and Pilgrim, A., eds, *Welfare Policy from Below* (Aldershot: Ashgate)

Rosdahl, A. and Weise, H. (2001) 'When all must be active: Workfare in Denmark' in Lødemel, I., and Trickey, H., eds, *An offer you can't refuse: Workfare in international perspective* (Bristol: Policy Press)

Rosenhaft, E. (1994) 'The historical development of German social policy' in Clasen, J.F. and Freeman, R. eds, *Social Policy in Germany* (Hemel Hempstead: Harvester Wheatsheaf)

Rubery, J. (2002) 'Shifting of risks and responsibilities in labour markets' in Auer, P. and Daniel, C., eds, *The Future of Work, Employment and Social Protection: The search for new securities in a world of growing uncertainties* (Geneva: ILO)

Rubery, J., Smith, M. and Fagan, C. (1999) *Women's Employment in Europe: Trends and prospects* (London: Routledge)

Sarfati, H. and Bonoli, G. (2002) *Labour Market and Social Protection Reforms in International Perspective: Parallel or converging tracks?* (Aldershot: Ashgate)

Scharpf, F.W. (2002) 'New challenges to welfare states' in Auer, P. and Daniel, C., eds, *The Future of Work, Employment and Social Protection: The search for new securities in a world of growing uncertainties* (Geneva: ILO)

Scharpf, F.W. and Schmidt, V.A., eds (2000) *Welfare and Work in the Open Economy* (Oxford: Oxford University Press)

Schekktat, R. (1997) 'Employment protection and labour mobility in Europe: An empirical analysis using the EU's labour force survey', *International Review of Applied Economics* 11/1: 105–14

Schmidt, V. (2000) 'Values and discourses in the politics of adjustment' in Scharpf, F.W. and Schmidt, V.A., eds, *Welfare and Work in the Open Economy* (Oxford: Oxford University Press)

Schwartz, H. (2001) 'Round up the usual suspects! Globalisation, domestic politics and welfare state change' in Pierson, P., ed., *The New Politics of the Welfare State* (Oxford: Oxford University Press)

Sigg, R. and Behrendt, C. (2002) *Social Security in the Global Village* (London and New Jersey: Transaction Publishers)

Simmonds, D. and Emmerich, M. (1996) *Regeneration Through Work: Creating Jobs in the Social Economy* (Manchester: Centre for Local Economic Strategies)

Sinclair, D. (1995) 'The importance of sex for the propensity to unionise', *British Journal of Industrial Relations* 33/2: 173–90

Solow, R.A. (1998) *Lectures on Work and Welfare* (Princeton: Princeton University Press)

Standing, G. (1997) 'The New Insecurities' in Anderson, P. and Gowan, P., eds, *The Question of Europe* (London: Verso)

—— (1999) *Global Labour Flexibility: Seeking distributive justice* (Basingstoke: Macmillan)

Stephens, J. (2001) 'Scandinavian Welfare States' in Sykes, R., Palier, B. and Prior, P., eds (2001) *Globalisation and European Welfare States: Challenges and change* (Basingstoke: Palgrave)

Stephens, P. (2001) 'The Blair Government and Europe', *Political Quarterly* 72/1: 67–75

Stewart, M.B. (1999) 'Low Pay in Britain' in Gregg, P. and Wadsworth, J., eds, *The State of Working Britain* (Manchester: Manchester University Press)

Strange, G. (1997) 'The British labour movement and Economic and Monetary Union in Europe', *Capital and Class* 63: 85–114

Supiot, A. (2003) 'Governing work and welfare in a global economy' in Zeitlin, J. and Trubeck, D., eds, *Governing Work and Welfare in a New Economy*: 376–406 (Oxford: Oxford University Press)

Swedish Ministry of Labour (1988) *Swedish Labour Market Policy* (Stockholm: Swedish Ministry of Labour)

Sweeney, K. (1996) 'Destination of leavers from claimant unemployment', *Labour Market Trends*, October: 443–52

Sykes, R., Palier, B. and Prior, P., eds (2001) *Globalisation and European Welfare States: Challenges and change* (Basingstoke: Palgrave)

Tampke, J. (1981) 'Bismarck's social legislation: A genuine breakthrough?' in Mommsen, W.J., ed., *The Emergence of the Welfare State in Britain and Germany* (London: German Historical Institute)

Taylor, G. and Mathers, A. (2002) 'The politics of European integration: A European labour movement in the making?' *Capital and Class* 75: 39–60

Taylor-Gooby, P. (2001) 'Sustaining state welfare in hard times: Who will foot the bill?', *Journal of Social Policy* 11/2: 133–42

TELCO (The East London Communities Organisation) (2001) *Mapping Low Pay in East London* (London: TELCO/Queen Mary College Department of Geography, University of London)

Therborn, Goran (1986) *Why Some Peoples are More Unemployed than Others: The strange paradox of growth and unemployment* (London: Verso)

Threlfall, M. (2002) 'The European Union's social policy focus: From labour to welfare and constitutionalised rights?' in Sykes, R., Bochel, C. and Ellison, N., eds, *Social Policy Review 14: Developments and debates (2001–2)* (Bristol: Policy Press)

Tonge, J. (1999) 'New packaging, old deal? New Labour and employment policy innovation', *Critical Social Policy* 19/2: 217–32

Torfing, J. (1999) 'Workfare with welfare: recent reforms of the Danish welfare state', *Journal of European Social Policy* 9/1: 5–28

Towers, B. and Terry, M. (1999) 'Editorial: Unemployment and the social dialogue', *Industrial Relations Journal* 30/4: 272–6

Trades Union Congress (2001) *Permanent Rights for Temporary Workers* (London: TUC)

—— (2002) *TUC Briefing Paper: New Deal Sanctions* (London: TUC)

Tremlett, N. and Collins, D. (1999) *Temporary Employment in Great Britain*, Department for Education and Employment, Research Report 100 (Sheffield: DfEE)

Treu, T. (1992) 'Labour flexibility in Europe', *International Labour Review* 4/5: 497–572

Turok, I. (2000), 'Memorandum of evidence' in House of Commons Education and Employment Committee, *Fourth Report, Minutes of Evidence and Appendices, 'Employability and Jobs: Is There a Jobs Gap?'* (London: HMSO)

Ullman, H.P. (1981) 'German industry and Bismarck's social security system' in Mommsen, W.J., ed., *The emergence of the welfare state in Britain and Germany* (London: German Historical Institute)

Unemployment Unit (1988) *Training or workfare? The New Job Training Scheme in London* (London: Unemployment Unit [later renamed the Centre for Social Inclusion])

—— (2000) 'New figures measure option performance', *Working Brief* (Aug./Sept.): 8–10

Unemployment Unit and Youthaid (2000) *New Deal Handbook* (London: Unemployment Unit/Youthaid [later renamed the Centre for Social Inclusion])

UNISON (1996) *Hillingdon Update*, issue 1, Winter (London: UNISON Health Care)

Visser, J. (2002) 'Why fewer workers join unions in Europe: A social custom explanation of membership trends', *British Journal of Industrial Relations* 40/3: 403–30

Voges, W., Jacobs, H. and Trickey, H. (2001) 'Uneven development – local authorities and workfare in Germany' in Lødemel, I. and Trickey, H., eds, *An Offer You Can't Refuse: Workfare in international perspective* (Bristol: Policy Press)

Wacquant, L. (2001) 'Blairism: Trojan horse of Americanisation?' in Rahkonen, K. and Lausti, T., eds, *Blairism – a beacon for Europe?* (Helsinki: Renvall Institute)

Wahl, A. (2001) 'Social dialogue, social pacts, or a social Europe?' in Abramsky, K., ed., *Restructuring and Resistance: Diverse voices of struggle in Western Europe* (London: K. Abramsky)

Walby, Sylvia (2002) 'Gender and the New Economy: Regulation or deregulation?', paper presented to ESRC seminar 'Work, life and time in the new economy', London School of Economics, October

Walsh, K., Atkinson, J. and Barry, J. (1999) *The New Deal Gateway: A labour market assessment*, Employment Service Research Report, ESR 24 (Sheffield: Employment Service)

Walwei, Ulrich (1998) *Moglichkeiten und Grenzen der Schaffung eines Neidriglohnsektors, Ein Thesenpapier zur aktuellen Diskussion um eine starkere Lohnspreizung*, IAB Werkstattbericht 5/98, Nurnberg

Watkinson, P. (1999) 'Green for Stop: Training, Education and Employment', *'t'-mag* (June): 20–5 (Redruth, Cornwall: 't'-Magazine)

Went, R. (2000) *Globalisation: Neoliberal challenge, radical responses* (London: Pluto Press)

White, L. (1999) 'Quality childcare for low income families' in Handler, J. and White, L., eds, *Hard Labor: Women and work in the post welfare era*: 116–42 (New York: M.E. Sharpe)

White, M. and Forth, J. (1998) *Pathways Through Unemployment: The effects of a flexible labour market* (Layerthorpe: York Publishing Services for Joseph Rowntree Foundation)

White, M. and Lakey, J. (1992) *The Restart Effect* (London: Policy Studies Institute)

Wilkinson, F. (2000) 'Inflation and employment: Is there a third way?' *Cambridge Journal of Economics* 24: 643–70

—— (2001) 'The theory and practice of wage subsidisation: Some historical reflections' in Bennett, F. and Hirsh, D., eds, *The Employment Tax Credit and Issues for the Future of In-Work Support* (York: Joseph Rowntree Foundation)

Wilks, S. (1996) 'Class compromise and the international economy: The rise and fall of Swedish Social Democracy', *Capital and Class* 58: 89–112

Wiseman, M. (2001) 'Making work for welfare in the United States' in Lødemel, I. and Trickey, H., eds, *An Offer You Can't Refuse: Workfare in international perspective* (Bristol: Policy Press)

Wittman, L. (1998) *In Our Own Words: Mothers' needs for successful welfare reform* (Wisconsin: University of Wisconsin, mimeo)

Wood, D. and Smith, P. (1987) *Employers' Labour Use Strategies: First report on 1987 Survey*, DfEE research report (Sheffield: Department for Education and Employment)

Wood, S. (2001) 'Labour market regimes under threat? Sources of continuity in Germany, Britain and Sweden' in Pierson, P. ed., *The New Politics of the Welfare State* (Oxford: Oxford University Press)

Woods, N., ed. (2000) *The Political Economy of Globalisation* (Basingstoke: Macmillan)

Web Sites

Much of the source material in this book comes from the Internet. The following sites may assist the reader to keep up to date:

INTERNATIONAL ORGANISATIONS

OECD: <http:// www.oecd.org>
European Union: <http://europa.eu.int>
European Industrial Relations Observatory (run by the European Foundation for the Improvement of Living and Working Conditions): <http://www.eiro. eurofound.ie>

NATIONAL GOVERNMENTS:

Belgian Ministry of Labour: <www.worldlii.org/catalog/51057.html>
French Ministry of Labour: <www.travail.gouv.fr/etranges/english_v.html>
Swedish Ministry of Labour: <http://www.ams.se/englishfs.asp?C1=223>
Danish Ministry of Labour: <www.bm.dk/english/default.asp>
UK: Department of Trade and Industry: < www.dti.gov.uk>
UK: Office for National Statistics: <www.statistics.gov.uk>
UK: general portal for government departments: <www.ukonline.gov.uk>

NGOS/SOCIAL MOVEMENTS:

Basic Income European Network: <www.basicincome.org>
Trades Union Congress: <www.tuc.org.uk>
Centre for Economic and Social Inclusion: <www.cesi.org.uk>
Euromarches: <www.euromarches.org>
AC! (Agir ensemble contre le chomage et la précarité): <www.ac.eu.org>
Workfare discussion list archive: <www-pluto.informatik.uni-oldenburg. de>

Index

Compiled by Sue Carlton